The Gnostic Treatise on Resurrection
from Nag Hammadi

HDR
HIR

Harvard Theological Review
Harvard Dissertations in Religion

edited by
George W. MacRae
Harvey Cox

Number 12

The Gnostic Treatise on Resurrection from Nag
Hammadi
by
Bentley Layton

The Gnostic Treatise on Resurrection from Nag Hammadi

Edited with Translation and Commentary by
Bentley Layton

Scholars Press

Distributed by
Scholars Press
PO Box 5207
Missoula, Montana 59806

The Gnostic Treatise on Resurrection from Nag Hammadi

Bentley Layton
Yale University

Library of Congress Cataloging in Publication Data

Treatise on resurrection. English & Coptic.
   The gnostic treatise on resurrection from Nag
Hammadi.

   (Harvard dissertations in religion ; no. 12)
   English or Coptic.
   Originally presented as the author's thesis, Harvard,
1971.
   Includes bibliographical references and index.
   1. Gnosticism. 2. Resurrection. I. Layton Bentley. II.
Title. III. Series.
BT1390.T7313   1979   232'.5   79-18521
ISBN 0-89130-341-3
ISBN 0-89130-342-1 pbk.

Printed in the United States of America
1   2   3   4   5
Edwards Brothers, Inc.
Ann Arbor, Michigan 48104

PARENTIBVS · OPTIMIS

CONTENTS

PREFACE

Research on this book was begun at the Griffith Institute, Oxford, in autumn 1969 and was completed somewhat later in Cambridge, Massachusetts. The manuscript was presented to Harvard University in 1971 for the degree of Ph.D. When the editors of this series kindly invited me to publish it here, it was decided that the original text should appear without the addition of substantial new material. It is therefore printed in nearly original form.

I have, however, ventured to rewrite the English translation, partly to make it clearer and more accurate, and partly to give myself fuller rein in expressing the author's argument. The extensive use of paraphrase in my translation (and so the addition of a strict literal version in the bottom register of the page) is made necessary by our ancient author's approximation to that extraordinarily odd rhetoric called the Greek diatribe. Any reader who has tried to render the Discourses of Epictetus into English will understand perfectly well the nature of this difficulty and recognize the impossibility of reproducing anything like the original phrases or style.

I had the good fortune in 1972 to collate the manuscript while in Cairo; this resulted in some minor corrections in the transcription. Furthermore I have incorporated new solutions to two textual cruces (at 41 and 77), recently communicated to me by Professor H. J. Polotsky. To him I express heartfelt thanks.

Some additional items of bibliography on the Treatise have accumulated in the intervening years, but none along the lines of interpretation followed here; the appearance of David

Scholer's complete <u>Nag</u> <u>Hammadi</u> <u>Bibliography</u>[1] now makes it superfluous to list them. The best photographic facsimile of the text will be found in <u>The</u> <u>Facsimile</u> <u>Edition</u> <u>of</u> <u>the</u> <u>Nag</u> <u>Hammadi</u> <u>Codices</u> . . . <u>Codex</u> <u>I</u> (Leiden: Brill, 1977).

Abbreviations of ancient Greek authors and texts are mostly those of Liddell-Scott-Jones, <u>Greek-English</u> <u>Lexicon</u>.

My most sincere thanks are due to all those who have helped me, and in particular to the Society of Fellows of Harvard University for generous support of several kinds during my research; to the A. Whitney Griswold Fund; to the Very Reverend Dr. Henry Chadwick and the senior common room of Christ Church College, Oxford, for hospitality and encourage-ment, as also to the Griffith Institute, the Ecole Biblique et Archéologique Française de Jérusalem, and the British School of Archaeology in Jerusalem; to Professors Helmut Koester (my academic advisor at Harvard), Thomas O. Lambdin, George W. MacRae, B. S. Page, Zeph Stewart, and John Strugnell for their great kindness in reading parts of my work in manuscript and for many useful suggestions; to Professor G. M. Browne for palaeographical advice; to Professor H. J. Polotsky for help on matters of Coptic grammar (though not, in the first instance, on this text); and to Madame Sameeha Abd el-Shaheed, Dean Krister Stendahl, and the late Professor Richard Walzer for assistance of one sort or another. I should finally wish to call attention to the continuing value of my predecessors' commentaries, which this study neither duplicates nor tries to replace.

---

[1]<u>Nag</u> <u>Hammadi</u> <u>Bibliography</u> <u>1948-1969</u> (Nag Hammadi Studies, 1; Leiden: Brill, 1971), with annual supplements in <u>Novum</u> <u>Testamentum</u> starting with vol. 13 (1971) for the year 1970: sub 'Coptic Gnostic Library: I, <u>3</u>'.

INTRODUCTION

This volume contains a new critical edition and translation, with commentary, of an anonymous gnostic work probably
belonging to the second century A.D. and entitled <u>Treatise</u> <u>on</u>
<u>Resurrection</u>.[1] To no small degree the historical importance of
the treatise lies in its detailed and sympathetic exposition of
a celebrated heresy attacked by the author of the Pastoral
Epistles (2 Tim. 2.17), <u>resurrectionem</u> <u>esse</u> <u>iam</u> <u>factam</u>. Many
New Testament critics now hold that the Pastoral Epistles were
composed some time in the second century; and it is not incon-
ceivable that in some way the Pastorals themselves constitute
an external testimony to the very text edited here. The text
is part of the Coptic Gnostic Library of Nag Hammadi
(Chenoboskion), occupying pp. 43-50 of Codex I, the Jung
Codex, now kept at the Coptic Museum in Old Cairo.

In writing the commentary (the most important part of the
present volume) my principal aim has been to make clear the
author's language and logic and to demonstrate the coherence
of his argument, tasks left largely undone by earlier commentators. The purpose of the commentary is thus to lay a more
solid groundwork for those who wish to make use of the <u>Treatise</u>
in historical research. As the commentary deals only with
matters of interpretation it can be easily used by readers who
have no Coptic (I call attention also to Grammatical Appendix
2 in which the author's use of Greek connective particles is
studied in detail; it is meant to be an exegetical tool). I
have also tried to indicate which elements in the treatise can
be considered commonplace for its age and milieu and which less

---

[1]Also known as <u>Epistle</u> <u>to</u> <u>Rheginus</u>.

1

so.

Though probably composed in Greek the <u>Treatise</u> <u>on</u>
<u>Resurrection</u> comes down to us only in a Subachmimic Coptic
translation, attested by a single manuscript found near Nag
Hammadi in Upper Egypt in 1945. Of its author and date we
hear nothing in the manuscript (which itself dates to perhaps
the fourth century). But the recipient or dedicatee, a certain Rheginus (the name is commonplace), is mentioned more
than once in the treatise, as are 'his brethren' from whom he
is urged to withhold none of the teachings, 'for what I have
taught you has power to be of benefit: many people are awaiting what I have written for you'. There is much convention in
the author's pose, but nothing leads us to doubt that we have
here a doctrinal exposition actually sent from one historical
person to another with the purpose of communicating vital
information about salvation--or 'resurrection'--of the spiritual element in man.

About the date of the Coptic translation little can be
said. As for that of the original composition in Greek, the
thought expressed in the <u>Treatise</u> is best paralleled in the
later second century. I have tried to illustrate points of
contact which it shares with the thought of that century in
various ways. Among the authors of the second century,
Christian and pagan, there is a particular wealth of parallel
material from the very end of the century in Clement of
Alexandria, a source untapped by previous commentators.
Clement's immersion in Platonism--and such other philosophical
ideas as were discussed in Platonic circles[2]--his first-hand
acquaintance with Valentinianism and other forms of gnosticism
(indeed his admiration for them) and his concern with the same
issues as those of the <u>Treatise</u> make his works, especially the
<u>Stromateis</u>, a natural context for similar expressions. These,
like the other contemporary parallels, help confirm the wording

---

[2]Clement's knowledge of the Platonic text is balanced by
his extensive acquaintance with the Bible and the Jewish
Platonist Philo (cf. Stählin's first apparatus) and his pro-
fessional if shallow knowledge of current philosophical
schools. Clement, like the Apologist Justin, speaks of his
<u>philosophische</u> <u>Reisen</u> (<u>Stro</u>. I. 11.1-2), implying control of
more than one school tradition and the superiority of Christian
Platonism to them all.

of the Greek model which underlies the extant Coptic version
and also demonstrate what may be considered normal modes of
expression in this kind of literature.

But in fact Clement's own theology is different from our
author's, as I have occasionally noted in the commentary. Thus
it is the residue of ideas not easily paralleled in Clement or
other non-gnostic writers which is, finally, what is striking
about our author's thought. This residue includes the doctrine
of a preexistent heavenly Fulness (Pleroma), somehow presently
dispersed in a totally alien world in the form of 'minds' and
driving now toward reintegration of its 'lacking' members.
Otherwise the author's presuppositions are dualist, Platonizing,
gnostic in the broader sense and, in a way to be discussed in
chapters II and III, predestinarian (predestination of mind to
survive bodily death).

Besides Clement's Christian gnosticizing Platonism the
Platonic corpus itself--which in part was seriously read in
the first and second centuries--throws much light upon our
treatise. Whether the author is directly acquainted with Plato
cannot be determined. But the coherence of his thought depends
on certain striking ideas and distinctions found in Plato or
his sources (e.g., Orphism), and here given new poignancy in
the context of heightened dualism and of the gnostic concept
of pleromatic reintegration. Professor Nock has called the
gnostic, or gnosticizing, aspects of early Christianity a
'Platonism run wild': one should not forget that close under
the surface of much supposedly gnostic language lies material
familiar from the most-read passages of Plato.

To a large extent, then, such a Platonic 'koine' constitutes the intellectual environment of the age. I have tried to
illustrate that environment also at the social level by citation of commonplaces from roughly contemporary funerary
inscriptions found all around the Mediterranean basin. These
constitute a tradition in themselves, partly influencing and
partly influenced by the related consolatio literature and
transmitted by a fairly conservative line of tradesmen. If
these inscriptions are not direct personal expressions of
popular sentiment about life, death, and the possibility of
afterlife they nonetheless can tell us what was an acceptable

and normal way to speak of the ultimate end of man's earthly career, a way of speaking that was familiar to nearly all. Here too the Platonizing koine makes itself felt.

Two earlier commentaries upon the Treatise take approaches quite different from mine. The first editors[3] cite what they consider parallels from Valentinian tradition. If these amply demonstrate that the treatise is of gnostic character in its language, they do not prove that it is necessarily Valentinian. That would best be demonstrated, if indeed it could be, by examination of the philosophical system of the text. Language alone is deceptive: our author refers (36) to 'lordships and divinities', θειότητες, cf. Col. 1.16. Now θειότης in this context, says Theodoret (Haer. fab. comp. I. 7), is specifically (if not uniquely) Valentinian. Yet on the other hand our author often calls the Savior 'lord': and this--as Professor van Unnik points out, quoting Irenaeus[4]--supposedly was not the practice of Valentinianism. One wonders how far such rigid canons of diction will really get us. As for the editors' worthy attempt to attribute the work to the master Valentinus (his writings in Greek are otherwise virtually lost, a meager 63 lines are collected in W. Völker's Quellen zur Geschichte der christlichen Gnosis, 1932), their arguments have been severely criticized by Peel.[5] There seems, in truth, to be no sure path behind the several Valentinian traditions attested by the Fathers back to a primitive system of the founder. Certainly none of those reported strikingly coincides in thought or language with the treatise studied here. The genetic approach to the development of Valentinian myth might in any case be questioned on principle.[6] For the moment then we must consider the Treatise for what it says and implies in

---

[3]M. Malinine et al., 1963.

[4]JEH 15 (1964) 148; Irenaeus Haer. I. 1.3 [1.1 H.]; cf. I. 2.6 [1.4 H.].

[5]De Resurrectione (1969) pp. 156-178.

[6]Nock's remarks on the non-existence of a gnostic Ursystem would seem to hold good even for a widespread movement like Valentinianism: Early Gentile Christianity and its Hellenistic Background, preface to the second edition, 1964, p. xiv.

itself, and hope that the publication and study of other
gnostic texts may later clarify the taxonomy of gnostic philosophies in the second and third centuries A.D.

But we shall always be condemned to some uncertainty in
the present case, for the Treatise is by no means a full
representation of its author's thought. He himself refers to
its simplicity, its avoidance of any but basic matters, and he
speaks as a pedagogue to a beginning pupil. He also offers in
conclusion to follow up with a more detailed elaboration of the
'deeper' points. We cannot know, then, what more elaborate
system--perhaps one close to the Valentinian myths known from
other sources--was to be given in the subsequent stage of
instruction. It may be of service to quote Richard Harder's
dictum on Plotinus[7]: 'Der Denker spricht nicht immer alles
aus was er weiss, man darf dann nicht sagen, er habe es "noch"
nicht gewusst'.

Professor Peel's commentary heavily emphasizes Biblical
parallels. These again are parallels of language, rarely
touching upon fundamental structures of the author's thought.
I must confess to finding few of them at all striking when a
wider view of the Greek language is introduced. Furthermore
Peel's method forces him to all but ignore the patently
Platonic cast of the work and to deemphasize its internal
consistency and development. For his view that there are
significant contacts between the Coptic text and that of the
Sahidic New Testament, I see no evidence at all.

In conclusion I should note that my translation differs
very substantially from previous ones, so that the system of
the author's thought will now seem quite different from what
it was formerly supposed to be. The basis for my understanding
of the Coptic text is presented in a series of grammatical
notes and associated appendices. As the new texts appear it
becomes ever clearer how much research in Coptic grammar lies
before us and how rich and rewarding these labors will be.
ὁ μὲν θερισμὸς πολύς, οἱ δὲ ἐργάται ὀλίγοι.

---

[7]Plotins Schriften, 2nd edition, 1966, vol. Ib
(Anmerkungen), p. 370, on I 6.1, 37-40.

I

TEXT AND TRANSLATION

Sigla

unci [ ]	*lacunam,* $\langle$ $\rangle$ *omissionem indicant.*
A̦A̦A̦A̦	*litterae incertae.*
{AAA}	*litterae delendae.*
⟦ AA ⟧	*lectio ante correctionem.*
cod.	*lectio codicis. tractatus noster (CG I,4) quartus est in codice papyraceo cairense gnostico (Jungiano) I, musei coptici babylonis 11597, 11640, saec. iv p.C.n., pag. 43-[50].*
edd. pr.	*De Resurrectione ediderunt Michel Malinine, Henri-Charles Puech, Gilles Quispel, Walter Till adiuuantibus R. McL. Wilson, Jan Zandee (Zürich, Stuttgart: Rascher, 1963).*
Barns	*J. W. B. Barns, Journal of Theological Studies, n.s. 15 (1964) 162-166.*
Polotsky	*H. J. Polotsky (uerbo).*

1 ογ ϩαειⲛⲉ ⲡⲁϣⲏⲣⲉ ⲣⲏⲅⲓⲛⲟⲥ
   ⲉⲩⲱϣⲉ ⲁⲥⲃⲟ ⲁϩⲁϩ |
   ⲟⲩⲛⲧⲉⲩ ⲙ̄ⲙⲉⲩ ⲙ̄ⲡ|ⲥⲕⲟⲡⲟⲥ |
   ⲉⲩⲉⲙⲁϩⲧⲉ ⲛ̄ϩ̄ⲛ̄ⲍⲏⲧⲏⲙⲁ |
5 ⲉⲩϣⲁⲁⲧ ⲙ̄ⲡⲉⲩⲃⲱⲗ
   ⲁⲩⲱ ‖ ⲉⲩϣⲁⲛⲙⲉⲉⲧⲉ ⲁⲛⲉⲉ|
   ϣⲁⲩ|ⲙⲉⲩⲉ ⲁϩ̄ⲛ̄ⲙ̄ⲛ̄ⲧⲛⲁϭ ⲛ̄ϩⲣⲏ|ⲓ̈ ⲛ̄ϩⲏⲧⲟⲩ
   ⲛ̄ⲧⲙⲉⲩⲉ ⲛ̄ⲇⲉ ⲉⲛ |
   ϫⲉ ⲁⲩⲁϩⲉ ⲁⲣⲉⲧⲟⲩ ⲙ̄ⲫⲟⲩⲛ ⲙ̄|ⲡⲗⲟⲅⲟⲥ
      ⲛ̄ⲧⲙⲏⲉ
10 ⲉⲩϣ|ⲛⲉ ‖ ⲛ̄ϩⲟⲩⲟ ⲁⲡⲉⲩⲙ̄ⲧⲁⲛ
   ⲡⲉⲉ| ⲛ̄ⲧⲁ ϩⲛ̄ϫ|ⲧ̄ϥ ϩⲓⲧⲙ̄ ⲡ̄ⲛ̄ⲥⲱ|ⲧⲏⲣ ⲡ̄ⲛ̄-
      ϫⲁⲉ|ⲥ ⲡⲉⲭⲣⲏⲥⲧⲟⲥ
   *ⲛ̄ⲧⲁ ϩⲛ̄ϫ|ⲧ̄ϥ
   ⲛ̄ⲧⲁⲣⲉⲛⲥⲟⲩ|ⲱⲛ ⲧⲙⲏⲉ
14 ⲁⲩⲱ ⲁⲛⲙ̄ⲧⲁⲛ | ⲙ̄ⲙⲁⲛ ⲁ ϩⲣⲏⲓ̈ ⲁϫⲱⲥ

30

35

*44

———

3 ⲥⲕⲟⲡⲟⲥ: C¹ corr. ex ⟦ⲕ⟧.

43:25   [1]There are certain persons, my child Rheginus,
who wish to become learned: [3]that is their aim when
they set out to solve unsolved problems, [6]and if they
succeed they regard themselves highly. [8]But I do not
think their results lie within the account of the
truth; [10]rather, it is recreation,[a] a kind of repose,[a]
that they are after. [11]Repose -- true repose -- we
obtained from our Savior, our Lord, the Excellent:
[12]we obtained it when we gained acquaintance with the
truth and rested our confidence upon it.

---

[a]recreation . . . repose: two senses of Greek anapausis.

[LITERAL TRANSLATION]

      [1]There are some, my son ʿΡηγῖνος, [2]who wish to learn about
many (things). [3]They have this σκοπός, [4]mastering ζητήματα [5]that
lack their solution. [6]And if/when they succeed at these, [7]they
think greatnesses within themselves. [8]But (δέ) I do not think
[9]that they have stood within the λόγος of the truth. [10]It is
rather their rest that they are seeking. [11]As for this, it is
from our σωτήρ, our lord, the χρηστός, that we received it.
[12]The time we received it, [13]was when we came to know the truth
[14]and rested ourselves upon it (scil. the truth).

11

12

15 ⲀⲖⲖⲀ | ⲈⲠⲈⲒⲆⲎ ⲈⲔϢⲒⲚⲈ ⲘⲘⲀⲚ ‖ Ⲁ-   44 5
   ⲠⲈⲦⲈϢϢⲈ ⲌⲚ ⲞⲨⲌⲖⲀϬ | ⲈⲦⲂⲈ ⲦⲀ-
   ⲚⲀⲤⲦⲀⲤ|Ⲥ
   ⳨ⲤⲌⲈ|ⲈⲒ ⲚⲈⲔ
   ϪⲈ ⲞⲨⲀⲚⲀⲄⲔⲀⲒⲞⲚ | ⲦⲈ
   ⲀⲨⲰ ⲞⲨⲚ ⲌⲀⲌ ⲘⲘⲈⲚ Ⲟ|ⲈⲒ ⲚⲀⲠⲒⲤⲦⲞⲤ
     ⲀⲢⲀⲤ
   ⲌⲚⲔⲞⲨ‖ⲈⲒ ⲚⲆⲈ ⲚⲈⲦϬⲒⲚⲈ ⲘⲘⲀⲤ | 10
20 ⲈⲦⲂⲈ ⲠⲈⲈⲒ ⲘⲀⲢⲈ ⲠⲖⲞⲄⲞⲤ | ϢⲰⲠⲈ ⲚⲈⲚ
     ⲈⲦⲂⲎⲦⲤ
   Ⲛ|ⲦⲀⲌⲀ ⲠϪⲀⲈⲒⲤ Ⲣ̄ⲬⲢⲰ Ⲛ̄ⲈϢ | Ⲛ̄ⲤⲈ Ⲛ̄-
     Ⲛ̄ⲌⲂⲎⲨⲈ
   ⲈⲨϢⲞⲨ‖ⲞⲠ ⲌⲚ ⲤⲀⲢⲌ̄   15
   ⲀⲨⲰ Ⲛ̄ⲦⲀ|ⲢⲈⲨⲞⲨⲀⲚⲌϤ ⲀⲂⲀⲖ
   ⲈⲨϢⲎ|ⲢⲈ Ⲛ̄ⲚⲞⲨⲦⲈ ⲠⲈ
25 ⲀϤⲤⲘⲀⲌⲈ | ⲌⲚ Ⲡ̄|ⲦⲞⲠⲞⲤ
   ⲠⲈⲈⲒ ⲈⲦ ⲔⲌ|ⲘⲀⲤⲦ̄ Ⲛ̄ⲌⲎⲦϤ
   ⲈⲨϢⲈϪⲈ ‖ ⲀⲠⲚⲞⲘⲞⲤ Ⲛ̄Ⲧ⳨ⲢⲤ|Ⲥ   20
   ⲈⲈ|ϪⲞⲨ | Ⲛ̄ⲆⲈ ⲘⲘⲀⲨ ϪⲈ ⲠⲘⲞⲨ·
   ⲠϢⲎ|ⲢⲈ Ⲛ̄ⲆⲈ Ⲙ̄ⲠⲚⲞⲨⲦⲈ Ⲣ̄ⲎⲄ|ⲒⲚⲈ | ⲚⲈⲨ-
     ϢⲎⲢⲈ Ⲛ̄ⲢⲰⲘⲈ ⲠⲈ
30 ⲀⲨⲰ ⲚⲈϤⲈⲘⲀⲌⲦⲈ ⲀⲢⲀⲨ Ⲙ̄ⲠⲈ‖ⲤⲚⲈⲨ   25
   ⲈⲨⲚ̄ⲦⲈϤ Ⲙ̄ⲘⲈⲨ Ⲛ̄Ⲧ|ⲘⲚ̄ⲦⲢⲰⲘⲈ ⲘⲚ̄ ⲦⲘⲚ̄Ⲧ-
     ⲚⲞⲨ|ⲦⲈ
32 ϪⲈⲔⲀⲤⲈ ⲈⲨⲚⲀϪⲢⲞ ⲘⲘⲈⲚ | ⲀⲠⲘⲞⲨ Ⲁ-
     ⲂⲀⲖ ⲌⲒⲦⲘ̄ ⲠⲦⲢϤ|ϢⲰⲠⲈ Ⲛ̄ϢⲎⲢⲈ Ⲛ̄-
     ⲚⲞⲨⲦⲈ ‖

———

21 Ⲛ̄ⲦⲀⲌⲀ: Ⲛ̄ fort. corr. ex ⟦Ⲧ⟧.   25 ⲀϤⲌ i.e.
ⲀⲌϤ uel ⲌⲘⲀⲌⲈ i.e. ⲘⲀⲌⲈ (cf. 26 ⲌⲘⲀⲤⲦ̄).
ⲘⲀⲌⲈ: Ⲁ corr. ex ⟦Ⲉ⟧.

On Resurrection §§ 15 - 32

44:3 [15]However, since it is the essential points on resurrection after which you so sweetly inquire, I am writing to you. [17]For resurrection is a basic matter; and not only do many give it no credence, but few are they who understand and find it. [20]So let this be the topic of our discussion.

44:12 [21]How did the Lord handle the circumstances of this world? [22]While He was incarnate, and after He had revealed Himself to be a son of god,[a] [25]He walked about in this region (where you dwell) discoursing of the law of the natural order: I mean, of death. [29]Moreover, o Rheginus, the son of god was a son of man.[b] [30]And He was master of His circumstances in two respects -- having both humanity and divinity: [32]so that He might conquer death through being son of god,[a]

---

[a]or: a divine son.
[b]or: a human son.

---

[15]ἀλλὰ ἐπειδή it is what is necessary about the[x] ἀνάστασις for which you are asking us sweetly, [16]I am writing to you. [17]For it is an ἀναγκαῖον. [18]And many μέν are ἄπιστοι regarding it (scil. resurrection); [19]it is few δέ that find it. [20]Because of this let the λόγος be for us about it (scil. resurrection). [21]How did the lord χρῆσθαι the things? [22]Existing in σάρξ [23]and when he had revealed himself [24]being a son of god[y] [25]he walked in this τόπος, [26]this in which you dwell, [27]talking about the νόμος of the φύσις [28](I call it δέ 'the death'). [29]The son δέ of god, ʻΡήγινε, was a son of man.[z] [30]And he prevailed with respect to them both, [31]having the humanity and the divinity, [32]so that he might conquer μέν the death by his being/becoming a son of god,[y]

---

[x]Coptic grammar insists upon use of the definite article ("the") with all abstract nouns, where English will often omit it.

[y]or: a divine son.

[z]or: a human son.

33 ϩΙΤΟΟΤϤ ΔΕ ⲙ̄ΠϢΗΡΕ ⲙ̄ΠΡⲰⲘΕ ΕΡΕ ΤΑ-   30
  ΠΟΚΑΤΑⲤΤΑ|ⲤΙⲤ ΝΑϢⲰΠΕ ⲀϨΟΥΝ
  ⲀΠ|ΠΛΗΡⲰⲘⲀ
  ΕΠΕΙΔΗ Ν̄ϢⲀ|ⲢⲠ̄ ΕϤϢΟΟΠ ⲀΒⲀⲖ ϨⲘ̄
  ΠⲤⲀΝ||ΤⲠΕ Ν̄ⲤΠΕΡⲘⲀ Ν̄ΤⲘΗΕ   35

35 ΕⲘⲠⲀΤΕ ϯⲤΥⲤΤⲀⲤΙⲤ ϢⲰⲠΕ |
  ϨΝ̄ ΤΕΕΙ ⲀϨⲚ̄ⲘⲚ̄ΤⲬⲀΕΙⲤ ⲘⲚ̄ | ϨⲚ̄ⲘⲚ̄Τ-
  ΝΟΥΤΕ ϢⲰΠΕ
  ΕΝⲀ|ϢⲰΟΥ
  ϯⲤⲀΥΝΕ
  ϪΕ ΕΕΙΤΕΥΟ * Ⲙ̄ΠΒⲰⲖ ϨⲚ̄ ϨⲚ̄ϨΒΗΥΕ *45
  Ν̄ⲆΥⲤΚΟⲖΟΝ

40 ⲀⲖⲖⲀ ⲘⲚ̄ ⲖⲀΥΕ Ν̄ⲆΥⲤΚΟⲖΟΝ ϢΟΟΠ
  ϨⲘ̄ ΠⲖΟ|ΓΟⲤ Ν̄ΤⲘΗΕ
  ⲀⲖⲖⲀ ΕΠΕΙΔΗ Ε|ΤΡΕ ΠΒⲰⲖ Ν̄ΤⲀϤΕΙ   5
  ⲀΒⲀⲖ Ⲁ|ΤⲘΗΤΕ ⲀΤⲘ̄ⲔΕ ⲖⲀΥΕ
  ΕϤϨΗⲠ |
  ⲀⲖⲖⲀ ⲀΤΡΕϤΟΥⲰⲚϨ̄ ⲀΒⲀⲖ | Ⲙ̄ΠΤΗⲢϤ̄
  ϨⲀⲠⲖⲰⲤ ΕΤΒΕ Π|ϢⲰΠΕ
  ΠΒⲰⲖ ⲀΒⲀⲖ Ⲙ̄ⲘΕΝ ‖ Ⲙ̄ΠΠΕⲐⲀΥ ΠΟΥ-   10
  ⲰⲚϨ̄ ΔΕ Ⲁ|ΒⲀⲖ Ⲙ̄ΠΕΤⲤⲀⲦⲠ̄ ΤΕΕΙ ΤΕ |
  ΤΠΡΟΒΟⲖΗ Ν̄ΤⲘΗΕ ⲘⲚ̄ ΠΕ|ΠΝΕΥⲘⲀ

45 ΤΕⲬⲀΡΙ|Ⲥ ΤⲀ ΤⲘΗ|Ε ΤΕ
  ΠⲤⲰΤΗΡ ⲀϤϢⲘ̄ⲚⲔ̄ Ⲙ̄ΠⲘΟΥ   15
  Ν̄ⲔΗⲠ ΕΝ Ⲁ|ϨⲀⲦⲤⲀΥΝΕ |
  ⲀϤⲔⲰϢ Ν̄ΓⲀⲢ ⲀϨⲢΗΪ Ⲙ̄ΠⲔΟ|ⲤⲘΟⲤ
  ΕϢⲀϤΤΕⲔΟ

50 ⲀϤϢⲰⲦ[Ϥ] | ⲀϨΟΥΝ ⲀⲢⲀ|ⲰΝ Ν̄ⲀΤΤΕⲔΟ |

---

41 ΕΤΡΕ: lege ΕΤΒΕ (Polotsky).   50 rest. edd.
pr.

and that through the son of man might come to pass the
return (apokatastasis) to the Fulness (pleroma): [34]since
from the beginning He existed as a seed of the truth
from above, [35]before there came into being this cosmic
structure, [36]in which lordships and divinities have
become so numerous.

44:39   [38]I know that I am phrasing this explanation in
difficult terms. [40]Yet consider: nothing within the
account of the truth is truly difficult. [41]At any rate,
since He came forward for the sake of explanation, to
leave nothing obscure, rather to reveal in simple terms
everything about coming-into-being -- [44]the undoing of
evil and the manifestation of the superior part, these
are the offshoot of the truth and the spirit: [45]this
grace is bestowed by the truth. [46]The Savior swallowed
death. [47]You must not be unperceptive: [48]for I mean
that laying aside the perishable world, [50]He exchanged
it for an unperishing eternal realm.

---

[33]through δέ the son of the man the ἀποκατάστασις might come to
pass into the πλήρωμα, [34]ἐπειδή it is from the beginning that he
has existed from the above as a σπέρμα of the truth, [35]this
σύστασις not yet having come into being; [36]in the latter, lordships and divinities have come to exist, [37]being numerous. [38]I
know [39]that it is in δύσκολα things that I am putting forth the
explanation. [40]ἀλλά nothing δύσκολον exists in the λόγος of the
truth. [41]ἀλλά ἐπειδή it is for the sake of the explanation that he/
it came into the midst, [42]so as not to leave anything being
hidden, [43]ἀλλά so he might reveal the whole ἁπλῶς about coming-
into-being/being,[x] [44]the dissolution μέν of the evil, the
manifestation δέ of the best/the chosen, this is the προβολή of
the truth and the πνεῦμα. [45]The χάρις belongs to the truth.
[46]The σωτήρ swallowed the death. [47]You must not be ignorant.
[48]For (γάρ) he laid down the κόσμος [49]that perishes, [50]he exchanged
it for an imperishable αἰών,

---

[x]"Coming-into-being" and "being" are the same word in Coptic.

45:19-46:2

51 ⲁⲣⲱ ⲁϥⲧⲟⲣⲛⲁⲥ̄ϥ
ⲉⲁϥⲱ‖ⲙ̄ⲛ̄ⲕ̄ ⲙ̄ⲡⲉⲧⲟⲩⲁⲛⲍ̄ ⲁⲃⲁⲗ | ⲁⲃⲁⲗ   20
ⲍⲓⲧⲟⲟⲧ̄ϥ ⲙ̄ⲡⲁⲧⲛⲉⲩ | ⲁⲣⲁϥ
ⲁⲣⲱ ⲁϥϯ ⲛⲉⲛ ⲛ̄ⲧⲉⲍⲓⲏ ⲛ̄ⲧⲛ̄ⲙ̄ⲛ̄ⲧⲁⲧⲙⲟⲩ
ⲧⲟ|ⲧⲉ ⲇⲉ ⲛ̄ⲑⲉ
55 ⲛ̄ⲧⲁⲍⲁ ⲡⲁⲡⲟⲥⲧⲟ‖ⲗⲟⲥ ⲭⲟⲟⲩ   25
ⲭⲉ ⲁⲛϣ̄ⲡ̄ ⲍⲓⲥⲉ | ⲛ̄ⲙⲙⲉϥ
ⲁⲣⲱ ⲁⲛⲧⲱⲱⲛ | ⲛ̄ⲙⲙⲉϥ
ⲁⲣⲱ ⲁⲛⲃⲱⲕ ⲁⲧⲡⲉ | ⲛ̄ⲙⲙⲉϥ
ⲉ|ϣⲡⲉ ⲧ̄ⲛ̄ϣⲟ|ⲟⲡ ⲛ̄ⲇⲉ
60 ⲉⲛⲟⲩⲁⲛⲍ̄ ⲁⲃⲁⲗ ⲍ̄ⲙ̄ ‖ ⲡⲓⲕⲟⲥⲙⲟⲥ   30
ⲉⲛⲣ̄ⲫⲟⲣⲉⲓ ⲙ̄|ⲙⲁϥ
ⲉⲛϣⲟⲟⲡ ⲛ̄ⲁⲕⲧⲓⲛ | ⲙ̄ⲡⲉⲧⲙ̄ⲙⲉⲩ
ⲁⲣⲱ ⲉⲩⲉ|ⲙⲁⲍⲧⲉ ⲙ̄ⲙⲁⲛ ⲁⲃⲁⲗ ⲍⲓ-
ⲧⲟ|ⲟⲧ̄ϥ ϣⲁ ⲡ̄ⲛ̄ϣⲱⲧⲡ
ⲉⲧⲉ ⲡⲉ‖ⲉⲓ ⲡⲉ ⲡⲉⲛⲙⲟⲩ ⲍⲙ̄ ⲡⲉⲉⲓⲃ‖ⲟⲥ   35
65 ⲉⲩⲥⲱⲕ ⲙ̄ⲙⲁⲛ ⲁⲧⲡⲉ ⲁ|ⲃⲁⲗ ⲍⲓⲧⲟⲟⲧ̄ϥ
ⲛ̄ⲑⲉ ⲛ̄ⲛⲓⲁⲕⲧⲓⲛ | ⲍⲓⲧⲙ̄ ⲡⲣⲏ
ⲉⲛⲥⲉⲉⲙⲁⲍⲧⲉ ⲙ̄ⲙⲁⲛ ⲉⲛ ⲍⲓⲧⲛ̄ ⲗⲁⲩⲉ
ⲧⲉⲉⲓ ⲧⲉ ‖ ⲧⲁⲛⲁⲥⲧⲁⲥⲓⲥ ⲛ̄ⲡⲛⲉⲩⲙⲁ-
*ⲧⲓⲕⲏ   *46   40
68 ⲉⲥⲱⲙ̄ⲛ̄ⲕ̄ ⲛ̄ⲧⲯⲩⲭⲓⲕⲏ | ⲍⲟⲙⲟ|ⲱⲥ ⲙ̄ⲛ̄
ⲧⲕⲉⲥⲁⲣⲕⲓⲕⲏ |

On Resurrection §§ 51 - 68

[51]And He raised Himself up[a] (having "swallowed" the visible by means of the invisible), [53]and gave us the way to our immortality.

45:23   [54]So then, as the Apostle said of Him, [56]we have suffered with Him, and arisen with Him and ascended into heaven with Him.[b]

45:28   [59]Now since we are manifestly present in this world, the world is our garment that we wear. [62]From Him (the Savior) we radiate like rays; [63]and being held fast by Him until our sunset (that is, until our death in the present life), we are drawn up to heaven by Him as rays are drawn by the sun, restrained by nothing. [67]This is resurrection of the spirit (spiritual resurrection), [68]which "swallows" resurrection of the soul along with resurrection of the flesh.

---

[a]or: and He arose.
[b]or simply: and ascended with Him.

---

[51]and he raised himself up/and arose, [52]having swallowed the manifest by means of the unseen. [53]And he gave us the way to/of our immortality. [54]τότε moreover, as [55]the ἀπόστολος said of him, [56]we have suffered with him, [57]and we have arisen with him, [58]and we have gone to the sky with him. [59]Since/If we exist δέ [60]being manifest in this κόσμος [61]it/he is what we φορεῖν. [62]It is of that one that we are ἀκτῖνες. [63]And being held by him/it until our sinking, [64]that is, our death in this βίος, [65]it is as ἀκτῖνες (are drawn) by the sun that we are drawn to the sky by him/it, [66]not being held by anything/anyone. [67]This is the πνευματική ἀνάστασις, [68]devouring the ψυχική, ὁμοίως with also the σαρκική.

46:3-19

69 ⲉ|ϣⲡⲉ ⲟⲩⲛ ⲟⲩⲉⲉ| ⲛ̄ⲇⲉ
70 ⲉⲙ̄ϥ̄|ⲡ|ⲥⲧⲉⲩⲉ ⲉⲛ
ⲙ̄ⲛ̄ⲧⲉϥ ⲙ̄ⲙⲉⲩ ⲙ̄‖ⲡⲣⲡⲉ|ⲑⲉ·   46⁵
ⲡⲧⲟⲡⲟⲥ ⲅⲁⲣ ⲛ̄ⲧⲡ|ⲥⲧ|ⲥ ⲡⲉ ⲡⲁϣⲏⲣⲉ
ⲁⲣⲱ ⲡⲁ ⲡ̄ⲣ|ⲡⲉ|ⲑⲉ ⲉⲛ ⲡⲉ
ⲡⲉⲧⲙⲁⲟⲩⲧ ⲛⲁ|ⲧⲱⲱⲛ
75 ⲁⲣⲱ ⲟⲩⲛ ⲡⲉⲧⲣ̄ⲡ|ⲥⲧⲉⲩⲉ|ⲉ ⲍ̄ⲛ̄ ⲛ̄ⲫ|ⲗⲟ-
        ⲥⲟⲫⲟⲥ ⲉⲧⲛ̄ⲛ|ⲙⲁ |
ⲁⲗⲗⲁ ϥ̄ⲛⲁⲧⲱⲱⲛ   10
ⲁⲣⲱ ⲡⲫ|ⲗⲟ|ⲥⲟⲫⲟⲥ ⲉⲧⲛ̄ⲛ|ⲙⲁ ⲙ̄ⲡⲱⲣ ⲁ-
        ⲧⲣⲉϥ|ⲡ|ⲥⲧⲉⲩⲉ ⲟⲩⲣⲉϥⲕⲧⲟ ⲙ̄ⲙⲁϥ
        ⲟⲩ|[ⲁ]ⲉⲉⲧϥ
ⲁⲣⲱ ⲉⲧⲃⲉ ⲧⲛⲡ|ⲥⲧ|ⲥ ⟨---⟩ |
[ⲁ]ⲍ̄ⲛ̄ⲥⲟⲩⲛ̄ ⲡϣⲏⲣⲉ ⲛ̄ⲅⲁⲣ ⲙ̄‖ⲡⲣⲱⲙⲉ   15
80 ⲁⲣⲱ ⲁⲍⲛ̄ⲡ|ⲥⲧⲉⲩⲉ |
ϫⲉ ⲁϥⲧⲱⲟⲩⲛ ⲁⲃⲁⲗ ⲍ̄ⲛ̄ ⲛⲉⲧ|ⲙⲁⲟⲩⲧ
ⲁⲣⲱ ⲡⲉⲉ| ⲡⲉⲧⲛ̄ϫⲟⲩ | ⲙ̄ⲙⲁϥ
83 ϫⲉ ⲁϥϣⲱⲡⲉ ⲛ̄ⲃⲱⲗ | ⲁⲃⲁⲗ ⲙ̄ⲡⲙⲟⲩ

---

70 i.e. ⲉⲛϥ ... ⲉⲛ.   73 ⲡ̄ⲣ̄: litt. rho imper-
fecta.   74 ⲙⲁⲟⲩⲧ: ⲁ corr. ex [[ⲟ]].   76-77
ⲁⲗⲗⲁ ... ⲁⲣⲱ: ⲁⲣⲱ ... ⲁⲗⲗⲁ coni. Barns.
77 lege ⲁⲩⲣⲉϥⲕⲧⲟ (Polotsky).   78 loc. corruptus.

On Resurrection §§ 69 - 83

46:3
[69]Now if there is anyone who is not a believer, he cannot be convinced. [72]For it is the domain of faith, my child, and not that of argumentation, to assert that [74]the dead will arise.

46:8
[75]And suppose that amongst the scholars here, there is one who believes? [76]Why then, he will arise. [77]And as for the scholar here, let him not trust in one who has caused his own conversion to faith. And because of our faith.[a]

46:14
[79]For we are personally acquainted with the son of man, and have come to believe that He arose from the dead. [82]And He is the one of whom we say: He became death's undoing.

---

[a]An incomplete sentence. Some words must have been accidentally omitted.

---

[69]If there is anyone δέ [70]who does not πιστεύειν, [71]he does not have the πείθεσθαι/πείθειν.[x] [72]For (γάρ) it is the τόπος of the πίστις, my son, [73]and not that of the πείθεσθαι/πείθειν,[x] [74]he who/that which is dead will arise. [75]And is there/there is[y] one who πιστεύειν in the φιλόσοφοι that are here? [76]άλλά he will arise. [77]And the φιλόσοφος that is here let him not πιστεύειν in one who turns himself. [78]And ‹...› because/for the sake of our πίστις. [79]For (γάρ) we have become acquainted with the son of the man, [80]and we have πιστεύειν [81]that he arose out of those who/that are dead. [82]And he is the one about whom we say: [83]he became (the) dissolution of the death.

---

[x]The active and middle-passive of this verb are indistinguishable in the Coptic.

[y]Here, as also in many Greek sentences, there is no formal indication of whether the sentence is affirmative or interrogative.

84	ⲍⲱⲥ ⲟⲩⲛⲁϭ ‖ ⲡⲉ ⲡⲉⲧⲟⲩⲣ̄ⲡ︦|ⲥⲧⲉⲩⲉ ⲁⲣⲁϥ̂ 46 20
85	ⲍⲛ̄|ⲛⲁⲧ ⲛⲉ ⲛⲉⲧⲣ̄ⲡ︦)ⲥⲧⲉⲩⲉ
	ⲛ̄ϥ︦ⲛⲁ|ⲧⲉⲕⲟ ⲉⲛ ⲛ̄ϭⲓ ⲡⲙⲉⲩⲉ ⲛ̄ⲛⲉ|ⲧⲟⲩⲁⲭ
	ⲛ̄ϥ︦ⲛⲁⲧⲉⲕⲟ ⲉⲛ ⲛ̄ϭⲓ	ⲡⲛⲟⲩⲥ ⲛ̄ⲛⲉⲧⲁⲍⲥⲟⲩ-
	ⲱⲱⲛ̄ϥ̄ ‖
	ⲉⲧⲃⲉ ⲡⲉⲉⲓ ⲧⲛ̄ⲥⲁⲡ ⲁⲍⲟⲩⲛ	ⲁⲡⲟⲩⲭⲉ- 25
	ⲉ̄ⲓ ⲙ̄ⲛ ⲡⲥⲱⲧⲉ
	ⲉ|ⲁⲍⲟⲩⲧⲁϣ︦ⲛ ⲭⲓⲛ ⲛ̄ϣⲁⲣⲡ︦	ⲁⲧⲣ̄ⲛ̄ⲧⲙ̄-
	ⲍⲁⲉⲓⲉ ⲍⲛ̄ ⲧⲙ̄ⲛⲧ|ⲁⲑⲏⲧ ⲛ̄ⲛⲉⲧⲟⲉⲓ
	ⲛ̄ⲁⲧⲥⲁⲩⲛⲉ ‖
90	ⲁⲗⲗⲁ ⲉⲛⲁⲉⲓ ⲁⲍⲟⲩⲛ ⲁⲧⲙ̄ⲛⲧ|ⲣⲙ̄ⲍⲏⲧ 30
	ⲛ̄ⲛⲉⲧⲁⲍⲥⲟⲩⲱⲛ ⲧ|ⲙⲏⲉ
	ⲧⲙⲏⲉ ϭⲉ ⲉⲧⲟⲩⲣⲁⲉ̄ⲥ ⲁ̄ⲣⲁⲥ
	ⲙ̄ⲛ ϣϭⲁⲙ ⲛ̄ⲕⲁⲁⲥ ⲁ̄ⲃⲁⲗ
	ⲟⲩⲧⲉ ⲛⲉⲥϣⲱⲡⲉ
	ⲟⲩ‖ⲭⲱⲣⲉ ⲡⲉ ⟨ⲡ⟩ⲥⲩⲥⲧⲏⲙⲁ ⲙ̄ⲡ|ⲡⲗⲏ- 35
	ⲣⲱⲙⲁ
95	ⲟⲩⲕⲟⲩⲉⲓ ⲡⲉ ⲡⲉⲛ|ⲧⲁⲍⲃⲱⲗ ⲁⲃⲁⲗ
	ⲁϥϣⲱⲡⲉ	ⲙ̂ⲕⲟⲥⲙⲟⲥ
97	ⲡⲧⲏⲣ︦ϥ ⲛ̄ⲇⲉ ⲡⲉ	ⲡⲉⲧⲟⲩⲉⲙⲁⲥⲧⲉ
	ⲙ̂ⲙⲁϥ

---

84 ⲡⲉⲡⲉⲧ post corr.: ⲡ² add. librarius.
85 ⲍⲛ̄ⲛⲁⲧ⟨ⲙⲟⲩ⟩ coni. edd. pr.   91 ϭⲉ:
ϭ corr. ex ⟦ⲧ⟧.   94 ⟨ⲡ⟩ edd. pr.   96 i.e.
ⲛ̄ⲕⲟⲥⲙⲟⲥ.

On Resurrection §§ 84 - 97

46:19 [84]Even as the object of belief is great, great too are the believers: [86]the thought of those who are saved will not perish, [87]the mind of those who have personal acquaintance with such an object will not perish. [88]Thus: we are chosen for salvation and ransom, [89]having been set apart from the beginning, so that we might not stumble in the folly of the ignorant, [90]but might enter[a] into the wisdom of those who are personally acquainted with the truth.

46:32 [91]Indeed that truth, to which they are wakeful, cannot be brought to naught; [93]and it will not.[b] [94]The structure of the Fulness is mighty. [95]That which broke loose[c] and became the universe is trifling. [97]But what is held fast is the Entirety:

---

[a]or: ignorant. Rather, we shall enter.
[b]or: nor does it partake of coming-into-being.
[c]or: perished.

---

[84]ὡς great is he who/that which πιστεύεσθαι (=is believed in), [85]great are those who/the things that πιστεύειν. [86]The thinking of those who/the things that are saved will not perish. [87]The νοῦς of those who/the things that have known it/him will not perish. [88]Because of/for the sake of this/him, we are chosen into the salvation and the ransom, [89]having been set apart since the first, so as not to fall in(to) the mindlessness of those who/the things that lack knowledge (=personal acquaintance), [90]ἀλλά that we might go into the intelligence[x] of those who/the things that have become acquainted with the truth. [91]The truth, then, towards which they are wakeful [92]cannot be dissolved/let go of. [93]οὐδέ it will not happen.[y] [94]The σύστημα of the πλήρωμα is strong. [95]That which came loose/perished [96]and became (a) κόσμος is trifling. [97]It is the all δέ that is held.

---

[x]or: ἀλλά it is into the intelligence . . . that we shall go.
[y]or: it does not come into being.

98 ⲙ̅ⲡⲉϥ*ϣⲱⲡⲉ   *47
   ⲛⲉϥϣⲟⲟⲡ ⲡⲉ
100 ϩⲱⲥⲧⲉ ⲙ̅ⲡⲱⲣ ⲁⲣⲇⲓⲥⲧⲁⲍⲉ ⲉⲧⲃⲉ |
    ⲧⲁⲛⲁⲥⲧⲁⲥⲓⲥ ⲡⲁϣⲏⲣⲉ ⲣⲏⲅⲓⲛⲉ |
    ⲉⲓϣⲡⲉ ⲛⲉⲕϣⲟⲟⲡ ⲛ̅ⲅⲁⲣ ⲉⲛ ‖ ϩⲛ ⲥⲁⲣⲝ̅   5
    ⲁⲕϫⲓ ⲥⲁⲣⲝ̅
    ⲛ̅ⲧⲁⲣⲉⲕ|ⲉⲓ ⲁϩⲟⲩⲛ ⲁⲡⲓⲕⲟⲥⲙⲟⲥ
    ⲉⲧⲃⲉ | ⲉⲩ ⲛ̅ⲕⲛⲁϫⲓ ⲉⲛ ⲛ̅ⲧⲥⲁⲣⲝ̅
105 ⲉⲕϣⲁⲛ|ⲃⲱⲕ ⲁϩⲣⲏ̈ⲓ ⲁϩⲟⲩⲛ ⲁⲡⲁ|ⲓⲱⲛ |
    ⲡⲉⲧⲥⲁⲧⲡ̅ ⲁⲧⲥⲁⲣⲝ̅ ⲡⲉⲧϣⲟ‖ⲟⲡ ⲛⲉⲥ   10
    ⲛ̅ⲁⲓⲧⲓⲟⲥ ⲙ̅ⲡⲱⲛϩ̅ |
    ⲡⲉⲧϣⲱⲡⲉ ⲉⲧⲃⲏⲧⲕ̅ ⲙⲏ ⲙ̅|ⲡⲱⲕ ⲉⲛ ⲡⲉ
    ⲡⲉⲧⲉ ⲡⲱⲕ ⲡⲉ | ⲙⲏ ⲛ̅ϥϣⲟⲟⲡ ⲉⲛ
    ⲛ̅ⲙ̅ⲙⲉⲕ |
    ⲁⲗⲗⲁ ⲉⲕⲛ̅ⲛⲓ|ⲙⲁ
110 ⲉⲩ ⲡⲉ ⲉⲧⲕ‖ϣⲁⲁⲧ ⲙ̅ⲙⲁⲩ   15
    ⲡⲉⲉⲓ ⲡⲉ
    ⲛ̅ⲧⲁ|ⲕⲣⲥⲡⲟⲩⲇⲁⲍⲉ ⲁⲥⲃⲟ ⲁⲣⲁⲩ |
    ⲡⲭⲟⲣⲓ|ⲟⲛ ⲙ̅ⲡⲥⲱⲙⲁ
    ⲉⲧⲉ ⲡⲉⲉⲓ ⲡⲉ ⲧⲙ̅ⲛ̅ⲧϩⲗ̅ⲗⲟ
114 ⲁⲩⲱ ⲕ|ϣⲟⲟⲡ ⲛ̅ⲧⲉⲕⲟ

---

108 possis et ⲛ̅ⲙ̅ⲙⲉⲓ uel ⲛ̅ⲙ̅ⲙⲉⲛ.   114 ⲕ-
ϣⲟⲟⲡ: ⲕ corr. ex ⟦ⲛ̅⟧.

On Resurrection §§ 98 - 114

47:1 ^{98}it did not come into being; ^{99}it simply was. ^{100}So do not be doubtful about resurrection, my child Rheginus. ^{101}Now (you might wrongly suppose) granted you did not preexist in flesh -- indeed, you took on flesh when you entered this world -- ^{104}why will you not take your flesh with you when you return to the realm of eternity? ^{106}It is the element superior to the flesh that imparts vitality to it; (furthermore, you might suppose) does not whatever comes into being for your sake (viz. the flesh) belong to you? ^{108}So may we not conclude that whatever is yours will coexist with you?

47:14 ^{109}Nay rather while you are here, what is it that you are alienated from? ^{111}Is this what you have endeavored to learn about: the bodily envelope?^{a} i.e., old age? ^{114}And are you -- the real you -- mere corruption?

---

^{a}Possibly a phrase has dropped out after this word.

---

^{98}It did not become. ^{99}It existed.

^{100}ὥστε do not διστάζειν about the ἀνάστασις, my son 'Ρήγινε. ^{101}Now (γάρ) since/if you did not exist in σάρξ -- ^{102}you took σάρξ ^{103}when you came into this κόσμος -- ^{104}why will you not take the σάρξ ^{105}when/if you go back into the αἰών? ^{106}It is that which/he who is superior to the σάρξ that exists for it (σάρξ) as (an) αἴτιος of the life. ^{107}That which comes into being for your sake, μή is it not yours? ^{108}That which is yours, μή does it not exist with you? ^{109}ἀλλά you being here, ^{110}what is it that you are cut off from? ^{111}Is it/it is this^{x} ^{112}that you have σπουδάζειν to learn about, the χόριον of the σῶμα? ^{113}That is, the old age?^{x} ^{114}And do you exist/you exist^{x} as corruption?

---

^{x}Here, as also in many Greek sentences, there is no formal indication of whether the sentence is affirmative or interrogative.

115 ογντεκ ⲙ‖ⲙⲉⲩ ⲛ̄ⲧⲁⲡⲟⲩⲥⲓⲁ ⲛ̄ⲟⲩⲍ̅ⲏⲩ | ²⁰
ⲛ̄ⲕⲛⲁ† ⲛ̄ⲅⲁⲣ ⲉⲛ ⲙ̄ⲡⲉⲧ|ⲥⲁⲧⲡ
ⲉⲕϣⲁⲛⲃⲱⲕ·
ⲡⲉⲑⲁⲩ | ογντⲉⲩ ⲙ̄ⲙⲉⲩ ⲙ̄ⲡϭⲱϫⲃ̅ |
ⲁⲗⲗⲁ ογⲛ ⲍⲙⲁⲧ ⲁⲣⲁⲩ

120 ⲙ̄ⲛ ⲗⲁ‖ⲁⲧⲉ ϭⲉ ⲥⲱⲧ ⲙ̄ⲙⲁⲛ ⲁⲃⲁⲗ | ²⁵
ⲛ̄ⲛ|ⲙⲁ
ⲁⲗⲗⲁ ⲡⲧⲏⲣ̅ϥ̅ ⲉⲧⲉ ⲁ|ⲛⲁⲛ ⲡⲉ
ⲧ̄ⲛⲟⲩⲁϫ
ⲁⲍ̄ⲛⲁ̄ⲓ | ⲙ̄ⲡⲟⲩϫⲉⲉⲓ ϫⲓ̄ⲛ ⲣⲁⲣⲏ̄ϫ̄ϥ | ⲍⲁ
ⲑⲁⲏ
ⲙⲁⲣⲛ̄ⲙⲉⲩⲉ ⲛ†ⲍⲉ‖ⲉⲥ ³⁰

125 ⲙⲁⲣⲛ̄ⲁϫⲓ ⲛ̄†ⲍⲉⲉⲥ
ⲁⲗⲗⲁ | ογⲛ ⲍⲁⲉⲓⲛⲉ ογⲱϣⲉ ⲁⲙ̄|ⲙⲉ
ⲛ̄ⲁⲍⲣⲉ ⲡϣⲓⲛⲉ ⲉⲧⲃⲉ | ⲛⲉⲧογϣⲓⲛⲉ
ⲉⲧⲃⲏⲧⲟⲩ
ⲉⲓⲱ|ⲡⲉ ⲡⲉⲧⲟⲩⲁϫ ⲉⲩϣⲁⲛⲕⲱ‖ⲉ ⲛ̄ⲥⲱⲩ ³⁵
ⲙ̄ⲡⲉⲩⲥⲱⲙⲁ
ⲉⲩⲛⲁ|ⲟⲩϫⲉⲉⲓ ⲛ̄ⲧⲟⲩⲛⲟⲩ
ⲙ̄ⲡⲣⲧⲣⲉ | ⲗⲁⲩⲉ ⲣ̄ⲁⲓ|ⲥⲧⲁⲍⲉ ⲉⲧⲃⲉ
ⲡⲉⲉⲓ |

130 ⲛ̄ⲛⲉⲥ ⲛ̄ⲍⲉ ϭⲉ ⲛ̄ⲙⲉⲗⲟⲥ ⲉⲧⲟⲩ|ⲁⲁⲛ̄ⲍ̄
ⲁⲃⲁⲗ ⲉⲧⲙⲁⲟⲩⲧ ⲛ̄ⲥⲉ*ⲛⲁⲟⲩϫⲉⲉⲓ ⲉⲛ *48

131 ϫⲉ ⲛ̄ⲙⲉⲗ[ⲟ]ⲥ ⲉ|ⲧⲁⲁⲛ̄ⲍ̄ ⲉⲧϣⲟⲟⲡ ⲛ̄ⲍⲣⲏ̈
ⲛ̄|ⲍⲏⲧⲟⲩ ⲛⲉⲩⲛⲁⲧⲱⲟⲩⲛ ⲡⲉ·

---

119 ⲁⲣⲁⲩ: ⲣ corr. ex [ϥ]. 123 i.e. ? ⲣⲁ ⲁⲣⲏ-
ϫ̄ϥ. ⲍⲁ: sahid. ϣⲁ. 127 ⟨ϫⲉ⟩
ⲉⲓϣⲡⲉ edd. pr., fort. recte. 128 ⲉⲩⲛⲁ:
ⲉ supra uersum add. 131 rest. edd. pr. ues-
tig. litt. ⲙⲉⲩⲉ non conuenit.

On Resurrection §§ 115 - 131

47:19   [115]You can count absence -- or in another sense of
that word, deficit[a] -- as your profit. [116]For you will
not pay back the superior element when you depart.
[118]The inferior element takes a loss; but what it owes
is gratitude. [120]Nothing then buys us back, or ransoms
us, while we are here; yet the Entirety, and we as
members of it, are saved. [123]We have had salvation
from start to finish. [124]Let us think in this way.
[125]Let us accept in this way.

47:30   [126]However, certain persons desire to know -- in
the investigation of their investigations -- whether
one who is saved will, upon taking off his body, be
immediately saved: [129]let no one doubt this!

47:38   [130]"Surely, then" (so might run the argument) "the
dead, visible members will be preserved: [131]for the
living, interior members are supposed to arise."

---

[a]absence . . . deficit, two meanings of the Greek word
apousia.

---

[115]You have the ἀπουσία as a profit. [116]For (γάρ) you will not
give (back) what/him who is superior/choice [117]when/if you go.
[118]What/he who is worst/bad has the diminution. [119]ἀλλά it owes
thanks/grace/gifts. [120]Nothing/no one then buys us back from
here/here. [121]ἀλλά the all, which is us, [122]are saved. [123]We
have gotten the salvation from limit to end. [124]Let us think in
this manner. [125]Let us accept in this manner. [126]ἀλλά some wish
to know, in the investigation of the things that they are investi-
gating, [127]whether he who/that which is saved, if he/it lays
aside his/its σῶμα, [128]will immediately be saved. [129]Let no one
διστάζειν about this. [130]How can it be, then, that the visible,
dead μέλη will not be saved? [131]For the living μέλη that exist in
them would arise.

48:3-28

132 ⲉⲩ | ϭⲉ ⲧⲉ ⲧⲁⲛⲁⲥⲧⲁⲥⲓⲥ
ⲡϭⲱⲗⲡ̄ ‖ ⲁⲃⲁⲗ ⲡⲉ ⲛ̄ⲟⲩⲁⲉⲓϣ ⲛ|ⲙ ⲛ̄|ⲛⲉ- 48⁵
ⲧⲁⲍⲧⲱⲟⲩⲛ
ⲉ|ϣⲡⲉ ⲁⲕⲣ̄|ⲡⲙⲉⲩⲉ ⲛ̄ⲅⲁⲣ

135 ⲉⲕⲱϣ ⲍ̄ⲙ̄ ⲡⲉⲩ|ⲁⲅⲅⲉⲗ|ⲟⲛ
ⲭⲉ ⲁⲍⲏⲗⲉ|ⲁⲥ ⲟⲩ|ⲱⲛ̄ⲍ̄ ⲁⲃⲁⲗ ⲁⲣⲱ
ⲙⲱⲣⲥⲏⲥ ‖ ⲛ̄ⲙ̄ⲙⲉϥ 10
ⲙ̄ⲡⲱⲣ ⲁⲙⲉⲩⲉ ⲁⲧⲁ|ⲛⲁⲥⲧⲁⲥⲓⲥ
ⲭⲉ ⲟⲩⲫⲁⲛⲧⲁⲥⲓⲁ | ⲧⲉ
ⲟⲩⲫⲁⲛⲧⲁⲥⲓⲁ ⲉⲛ ⲧⲉ

140 ⲁⲗⲗⲁ | [ⲟ]ⲩⲙⲏⲉ ⲧⲉ
ⲛ̄ⲍⲟⲩⲟ ⲛ̄ⲇⲉ ⲟⲩ|ⲡⲉⲧⲉⲥϣⲉ ⲡⲉ ⲁⲭⲟⲟⲥ
ⲭⲉ ⲟⲩ‖ⲫⲁⲛⲧⲁⲥⲓⲁ ⲡⲉ ⲡⲕⲟⲥⲙⲟⲥ | ⲛ̄- 15
ⲍⲟⲩⲟ ⲁⲧⲁⲛⲁⲥⲧⲁⲥⲓⲥ
ⲧⲉⲉⲓ | ⲉⲛⲧⲁⲥϣⲱⲡⲉ ⲁⲃⲁⲗ ⲍⲓ|ⲧⲟ|ⲟⲧϥ̄
ⲙ̄ⲡⲉⲛⲭⲁⲉⲓⲥ ⲡⲥⲱ|ⲧⲏⲣ ⲓⲏ̄ⲥ ⲡⲉⲭⲣⲏⲥⲧⲟⲥ
ⲉⲧ‖ⲃⲉ ⲉⲩ ⲛ̄ⲇⲉ ⲉⲉⲓ|ⲧⲁⲙⲟ ⲙ̄|ⲙⲁⲕ 20

145 ⲛ̄ⲧⲉⲩⲛⲟⲩ ⲛⲉⲧⲁ|ⲁⲛ̄ⲍ̄ ⲥⲉⲛⲁⲙⲟⲩ
ⲡⲱⲥ | ⲉⲩⲁⲛ̄ⲍ̄ ⲍⲛ̄ ⲟⲩⲫⲁⲛⲧⲁ|ⲥⲓⲁ
ⲛ̄ⲣⲙ̄ⲙⲁⲉⲓ ⲁⲩⲣ̄ⲍⲏ‖ⲕⲉ 25
ⲁⲩⲱ ⲛⲛ̄ⲣ̄ⲙⲁⲉⲓ ⲁⲩⲱⲣ̄|ϣⲱⲣⲟⲩ
ⲡⲧⲏⲣϥ̄ ϣⲁⲣⲉⲃ‖ϣ̄ⲃⲉⲓⲉ

150 ⲟⲩⲫⲁⲛⲧⲁⲥⲓⲁ | ⲡⲉ ⲡⲕⲟⲥⲙⲟⲥ

148 ⲛⲛ̄ⲣ̄ⲙⲁⲉⲓ i.e. sahid. ⲛ̄ⲣ̄ⲣⲱⲟⲩ.

On Resurrection §§ 132 - 150

[132]But what is resurrection? It is the uncovering at any given time[a] of the elements that have "arisen."

48:6   [134]Now if you should recall having read in the Gospel[b] [136]that Elias appeared -- and Moses -- in His (Jesus') company, [137]do not suppose that resurrection is an apparition. [139]It is not an apparition; rather it is something real. [141]Instead, one ought to maintain that the world is an apparition, rather than resurrection,[c] which became possible through our Lord, the Savior, Jesus the Excellent.

48:19   [144]And what am I telling you? [145]Suddenly the living are dying ([146]surely they are not alive at all in this world of apparition!), [147]the rich have become poor, rulers overthrown: [149]all changes, the world is an apparition.

---

[a]or (quite differently): for all time.
[b]Mt 17:3, Mk 9:4, Lk 9:30.
[c]i.e. the world, rather than resurrection, is an apparition.

---

[132]What then is the ἀνάστασις? [133]It is the uncovering/ revealing at any given time/for all time of the things that/ those who have arisen. [134]For (γάρ) if/since you have remembered, [135]reading in the εὐαγγέλιον, [136]that Ἠλίας appeared, and Μωυσῆς, together with him, [137]do not think concerning the ἀνάστασις, [138]that it is a φαντασία. [139]It is not a φαντασία, [140]ἀλλά it is true/a truth. [141]Rather δέ it is necessary to say [142]that the κόσμος is a φαντασία, rather than the ἀνάστασις, [143]which came into being/came to pass through our lord, the σωτήρ, Ἰησοῦς, the χρηστός. [144]About what δέ am I informing you? [145]Suddenly/ immediately those who/the things that are alive are dying/will die. [146]πῶς are they alive in a φαντασία? [147]The rich have become poor [148]and the kings have been overthrown. [149]The all is wont to change. [150]The κόσμος is a φαντασία.

151 ⲝⲉⲕⲁⲥⲉ | ϭⲉ ⲛⲓⲣ̄ⲕⲁⲧⲁⲗⲁⲗⲉⲓ ⲥⲁⲛ‖ⲍ̄ⲃⲏ-   30
    ⲣⲉ ⲁⲡⲉⲅⲟⲩⲟ
    ⲁⲗⲗⲁ | ⲧⲁⲛⲁⲥⲧⲁⲥⲓⲥ ⲙ̄ⲛⲧⲉⲥ ⲙ̄ⲙⲉⲩ |
    ⲙ̄ⲡⲓⲥⲙⲁⲧ ⲛ̄ϯⲙⲓⲛⲉ
    ⲝⲉ | ⲧⲙⲏⲉ ⲧⲉ {ⲡⲉ}
    ⲡⲉⲧⲁⲍⲉ ⲁⲣⲉⲧϥ̄ ⟨ⲡⲉ⟩ |
155 ⲁⲩⲱ ⲡⲟⲩⲱⲛ̄ⲍ̄ ⲁⲃⲁⲗ ⲙ̄ⲡⲉ‖ⲧϣⲟⲟⲡ ⲡⲉ   35
    ⲁⲩⲱ ⲡⲩϣⲃⲉ‖ⲉ ⲡⲉ ⲛ̄ⲛⲍ̄ⲃⲏⲣⲉ ⲁⲩⲱ ⲟⲩ|ⲙⲉ-
    ⲧⲁⲃⲟⲗⲏ ⲁⲍⲟⲩⲛ ⲁⲩⲙ̄ⲛⲧ|ⲃ̄ⲣ̄ⲣⲉ
    ⲧⲙ̄ⲛⲧⲁⲧⲧⲉⲕⲟ ⲛ̄ⲅⲁⲣ * ⸢ⲥⲍⲉϯⲉ⸣ ⟦ⲁⲍⲣⲏⲓ̈⟧   *49
    ⲁⲡⲓⲧⲛ̄ ⲁⲭ̄ⲙ̄ | ⲡⲧⲉⲕⲟ
    ⲁⲩⲱ ⲡⲟⲩⲁⲉⲓⲛ ϥⲍⲉ|ϯⲉ ⲁⲡⲓⲧⲛ̄ ⲁⲭ̄ⲙ̄
    ⲡⲕⲉⲕⲉⲓ
    ⲉϥϣⲱⲙⲛ̄ⲕ ⲙ̄ⲙⲁϥ
160 ⲁⲩⲱ ⲡⲡⲗⲏ‖ⲣⲱⲙⲁ ϥϫ̄ⲱⲕ ⲁⲃⲁⲗ ⲙ̄ⲡⲉ-   5
    ϣ|ⲧⲁ
    ⲛⲉⲉⲓ ⲛⲉ ⲛ̄ⲥⲩⲙⲃⲟⲗⲟⲛ ⲙⲛ | ⲛ̄ⲧⲁⲛⲧⲛ̄ ⲛ̄-
    ⲧⲁⲛⲁⲥⲧⲁⲥⲓⲥ · |
    ⲛ̄ⲧⲁϥ ⲡⲉ ⲉⲧⲧⲁⲙⲓⲟ ⲙ̄ⲡⲡⲉ|ⲧⲛⲁⲛⲟⲩϥ
    ⲍⲱⲥⲧⲉ ⲙ̄ⲡⲱⲣ ⲁ‖ⲣ̄ⲛⲟⲉⲓ ⲙⲉⲣⲓⲕⲱⲥ ⲱ   10
    ⲣⲏⲅⲓ|ⲛⲉ
    ⲟⲩⲧⲉ ⲙ̄ⲡⲣ̄ⲣ̄ⲡⲟⲗⲓⲧⲉⲩⲉ|ⲥⲑⲁⲓ ⲕⲁⲧⲁ
    ⲧⲉⲉⲓⲥⲁⲣⲝ ⲉⲧⲃⲉ | ⲧⲙ̄ⲛⲧⲟⲩⲉⲓ
165 ⲁⲗⲗⲁ ⲁⲙⲟⲩ ⲁ|ⲃⲁⲗ ⲍ̄ⲛ ⲛ̄ⲙⲉⲣⲓⲥⲙⲟⲥ
    ⲙⲛ ⲛ̄|ⲙ̄ⲣ̄ⲣⲉ   15
166 ⲁⲩⲱ ⲏⲇⲏ ⲟⲩⲛⲧⲉⲕ ⲙ̄|ⲙⲉⲩ ⲛ̄ⲧⲁⲛⲁⲥⲧⲁⲥⲓⲥ

153-154 {ⲡⲉ} ... ⟨ⲡⲉ⟩ edd. pr.   157 rest.
edd. pr.   ⟦ⲁⲍⲣⲏⲓ̈⟧ litt. expunctae.   ⲁⲭ̄ⲙ̄
i.e. ⲁⲭ̄ⲙ̄.

On Resurrection §§ 151 - 166

48:28 ^{151}But let me not deprecate the circumstances of
this world at too great a length. ^{152}Simply: resurrection is not of this sort, ^{153}for it is real.

48:33 ^{154}It is what is constant:

And the revealing of what truly exists.

^{156}And it is what one receives in exchange for the
circumstances of this world:

And a migration into newness.

^{157}For incorruption [is streaming] down upon
corruption:

And light is streaming down upon darkness,
swallowing it.

^{160}And the Fulness is filling up its lack:
(^{161}these are the symbols and the likenesses of
resurrection;)

^{162}This is what brings about goodness.

49:9 ^{163}Therefore do not concentrate on particulars, o
Rheginus, nor live according to the dictates of this
flesh; do not, for the sake of oneness. ^{165}Rather,
leave the state of dispersion and bondage, ^{166}and then
you already have resurrection.

---

^{151}So that, then, I might not καταλαλεῖν against the things too
much. ^{152}ἀλλά the ἀνάστασις does not have such a quality. ^{153}For
it is the truth/the true. ^{154}It is what/he who stands. ^{155}And
it is the revealing of that which/he who exists. ^{156}And it is
the requital for the things and a μεταβολή into a newness. ^{157}For
(γάρ) the incorruption [is flowing] down upon the corruption.
^{158}And the light is flowing down upon the darkness, ^{159}swallowing
it. ^{160}And the πλήρωμα is filling up the lack. ^{161}These are the
σύμβολα and the resemblances of the ἀνάστασις. ^{162}It is that
which/he that creates the good. ^{163}ὥστε do not νοεῖν μερικῶς, ὦ
'Ρήγινε, ^{164}μήτε do not πολιτεύεσθαι κατά this σάρξ, for the sake/
because of the one-ness. ^{165}ἀλλά come out of the μερισμοί and
the bonds, ^{166}and ἤδη you have the ἀνάστασις.

167 ⲉⲓϣ|ⲡⲉ ⲡⲉⲧⲛⲁⲙⲟⲩ ⲛ̄ⲅⲁⲣ ⲏ̄ϥⲥⲁⲩ|ⲛⲉ ⲁⲣⲁϥ
    ⲟⲩⲁⲉⲉⲧϥ
    ϫⲉ ⲉϥ|ⲛⲁⲙⲟⲩ
    ⲕⲁⲛ ⲉϥϣⲁⲛⲣ̄ϩⲁϩ ‖ ⲛ̄ⲣⲁⲙⲡⲉ ϩ̄ⲙ ⲡⲉⲉⲓ-   20
    Ⲃⲓⲟⲥ
170 ⲥⲉ|ⲉⲓⲛⲉ ⲙ̄ⲙⲁϥ ⲁϩⲟⲩⲛ ⲁⲡⲉⲉⲓ |
    ⲉⲧⲃⲉ ⲉⲩ ⲛ̄ⲧⲁⲕ ⲛ̄ⲕⲛⲉⲩ ⲁⲣⲁⲕ | ⲉⲛ ⲟⲩⲁ-
    ⲉⲉⲧ̄ⲕ
    ⲉⲁⲕⲧⲱⲟⲩⲛ
    ⲁⲩ|ⲱ ⲥⲉⲉ|ⲓⲛⲉ ⲙ̄ⲙⲁⲕ ⲁϩⲟⲩⲛ ⲁⲡⲉ‖ⲉⲓ   25
    ⲉⲓϣⲡⲉ ⲟⲩⲛⲧⲉⲕ ⲙ̄ⲙⲉⲩ ⲙ̄|ⲡⲧⲱⲟⲩⲛ
175 ⲁⲗⲗⲁ ⲕϭⲉⲉⲧ
    ϩⲱⲥ | ⲉⲕⲛⲁⲙⲟⲩ
    ⲕⲁⲓⲧⲟⲓⲅⲉ ⲡⲏ ⲏ̄ϥⲥⲁⲩ|ⲛⲉ
    ϫⲉ ⲁϥⲙⲟⲩ
    ⲉⲧⲃⲉ ⲉⲩ ϭⲉ | ϯⲕⲱϩ ⲁⲃⲁⲗ ⲛ̄ⲥⲁ ⲧⲉⲕ-
    ⲙ̄ⲛⲧ‖ⲁⲧⲣ̄ⲅⲩⲙⲛⲁϩⲉ   30
180 ⲥⲱϩ ⲁⲡⲟⲩ|ⲉⲉⲓ ⲡⲟⲩⲉⲉⲓ ⲁⲧⲣⲉϥⲣ̄ⲁⲥⲕⲉⲓ |
    ⲛ̄ⲟⲩⲁⲡ̄ⲥ ⲛ̄ϩⲉⲉⲥ
    ⲁⲣⲱ ⲛ̄ⲥⲉ|Ⲃⲁⲗⲏ̄ϥ ⲁⲃⲁⲗ ⲙ̄ⲡⲓⲥⲧⲟⲓⲭⲉⲓⲟⲛ |
    ϫⲉⲕⲁⲥⲉ ⲛϥⲣ̄ⲡⲗⲁⲛⲁ
    ⲁⲗⲗⲁ ⲉϥ‖ⲛⲁϫⲓ ⲙ̄ⲙⲁϥ ⲟⲩⲁⲉⲉⲧϥ̄ ⲛ̄ⲕⲉ|-   35
    ⲥⲁⲡ ⲡⲉⲉⲓ ⲉⲧⲱⲣⲡ̄ ⲛ̄ϣⲟ|ⲟⲡ
184 ⲛⲉⲉⲓ ⲛ̄ⲧⲁϩⲓ|ϫⲓⲧⲟⲩ ⲁⲃⲁⲗ | ϩⲛ ⲧⲙⲛ̄ⲧ-
    ⲁⲧ̄ⲣ̄ⲫⲑⲟⲛⲉⲓ ⲙ̄ⲡⲁ*ϫⲁⲉⲓⲥ ⲓ̄ⲥ ⲡⲉ-   *50
    ⲭⲣⲏⲥⲧ[ⲟⲥ]

---

172 ⲉⲁⲕ: ⲁ corr. ex ⟦ⲕ⟧.

On Resurrection §§ 167 - 184

[167]For if the dying part (flesh) "knows itself," and knows that since it is moribund it is rushing towards this outcome (death) even if it has lived many years in the present life, [171]why do you (the spirit) not examine your own self and see that you have arisen? [173]And you are rushing towards this outcome (separation from the body) since you possess resurrection.

49:26   [175]Yet you persist as though you were dying, even though it is the former (the moribund flesh) that "knows" it has died. [179]Why then am I so lenient, except because of your inadequate training? [180]Everyone should practice in many ways to gain release from this element (the body), [182]so that he might not wander aimlessly [183]but rather might recover his former state of being.

49:37   [184]What I received through the generosity of my Lord, Jesus the Excellent,

---

[167]For (γάρ) if/since that which/he who is dying/is going to die knows its/his own self, [168](knowing) that, dying, [169]κἄν if it/he lives many years in this βίος, [170]it/he is being carried into this, [171]why do you not look at your own self, [172]that you have arisen? [173]And you are being carried into this, [174]since/ if you have the resurrection. [175]ἀλλά you remain [176]ὡς you are dying/going to die. [177]καίτοιγε that/that man knows [178]that it/he has died. [179]Why then do I forgive, except because of your ἀγυμνασία? [180]It behooves every man to ἀσκεῖν in a multitude of ways, [181]and be set free from this στοιχεῖον, [182]so that he might not πλανᾶν, [183]ἀλλά might take (back) his own self again, which originally existed. [184]These, which I have received from the ἀφθονία of my lord Ἰησοῦς the χρηστός,

185 [ⲁⲍⲓⲧ]ⲥⲉ|ⲃⲁⲕ ⲁⲣⲁⲩ ⲙⲛ ⲛⲉⲕⲥⲛ[ⲏⲩ] ⲛⲁ-
ⲱⲏ|ⲣⲉ
ⲉⲙⲡⲓⲕⲉ ⲗⲁⲣⲉ ⲛⲥⲱⲉⲓ ⲍⲛ | ⲛⲉⲧⲉⲥⲱⲉ
ⲁⲡⲧⲁⲭⲣⲉ ⲧⲏⲩⲧⲛ ‖
ⲉⲓⲱⲡⲉ ⲟⲩⲛ ⲟⲩⲉⲉⲓ ⲛⲇⲉ ⲥⲏⲍ | 5
ⲉϥⲱⲏⲕ ⲍⲛ ⲧⲁⲡⲁⲅⲅⲉⲗⲓⲁ ⲙ|ⲡⲗⲟⲅⲟⲥ
ⲧⲛⲁⲃⲁⲗϥ ⲁⲣⲱⲧⲛ
190 ⲉ|ⲣⲉⲧⲛⲱⲓⲛⲉ
ⲧⲛⲟⲩ ⲛⲇⲉ ⲙ|ⲡⲣⲣⲫⲑⲟⲛⲉⲓ ⲁⲗⲁⲣⲉ ⲉⲧⲏⲡ
ⲁ‖ⲣⲁⲕ   10
ⲉⲩⲛ ϭⲁⲙ ⲙⲙⲁϥ ⲛⲣ̅ⲱ|ⲫⲉⲗⲉⲓ
ⲟⲩⲛ ⲍⲁⲍ ϭⲱϣⲧ ⲁⲍⲟⲩⲛ | ⲁⲡⲉⲉⲓ
ⲡⲉⲉⲓ ⲛⲧⲁⲉⲓⲥⲍⲉⲉⲓ ⲙ|ⲙⲁϥ ⲛⲉⲕ
195 ⲛⲉⲉⲓ ⲧⲁⲙⲟ ⲙⲙⲁⲩ | ⲁⲧⲣⲏⲛⲏ ⲛⲍⲏⲧⲟⲩ
ⲙⲛ ⲧⲉⲭⲁⲣⲓⲥ ‖
ⲧⲱⲓⲛⲉ ⲁⲣⲁⲕ ⲙⲛ ⲛⲉⲧⲙⲁⲉⲓⲉ | ⲙⲙⲱⲧⲛ   15
ⲉⲧⲟⲉⲓ ⲙⲙⲁⲉⲓⲥⲁⲛ |

198   ⲡⲗⲟⲅⲟⲥ ⲉⲧⲃⲉ ⲧⲁ|ⲛⲁⲥⲧⲁⲥⲓⲥ

---

185 ⲁⲍⲓ-: possis et ⲇⲉⲓ-.
187 ⲉⲓⲱⲡⲉ: ⲉ¹ corr. ex ⟦ⲍ⟧.   191 ⲉⲧ: expectauerim
ⲉϥ.   194 ⲛⲧⲁᵘⲉⲓ cod., spatio relicto.   198
(tit.) ⲡ corr. ex ⟦ⲉ⟧.

[185]I have taught to you and your brethren (who are my children) without omitting any of the points necessary to strengthen you. [187]But if anything in my exposition is too profound, I shall explain it to you if you inquire.

50:8   [191]Since this is so, do not hesitate to share with any other members of your circle, for what I have taught you has power to be of benefit. [193]Many people are awaiting what I have written for you: [195]to them I address this lesson, to bring about "peace" among them "and grace." [196]I greet you and whoever, with fraternal love, love you.

TREATISE ON RESURRECTION

---

[185]I have taught to you[x] and your brothers, my children, [186]without having omitted anything among the things that are necessary for strengthening you (plural). [187]If something δέ is written [188]being deep in the ἀπαγγελία of the λόγος, [189]I shall interpret it for you (plural), [190]you (plural) asking. [191]Now δέ do not φθονεῖν any that belong to you (singular), [192]it/he having power to ὠφελεῖν. [193]Many are awaiting this, [194]which I have written for/to you (singular). [195]These I am teaching, for the εἰρήνη among them and the χάρις. [196]I greet you (singular) and those who love you (plural), [197]they being brother-loving.

    [198]The λόγος about the ἀνάστασις.

---

[x]Up to this point in the Treatise the word 'you' is always singular.

II

COMMENTARY

edd. = Malinine et al. (1963).

   * = Hypothetical retroversion from Coptic
      into Greek. E.g., <u>2</u> *πολλὰ *μαθεῖν.

Transliterated Greek (<u>3</u> <u>skopos</u>) or Greek without
an asterisk (<u>21</u> χρῆσθαι) is actually used in the
Coptic text. Ancient Coptic translators treated
such borrowed words as part of their own literary
language: usually it can be assumed that the
same word was taken over from the original Greek
composition. E.g., <u>38</u> χρῆσθαι *τοῖς *πράγμασι:
the verb χρησθαι is used in the Coptic text and
was almost certainly there in the Greek original;
while *τοῖς *πράγμασι has been retranslated by
myself from an equivalent Coptic phrase, and was
probably (but not necessarily) there in Greek.

II

COMMENTARY

(1-14) <u>There are some whose goal is wide learning and
the solution of unsolved problems.</u> Their approach does not
lead to the truth; rather they seek anapausis, intellectual
recreation. We however have gained another kind of anapausis,
true repose, from the Savior. For through Him we gained
acquaintance (gnosis) with the truth.

1 sq. The work begins on a note of rhetorical polemic. <u>There</u>
       <u>are</u> <u>certain</u> <u>persons</u> . . . <u>But</u> <u>I</u> <u>do</u> <u>not</u> <u>think</u> . . .
       This is a customary way of citing and rejecting earlier
       opinions; it is used, e.g., in the scholiastic tradition
       (the two-part formula <u>quidam</u> <u>dicant</u> . . . <u>nescientes</u>
       and Greek equivalents; cf. Ed. Fraenkel, <u>Kl</u>. <u>Beitr</u>.
       II.388). Edd. (M. Malinine et al. <u>De</u> <u>Res</u>. [1963] in
       loc.) aptly note its frequent occurrence in the open-
       ings of Patristic works; cf. Chr. Baur, <u>Initia</u> <u>patr</u>.
       <u>gr</u>. I.254, M. Vattasso, <u>Init</u>. <u>patr</u>. . . . <u>lat</u>. II.494.

1   <u>certain</u> <u>persons</u>] The anonymity of the supposed opponents
       is a part of the rhetorical commonplace, even when their
       identity is specifically known to the author; this pro-
       cedure serves to focus attention upon the author's own
       comments. Cf. Nock, <u>Sallustius</u> p. xxxviii n. 123.
       Thus Athenag. <u>Res</u>. 3, p. 51,30-52,1 Schw.:

            τινας καὶ τῶν ἐπὶ σοφίᾳ θαυμαζομένων, ἰσχυρὰς
            οὐκ οἶδ' ὅπως ἡγησαμένων τὰς παρὰ τῶν πολλῶν
            φερομένας διαπορήσεις.

37

38

(1)   9, p. 57,24f.: τοὺς καταφεύγοντας ἐπὶ τὰ τῶν ἀνθρώπων
ἔργα; 14, p. 65,5 πολλοί; 19, p. 71,25f. 'those who
differ on first principles'. Here the vagueness
expresses disdain.

my child] Or 'son' (Coptic is ambiguous). This is a
conventional mode of address in Eastern didactic literature (Festugière, Révélation d'Hermès I.335f.), including Jewish and Egyptian Greek works, and thus pace edd.
not necessarily the language of 'un fondateur et chef
d'école tel que l'était Valentin'; every teacher of
wisdom likes to think of himself as a potential chef
d'école. But in classical Greek literature, where the
convention is not used, such an expression might mean
something else altogether: Pla. Phdr. 237 B. Its
classical Greek meaning usually is more or less literal.
      Roman introductory treatises are typically
addressed to a son, but to a real one--if not to the
author's own, to that of a friend. Despite this important difference, the Latin tradition and that of Eastern
wisdom show, as a common style feature, the tendency to
repeat the vocative 'o my son', imparting a 'briefähn-
lich' quality (Norden, Hermes 40 [1905] 526 n. 1, on
Cato Ad Marcum filium), and thus invoking the tradition
of the dogmatic epistle. Of course nothing rules out
the possibility that in our text, Rheginos is the
author's actual son; he is certainly a historical
person. But this need not be so. For, as Clement of
Alexandria (Stro. I. 2.1) explains, υἱὸς δὲ πᾶς ὁ
παιδευόμενος καθ᾽ ὑπακοὴν τοῦ παιδεύοντος (he is eluci-
dating, for his puzzled Greek readers, Solomon's use of
υἱέ in Prov. 2.1, 3.1). Similarly he explains the convention in Stro. I. 1.2: ψυχῆς δὲ ἔγγονοι οἱ λόγοι
(Pla. Smp. 209 A-D). αὐτίκα πατέρας τοὺς κατηχήσαντάς
φαμεν. So in Paed. I. 1.1 ὦ παῖδες ὑμεῖς, cf. 4.1.

2   become learned] *πολλὰ *μαθεῖν or the like, answered at
7 by *μέγα *φρονεῖν.

(2)   Breadth of knowledge was an ideal of the fifth-
century Sophists (Gorgias, Hippias: cf. H.-I. Marrou,
Hist. of Educ. 54-56), and this Sophistic ideal became
one essential ingredient of Greek and eventually Roman
rhetorical education (Marrou 208). But the polemic
against it is equally old. Thus Plato (R. 475 DE, Amat.
137 B) distinguishes polymathy and study of the encycli-
cal arts from the task of true philosophy; here he bases
himself on older tradition (Heracl. fr. 40 Diels Fr.
Vorsokr., Democr. frr. 64, 65 Diels Fr. Vorsokr.). In
certain circles the distinction stuck and remained a
perpetual topic of discussion: Clement, who uses both
Platonic passages and Heraclitus, summarizes the matter
as follows (Stro. I. 93.5):

οὐδ' . . . τὴν ἐγκύκλιον παιδείαν συντελεῖν πρὸς
τἀγαθὸν . . . συνεργεῖν δὲ πρὸς τὸ διεγείρειν
καὶ συγγυμνάζειν πρὸς τὰ νοητὰ τὴν ψυχήν.

Thus Porph. Ad Marc. 9 says that apaideusia is the
mother of all passions; education οὐκ ἐθεωρεῖτο in the
acquisition of polymathia but in the relief (apallaksis)
of psychic passions.

        In actual practice the theoretical distinction
became blurred. By Hellenistic times some philosophy
was regularly included in rhetorical training. In
Cicero's day Plato came again to be admired as a writer
as well as thinker (literary references are given by
Nock, Sallustius p. xviii; the quantity and distribution
of papyrus fragments of Plato found in Egypt fully con-
firms this, cf. E. G. Turner, Gk. Papyri 81). And so
from the second century B.C., rhetoric claimed the right
to treat general theses or zêtêmata politika; later,
Philostratus (VS p. 480f.) would look back to distinguish ῥητορικὴ φιλοσοφοῦσα (deriving from Gorgias)
from a more 'historical' rhetoric (Aeschines). Not only
did rhetoric claim to philosophize; intellectuals like
Dio of Prusa, Favorinus and the earlier Carneades were
called 'ones who philosophized with the glory of
sophists', ἐν δόξῃ τοῦ σοφιστεῦσαι, VS p. 486-492.

(<u>2</u>)   On the training and career of these sophists in the
second century A.D., see G. W. Bowersock, <u>Greek</u> <u>Sophists</u>
8-9 et pass. Thus by the time of Platonists such as
Apuleius or Maximus of Tyre, who are roughly contemporary with our author, philosophy and rhetoric have
become truly fused in certain public careers and
intellectual efforts (thus an epitaph at Athens, Kaibel,
<u>Epigr</u>. 106: οὕνεκ' ἦν ῥήτωρ μὲν εἰπεῖν, φιλόσοφος δ' ἃ
χρῆ νοεῖν). A work attributed to Tertullian praises the
<u>style</u> of Valentinus: <u>sperauerat</u> <u>episcopatum</u> <u>Valentinus</u>,
<u>quia</u> <u>et</u> <u>ingenio</u> <u>poterat</u> <u>et</u> <u>eloquio</u> (<u>Adu</u>. <u>Val</u>. IV.1).

It is of interest, then, that our author comes
down hard on the side of an ancient tradition that sus-
pected philosophy for resorting to rhetorical tricks,
'argumentation' (or 'persuasion') as he puts it later
(<u>73</u>), and for its boundless curiosity about side issues
(on the danger of this, cf. Marcus Aurelius III. 12 and
14). The specific reference to <u>unsolved</u> <u>problems</u> at <u>5</u>
means more than just rhetorical themes. Later the
author attacks all 'scholars' (<u>philosophoi</u>) (69-78),
and he finally lumps together μερικῶς νοεῖν (<u>163</u>), perhaps meaning overinterest in specifics (such as the
<u>aporiae</u> which he dogmatically disposes of in the latter
half of the work), and life according to the dictates
of the flesh (<u>164</u>). Like Clement he includes all philosophical traditions under one heading (Clement's
'Greeks'); but although we may detect Platonizing
influence at work in our author's theology, as in
Clement's, his evaluation of the philosophical tradition is opposite to Clement's. Clement holds philosophy
to be a 'useful' propaedeutic, and with his wider historical scope thinks it even 'necessary until the advent
of the Lord' (<u>Stro</u>. I. 28.1); so too, polymathy is said
to be valuable in apologetics, <u>Stro</u>. VI. 65.1. All this
is generally condemned by our author; more specifically
he may also have in mind argumentative works on his
topic like Athenagoras <u>Res</u>., or even more so, Athenagoras' opponents (the τινὲς).

__3__   aim] Copt. has <u>skopos</u> (a usual metaphor for the immediate object of one's efforts; Clem. <u>Paed</u>. II. 83.1
contrasts this with <u>telos</u>, the long-range object).
These investigators have no more than a short-range
goal, <u>polymathia</u>:   ours (cf. below) is the view towards
eternal repose.

__4__   <u>problems</u>] Copt. has <u>zêtêma</u>, the usual term for objects
of philosophical investigation (Plato, Arist.), whence
its frequency in academic book titles. Clem. <u>Stro</u>. V.
5.2 sq., using Arist. <u>Top</u>. 105^{a}3-9, substitutes the
words ζήτησις and ζήτημα for Aristotle's πρόβλημα, θέσις
and ἐρώτημα. The word survives in Modern Gk. to mean
'controversial question', a flavor already obvious in
the koine of the NT. Thus Ps.-Cl. <u>Rec</u>. I.4 will give
'immortality' as a <u>zêtêma</u>. It and the corresponding
nomen actionis can also be used more loosely (Sallustius
attacks both Epicurean views [IX, p. 16,30 Nock] and
Christian polemic against sacrifices [XV, p. 28,8] as
<u>zêtêseis</u>).

__6__   <u>succeed</u>] 'Hit the mark', 'reach', *τυγχάνειν (Isoc. <u>Ant</u>.
271, <u>Panath</u>. 30-32).

__7__   <u>regard</u> . . . <u>highly</u>] *μέγα *φρονεῖν, 'are presumptuous'.
This is ironic: not arrogance itself, but failure to
produce meaningful results is condemned.

__9__   <u>results lie within</u>] Copt. 'they have stood within'. For
this metaphor LSJ cites Philod. <u>Oec</u>. p. 38 Jensen ὡς
ἵστασθαι δεῖ περὶ χρημάτων κτήσεως, and <u>Rh</u>. I.53 S.
οὐκ ὀρθῶς ἵστασθαι. The construction is common in Paul
with the preposition ἐν, almost meaning <u>se trouver</u>:
Rom.5.2, 1 Cor.16.13, Phil.1.27, 4.1, etc. So Clem.
<u>Stro</u>. IV. 168.2, where it is merely <u>variatio</u> upon εἶναι:
ὁ γὰρ ἐν ἀγνοίᾳ ὢν . . . ὁ δ' ἐν γνώσει καθεστώς . . .

(9)   account of the truth] I.e., not even within a mere
       account (λόγος) about the truth, not to speak of truth
       itself. Clem. uses the phrase precisely thus (mere
       'story about the truth') in Stro. VI. 149.3f.:

              οὕτως δὲ καὶ τὴν ἀλήθειαν μετίασιν οἱ πλείους,
              μᾶλλον δὲ τὸν περὶ ἀληθείας λόγον. οὐ γὰρ περὶ
              θεοῦ τι λέγουσιν, ἀλλὰ τὰ ἑαυτῶν πάθη ἐπὶ θεὸν
              ἀνάγοντες ἐξηγοῦνται. γέγονεν γὰρ αὐτοῖς ὁ βίος
              τὸ πιθανὸν ζητοῦσιν, οὐ τὸ ἀληθές· ἐκ μιμήσεως δὲ
              ἀλήθεια οὐ διδάσκεται, ἀλλ᾽ ἐκ μαθήσεως.

       Surely this phrase does not mean (as Peel suggests) the
       canonical scriptures: the Savior's teaching, which our
       author goes on to describe, is far from that. For the
       sentiment, cf. Stro. I. 81.4: φιλοσοφία δὲ . . . ἦλθε
       . . . μαθών τι τῆς ἀληθείας καὶ μὴ καταμείνας ἐν αὐτῇ,
       ταῦτα ἐνέπνευσε . . . So Athenag. Suppl. 7, p. 125,20ff.
       Geff. The opposite position is mentioned at 14, 'we
       gained acquaintance with the truth and rested our con-
       fidence upon it'.

10   recreation . . . repose] Probably *ἀνάπαυσις. There is
       a play on words: for us *ἀνάπαυσις is eternal 'repose'
       (cf. 11), for them merely 'recreation'. The latter
       sense of this word is well illustrated by Pla. Ti. 59 C:
       investigation of γένεσις for the sake of ἀνάπαυσις
       leads to ἀμεταμέλητος ἡδονή. Cf. Apophthegmata Patrum
       (MPG 65.85 C): μισήσατε πᾶσαν σαρκικὴν ἀνάπαυσιν
       ('leisure'). Clem. Stro. V. 19.1 attacks Gk. use of
       philosophy for self-gratification.

       are after] Perhaps *ζητοῦσι.

11   Repose - true repose] Text has simply a relative pro-
       noun, *ἥν. In the context of this verse the concept of
       repose becomes more profound. ἀνάπαυσις means 'rest',
       specifically 'from toil'. Everything depends on what
       the toil consists of. Cessation from labor is 'rest'

(11)   (or in malam partem, 'laziness'); accompanied by food,
        'refreshment', or by a more pleasant activity, 'recrea-
        tion' or 'diversion'; as alleviation of puzzlement,
        'satisfaction'; of stress or evils, 'relief' or
        'repose'; from waking, 'sleep'; etc. The word was
        especially favored as a metaphor in the religious and
        philosophical spheres: if this life was πόνος or
        ταραχή, there might be some escape, whether at death or
        by mental and moral elevation above the domain of toil.
        Thus Heraclitus, quoted by Plotinos IV. 8.1 (on descent
        of soul into body), fr. 84 Diels, Fr. Vorsokr. ὁ μὲν
        γὰρ Ἡρακλεῖτος, ὃς ἡμῖν παρακελεύεται ζητεῖν τοῦτο (how
        soul came to be in body), ἀμοιβάς τε ἀναγκαίας τιθέμενος
        ἐκ τῶν ἐναντίων ὁδόν τε ἄνω κάτω εἰπὼν καὶ μεταβάλλον
        ἀναπαύεται. This idea is of course an utter commonplace
        in antiquity, as the funerary inscriptions and consola-
        tory literature also attest. It is no surprise, then,
        that anapausis became something of a catchword in
        gnosticism, presupposing a dualism that is at once
        anthropological and cosmic: apokatastasis is return
        to the 'place of anapausis' (Stro. VII. 57.1; Pla. R.
        532 E). Proleptic eschatological anapausis is closely
        related to the concept of 'peace of mind', rest from
        ταραχή. In its weakest sense this is illustrated by
        Stro. I. 11.2: speaking of his last and best teacher,
        'the Sicilian bee', Clement remarks, ὑστάτῳ δὲ περιτυχών
        (δυνάμει δὲ οὗτος πρῶτος ἦν) ἀνεπαυσάμην. This same
        usage can also be explicitly eschatological (Stro. IV.
        149.8):

                ὁ δὲ ἐμοῦ ἀκούων, φησίν (Prov.1.33), ἀναπαύσεται
                ἐπ' εἰρήνῃ πεποιθὼς καὶ ἡσυχάσει ἀφόβως ἀπὸ παντὸς
                κακοῦ. . . . τούτῳ δυνατὸν τῷ τρόπῳ τὸν γνωστικὸν
                ἤδη γενέσθαι θεόν (Ps.82.6).

obtained] Cf. 184. The author claims to have something
new; but the way in which this was received goes
unexplained in the treatise. Complex speculative
systems and personal 'revelations' might be transmitted
in works attributed to one or another figure of the

(11)   religious past. Elsewhere, gnostics are known to have
        claimed access to a rival apostolic tradition by which
        their essential doctrines had been passed along in a
        more academic fashion (L. Cerfaux in RHE 50 [1955] 569ff.
        with H. v. Campenhausen, Kirchliches Amt 173; the καί
        is decisive). In this text, the Savior's destruction
        of death seems to be a result of his teaching (27).
        Clement's view on the matter is phrased in remarkably
        similar terms (Stro. I. 32.4):

   φαμὲν τοίνυν ἐνθένδε γυμνῷ τῷ λόγῳ τὴν φιλοσοφίαν
   (the Platonic school) ζήτησιν ἔχειν περὶ ἀληθείας
   καὶ τῆς τῶν ὄντων φύσεως (ἀλήθεια δὲ αὕτη, περὶ ἧς
   ὁ κύριος αὐτὸς εἶπεν ἐγώ εἰμι ἡ ἀλήθεια), τήν τε
   αὖ προπαιδείαν τῆς ἐν Χριστῷ ἀναπαύσεως γυμνάζειν
   τὸν νοῦν καὶ διεγείρειν τὴν σύνεσιν ἀγχίνοιαν
   γεννῶσαν ζητητικὴν διὰ φιλοσοφίας ἀληθοῦς. ἣν
   εὑρόντες, μᾶλλον δὲ εἰληφότες παρ' αὐτῆς τῆς
   ἀληθείας, ἔχουσιν οἱ μύσται.

The underlying idea is the impossibility of knowing the
ultimate without the intervention of some external
revelatory agency, an idea whose development in our
period has been traced by Nock in VC 16 (1962) 79ff.

the Excellent] Copt. has khrêstos. The spelling
χριστός does not occur in this text. Coptic manuscripts
of the classical period generally do not confuse
ΧΡΙСΤΟС with ΧΡΗСΤΟС , though the compendium
ΧС or ΧΡС is used to represent both, cf. Rahlfs, Abh.
Ak. Gött., phil.-hist. Kl., N.F. IV, 4 (1901) 18 (Berlin
Psalter). Our text is insistent upon the form in êta.
This avoids, perhaps deliberately, any implication that
the Savior is related to the Messianic 'Anointed' of
Jewish scripture; also Manichees are said by Alexander
of Lycopolis to have avoided the term χριστός in favor
of χρηστός (C. Manich. 24, p. 34,18 sq. Brinkm.).
        On Greek funerary inscriptions, χρηστός as an
epithet is commonly applied to slaves who served their
masters well, or to strangers (L. Robert, Etudes Anatol.

369). But any such specific nuance is unlikely in our
text.

There was widespread confusion among pagans as to
the correct spelling, hence the correct meaning, of
Christos and Christianos because of itacism. Christian
apologists were quick to seize upon this opportunity:
Justin Apol. I. 4.5 χριστιανοὶ γὰρ εἶναι κατηγορούμεθα·
τὸ δὲ χρηστὸν μισεῖσθαι, οὐ δίκαιον; so Theoph. Ant.
Autol. I. 12; Tert. Adv. nat. I. 3.8f. Christianum uero
nomen, quantum significatio est, de unctione interpreta-
tur: etiam cum corrupte a uobis Chrestiani pronuntiamur
. . . sic quoque de suauitate uel bonitate modulatum
est; Clem. Stro. II. 18.3 For the pagan confusion as
to these words, see Meyer, Ursprung und Anfänge³ III.
307 n. 1, using Blass, Hermes 30 (1895) 466ff., etc.

To summarize: khristos and khrêstos had perceptib-
ly different meanings, were pronounced alike, and were
synonymous only insofar as they both might be epithets
of Jesus. But we are not warranted to translate
khrêstos by 'Christ', as do the edd., however self-
conscious may be our author's pun. In any case Jesus
is meant, cf. 184.

13   gained acquaintance with] This is correlate to his self-
revelation, mentioned at 23.

the truth] This is the first principle, higher than the
Savior. In contrast Clement here follows the gospel of
John: God is unknowable, but the son who is truth
reveals him (Stro. IV. 156.1).

14   rested our confidence] Probably *ἐπαναπαύεσθαι, a pun:
(1) 'rely upon', hence receive peace of mind; (2) 'rest
upon' locatively, as opposed to those who cannot even
'station themselves within an account about it' (9; for
the verb in this sense, cf. Luke 10.6; C.H. IX. 10 τῇ
καλῇ πίστει); (3) 'refresh oneself in'.
Because of pronom. concord 'it' must = 'the truth'.

(15-20) <u>But your inquiry concerns the essentials of a
basic, if controversial and difficult, doctrine. Hence I am
justified in making a reply. So let this be my topic</u>:
'<u>resurrection</u>'.

Philosophical ζήτησις is vanity; truth can be had
('only', is the implication) through revelation by the Savior.
Why then write a <u>logos</u> of this controversial topic? First, as
a courtesy (since you ask 'sweetly', 'graciously', 'decently').
Second, because you ask for 'essential points' rather than
'many things' (<u>2</u>). Third, because without the author's
guidance its proper interpretation is difficult.

15   <u>essential points</u>] In fact the author offers to send an
          elaboration of these points once his <u>logos</u> is done (<u>187-
          190</u>); perhaps the present verse is merely a <u>captatio
          benevolentiae</u>. The text has 'what is necessary' (*ὅ τι
          *δεῖ, <u>scil</u>. νοεῖν). The idea that introductory pedagogy
          deals only with essentials is as old as encyclical
          paideia: Pla. <u>Hp</u>. <u>ma</u>. 286 A; so Athenag. <u>Res</u>. 23, p.
          77,6-9 Schw.:

               οὐ γὰρ τὸ μηδὲν παραλιπεῖν τῶν ἐνόντων εἰπεῖν
               πεποιήμεθα σκοπόν, ἀλλὰ τὸ κεφαλαιωδῶς ὑποδεῖξαι
               τοῖς συνελθοῦσιν ἃ χρὴ περὶ τῆς ἀναστάσεως φρονεῖν.

          <u>inquire</u>] Literally 'are asking us'. This is merely the
          authorial plural; the author moves freely between this
          and the sing.

17   <u>for</u>] *ὅτι or *διότι (epexegetical). Edd. take this to
          introduce <u>oratio</u>, but it seems to me that the author is
          defending himself against the suspicion of needless
          interest in learned problem-solving.

          <u>basic matter</u>] *ἀναγκαῖον. W. C. van Unnik (<u>JEH</u> 15
          [1964] 166) has noted the use of this word in Justin to

mean a tenet 'doctrinally essential' to the dogmatic
system of a given school of thought: Dial. 2.3 (219 A)
ἀναγκαίαν . . . τὴν μάθησιν. Dial. 2.5 (219 B) ταῦτα
τὰ μαθήματα . . . ἀναγκαῖα. From Clem. Stro. IV. iv-v,
we can see that this terminology derives from the
application (or misapplication) of Stoic ethical categories to different parts of philosophy: 21.1 penia
forces the soul to ἀποσχολεῖν τῶν ἀναγκαίων, τῆς
θεωρίας λέγω καὶ τῆς καθαρᾶς ἀναμαρτησίας. So too
Albinos Did. III, p. 153,31f. Herm.: rhetoric is not
προηγουμένον for a philosopher, ἀναγκαῖον δέ. Clem.
Stro. VII. 98.2 οὐκ ἀναγκαίας ἀρχάς; VI. 162.2f. (understand 'dogmata'). Athenag. Res. 11, p. 60,2f. Schw.:
ὁ μὲν γὰρ περὶ τῆς ἀληθείας λόγος ἀναγκαῖος ὢν πᾶσιν
ἀνθρώποις πρὸς ἀσφάλειαν καὶ σωτηρίαν. Similarly 11,
p. 60,18ff. Van Unnik (ibid. 153-167) notes the
centrality of this doctrine in second-century theology.

18   give no credence] Text has either 'are ἄπιστοι' or
      ἀπιστεύουσι. Thus Pla. Phd. 69 E-70 A; cf. also
      Athenag. Res. 1, p. 49,18f. Schw.

19   By implication: 'those who disbelieve will not attain
      it'. (But find, *εὑρίσκειν, is primarily meant
      intellectually: as Clem. Stro. IV. 27.3 τοῦτ' ἐστι τὸ
      εὑρεῖν τὴν ψυχήν, τὸ γνῶναι ἑαυτόν; Pla. Alc. I 109 E.)
      The thought is a commonplace of esoteric literature:
      van Unnik op. cit. 166.
           There is little difference in the text between
      finding the meaning of 'resurrection' and attaining it:
      for from the former follows the ascesis (180) that leads
      to attainment of spiritual resurrection. Pistis and
      gnosis tend to converge in our author's usage; the two
      related verbs interchange throughout 79-90 and πιστεύειν
      is contrasted only with πείθεσθαι (69ff.). On the other
      hand, one can *γινώσκειν not only truth (13 90), but the
      son of man (79). It is worth remembering that γινώσκειν,
      compared with ἐπίστασθαι, has distinct connotations of

acquaintance with a person rather than knowledge of a
proposition.

18-19 allude to Matt. 7.13-14. The Biblical
passage has been condensed and rewritten to avoid
interruption of the stylistic flow. Ancient Greek art-
prose generally avoided direct quotation if use of the
verbatim wording would result in stylistic disunity:
the canon is discussed by Norden, Kunstprosa 89-91.

20   discussion] Copt. has logos. Athenag. Res. 11, p. 59,
21ff. Schw. contrasts rational defence of the truth with
its mere exposition, ὁ περὶ τῆς ἀληθείας λόγος. Thus
our author.

(21-37) <u>How did the Savior conduct His earthly career?
After He revealed His divinity He taught about the inevitable
end of life in the natural order: bodily death. And He
mastered the affairs of life in this world by having both a
divine and a human aspect. Through the one He rose above
bodily death; through the other He caused the general return
(apokatastasis) to the realm of the heavenly Fulness. For He
had existed there as a seed of the truth, before the creation
of our world.</u>

<u>21</u>   The major exposition begins with a rhetorical question
      (classroom style).

      <u>Lord</u>] The author refers to him as 'the Lord' or 'the
      Savior' interchangeably.

      <u>handle the circumstances of this world</u>] χρῆσθαι *τοῖς
      *πράγμασι. In this common idiom (Isoc. <u>Arch</u>. 50; Clem.
      <u>Stro</u>. VI. 112.1), πράγματα usually connotes difficult or
      inherently obdurate events of public life. The follow-
      ing two clauses ('while . . . son of god') could also be
      taken as subordinate to <u>21</u>, further sharpening the scope
      of the question. In any case the real answer comes at
      <u>30</u>.

<u>22</u>   <u>was incarnate</u>] He existed before, in a discarnate state
      (<u>34</u>).

      <u>incarnate</u>] See below on <u>101</u>.

<u>23</u>   <u>revealed</u>] One of the Biblical episodes may be meant, for
      example, John 10.36: εἶπον· υἱὸς τοῦ θεοῦ εἰμι. This
      is followed by an account of Jesus' raising of Lazarus
      from the dead, Martha's confession (11.27f.), and the
      explicit statement that εἰρήκει δὲ 'Ιησοῦς περὶ τοῦ
      θανάτου αὐτοῦ, as below <u>27-28</u>. However, there is no
      other Johannine influence in our text, so perhaps the

Transfiguration is meant. See 134.

24   son of god] I.e., 'divine', 'from above'. Ignatius
          (Eph.20.2) uses this expression in a similar way.
          Otherwise 'god' is not mentioned in our text: the
          first principle is called 'truth', cf. on 13.

25   walked] 'Went about' as 1 Clem.17.1. Cf. Barn.10.11
          (ἐν τούτῳ τῷ κόσμῳ). The sense meaning 'live' (like
          politeuesthai) would require as its prepositional object
          some virtue, vice, or state of being, pace Peel.

          this region] Copt. has topos. A disdainful reference to
          the alien world of visible matter in which the soul must
          live out its carnate life. So Clem. Stro. II. 133.3,
          quoting a famous passage from Pla. Tht. (176 AB on
          ὁμοίωσις θεῷ), speaks of τὰ κακὰ ἀμφὶ τὴν θνητὴν φύσιν
          καὶ τόνδε τὸν τόπον.

26   The author implicitly draws an analogy between the
          Savior's incarnation and that of the believing mind.
          This analogy is central to his philosophical system;
          only later is it discussed explicitly. (Schenke, how-
          ever, takes this literally: Rheginos lives in
          Palestine--which seems to me irrelevant to the author's
          point; OLZ 60 [1965] 471-77.)

          dwell] Or 'remain' (Peel), unlike the Savior, who has
          departed.

27   discoursing of] Or possibly 'discoursing against'
          (Schenke); the Copt. is ambiguous. But the thrust of
          our author's philosophy is not to rail against death,
          rather to assert calmly its irrelevance to the imperish-
          able νοῦς.

(27)   law of the natural order] Copt. has 'nomos of phusis'.
This is merely the commonplace that all men must die,
death is ἀνάγκη. It has nothing to do with Stoic or
Academic speculation on the operations of universal
reason. If our author is conscious of the Stoic usage
of his phrase, the reference to it is purely ironic:
cf. the next line. Nor is Jewish law meant. Peel
cites a good parallel from Jos. Ant. 4.322: 'do not
grieve over death' ὡς κατὰ βούλησιν αὐτὸ πάσχοντας θεοῦ
καὶ φύσεως νόμῳ. In fact the sentiment is commonly
expressed in these terms, e.g., on epitaphs of the
period: Hoffmann, Sylloge 88 [B. Lier in Philologus 62
(1903) 586]: πάντων ἀνθρώπων νόμος ἐστὶ κοινὸς τὸ
ἀποθανεῖν.

It is especially well attested in Latin epitaphs
and the related literature:
Buecheler, Carmina 1021 mortua cum fueris, fati quod
        lege necesse est.
ibid. 436,14 sisti quae (scil. lex perennis) cunctos
        iubet ad uadimonia mortis.
ibid. 432 uota superuacua fletusque et numina diuum
        naturae leges fatorumque arguit ordo.
So in the Consolatio ad Liviam 360: omnia sub leges
mors uocat atra suas. Similarly worded is the idea that
death is a law of each man's own nature, the telos of
his existence: Buecheler 1567 mors etenim hominum
natura, non poena est; sim. 756. Lier (l.c.) considers
the former to derive from Seneca Rem. fort. II.1:
morieris: ista hominis natura est, non poena ('quae
sententia apud Senecam frequens est: Senec. epigr. I 7
[PLM IV 1 Baehrens]; cons. ad Helv. XIII 3 [sic]; quaest.
nat. VI 32,12').

natural order] Copt has phusis. The realm of growth and
change; thus within a dualistic framework, the realm of
coming-into-being. As pertaining to such, this law does
not affect what belongs to the realm of being. Clem.
Stro. III. 64.2f:

        φυσικῇ δὲ ἀνάγκη θείας οἰκονομίας γενέσει θάνατος

ἔπεται, καὶ συνόδῳ ψυχῆς καὶ σώματος ἡ τούτων
διάλυσις ἀκολουθεῖ. εἰ δὲ ἕνεκεν μαθήσεως καὶ
ἐπιγνώσεως ἡ γένεσις, ἀποκαταστάσεως δὲ ἡ διάλυσις.

28   This explanation of νόμος τῆς φύσεως as though an after-
      thought may be ironic, cf. on 27.

29   was a son of man] I.e., he became incarnate. In the
      rigidly dualist system of our text flesh is and remains
      completely devalued: through incarnation the pre-
      existent Savior was enabled to communicate his teaching
      to fellow minds. See on 33.
           29-37 forms one long piece of λέξις εἰρομένη. Note
      the chains of chiasmus.

30   was master of his circumstances] Text has simply
      *κρατεῖν (used absolutely), 'got the upper hand', 'was
      superior'. This answers the rhetorical question posed
      at 21.

32   conquer death] This image, which the author goes on to
      elaborate, belongs to second-century Christological
      speculation, in the same context as abstractions such
      as 'humanity' and 'divinity' (cf. Lampe, Lex. νικάω s.v.
      (2); Just. Apol. I. 63.16; Ir. Haer. III. 18.7 (19.6 H.),
      19.3 (20.3 H.); Clem. Protr. I. 6.1).

33   As incarnate He could deliver the teaching necessary for
      the νοῦς to detach itself from flesh and return to its
      metaphysical home.

      through the son of man] I.e., 'through the example and
      teaching of the Savior, while he was incarnate'.

      return . . . Fulness] Copt. has the usual gnostic
      technical terms, apokatastasis . . . plêrôma.

Of special interest is occurrence of the verb
ἀποκαθιστάναι in the Transfiguration pericope (cf. on
134 and following). But the emergence of this word as
a technical term for 'return of the soul' belongs to
the second century and is probably the invention of
gnosticism. The necessary components for its crystalli-
zation can be detected in various authors read in, or
belonging to, that century:

(1) The Platonic 'Great Year', cf. Plt. 272 E.

(2) Independently, the Stoic doctrine of cosmic
cycling and ecpyric universal regeneration, with the
accompanying term apokatastasis.

(3) Application of the latter term to the Platonic
'Great Year', first attested in Plutarch (cf. Dodds[2] on
Proclus Elem. 200).

(4) Comparison of the soul's cycling into and out
of bodies (an old idea in Greek thought) to cycles of
the kosmos: the soul's anapausis from bodily ponos is
compared to the peace of the Golden Age.

(5) Clement, discussing all these elements, brings
in Jewish speculation upon the Jubilee Year as well
(Stro. IV. 158.4 sq.). This, via reference to Pla. R.
x, is taken to mean the soul's ascent through the seven
planetary zones; in this way a purely spatial exegesis
is made of the temporal-spatial concept. As expected in
Clement a further purely eschatological exegesis thereof
is given (VII. 57.1 sq.), whereby the gnostic's psychic
ἀγωγή, such as described in the Symposium, is analogized
with ascent of the soul after death. The comparison of
psychic motion to that of the heavenly spheres is
already explicit in the Timaeus, and is described (for
different purposes) as being cyclical.

(6) Finally, an important catalytic element is the
suggestive language of Eph.4.11-13, with plêrôma and
henotês. See Stro. IV. 132.1 sq., VI. 73.3 (spiritually
the gnostic already has apokatastasis).

34   since etc.] He could return to the Fulness because he

(34)   had dwelt there once before. His cosmic career serves
       as a paradigm for every believing νοῦς.

       seed] Copt. has sperma. Valentinus' use of a similar
       phrase (fr. 1 Vö., Clem. Stro. II. 36.2) is not relevant
       since the context is different; probably Valentinus
       means something like the seeds sown by Justin's 'Sowing
       Reason'; cf. the Platonic demiurge (Ti. 41 C, E, 42 D).
       In any case, Valentinus speaks of an ἄνωθεν οὐσία, of
       which we hear nothing here.

       from above] A slight non-sequitur since it was 'above'
       that he preexisted thus, but the author speaks descrip-
       tively from his own vantage point here below. Or
       perhaps reference is made to the preexistent Savior's
       derivation from a 'higher', i.e., more abstract prin-
       ciple. While *ἄνωθεν can mean also 'from the beginning',
       the Coptic has not understood it thus.

35   came into being] It was by no means a universal Platonic
       dogma at this time that the world had ever come into
       being: Apuleius De Plat. I. viii, p. 91.12 Thomas;
       Albinos Did. XIV, p. 169,26ff. Herm. (contra Pla. Ti.
       28 B).

35-36 structure . . . divinities] The universe was commonly
       said to be a σύστημα θεῶν καὶ ἀνθρώπων. The tag seems
       to derive from Chrysippus (frr. 527-529 Arn. SVF). Cf.
       Philo Aet. 4. In our text σύστασις may be used rather
       than σύστημα because the moment of cosmic organization
       ('organizing') is spoken of; it also raises the question
       of eventual cosmic dissolution (contra dissolution, cf.
       Philo Aet.). But the two forms could also be used
       interchangeably for the resultant product of the action
       (loss of contrast between these two noun endings
       occurred generally through the Greek language).

36   lordships and divinities . . . numerous] This is ironic,

(36)   since the Savior is both 'Lord' and 'son of god', i.e.,
          divine. Perhaps it is also a disparagement of conven-
          tional religion. I do not think any weight should be
          placed upon this phrase since the author never returns
          to it; nor is the ascent of the soul (e.g., past a
          series of heavenly guardians) of any importance (68),
          since through proleptic spiritual resurrection the νοῦς
          comes under the full protection of the Savior until and
          up to its reabsorption at death (63).

          Belief in intermediary deities, daemones, and
          angels was commonplace in our period. They were a
          necessary bridge between the divine and human spheres
          (Sallustius XIII, p. 26,9sq. Nock with comments in loc.);
          or, if discontinuity between the two realms were felt,
          they would be malevolent forces (archons or astral
          deities). A passage in Colossians (1.16) combined with
          Pla. Ti. 41 A (cf. Athenag. Suppl. 6, p. 124,27ff.; 10,
          p. 128,4ff. Geff.) supplied conveniently orthodox termi-
          nology and warrant for the discussion of such minor
          divinities and endless fascination with their functions
          and identities. The lists and names vary from writer to
          writer, including those who use the canonical text (cf.
          Lampe, Lex. s.vv.). Thus I cannot follow the edd. in
          seeing a tendentious and peculiarly Valentinian text of
          Col.1.16 behind the present passage. Of more relevance
          is Theodoret's notice that the term θεότης, 'divinity',
          in such a context is peculiarly Valentinian (Haer. fab.
          comp. I. 7 apud Harvey ed., Ir. Haer. I. 4.5 [1.8 H.]).
          This meaning is not even glossed by Lampe, Lex., imply-
          ing its later rarity; cf. however, Clem. Exc. Theod.
          43.3 and Ir., Theod. l.c. Thus our author's use of this
          word possibly presupposes a Valentinian background, even
          if not a special Valentinian text form.

(38-68) <u>The accomplishment of the Savior was two-fold</u>:
<u>the vanquishing of death and the demonstration that there</u>
<u>exists within us a superior part</u>. <u>This grace was given by the</u>
<u>truth</u>. <u>The Savior 'swallowed' death, laying aside the perish-</u>
<u>able world, exchanging it for an incorruptible aeon and</u>
<u>'raising Himself' having 'swallowed' the visible realm by</u>
<u>power of the invisible realm</u>. <u>And He taught us the way to</u>
<u>immortality</u>. <u>We have undergone this like Him--suffered,</u>
<u>arisen, ascended</u>. <u>In our present state we wear Him like a</u>
<u>garment; He is as it were the sun, and we are His rays,</u>
<u>stretched up to heaven until our setting (bodily death), when</u>
<u>the 'sun' will withdraw his rays</u>. <u>This is spiritual resurrec-</u>
<u>tion: it 'swallows' fleshly and psychic resurrection</u>.

<u>38-43</u>   So much then for the presuppositions of the doctrine.
          Like a good lecturer our author pauses before the next
          and major part of his exposition.

<u>39</u>   <u>explanation</u>] Scil., of <u>anastasis</u>. *(ἀνά)λυσις is the
          usual Gk. term since Arist. (<u>EN</u> 1146^{b}7; 1153^{b}5; 1112^{b}23;
          Plut. <u>Rom</u>. 12).

          <u>difficult terms</u>] Text has δύσκολα *πράγματα. Resumed
          at <u>187-188</u>.

<u>40</u>   <u>account of the truth</u>] As at <u>9</u>. This explicitly contra-
          dicts a view that was commonplace among the learned.
          As Sallustius (III, p. 4,14 Nock) says, τὸ διὰ μύθων
          τἀληθὲς ἐπικρύπτειν is beneficial because it prevents
          the foolish from despising philosophy and compels the
          wise to study it. Nock, <u>Sallustius</u> xliv-xlv, traces
          this idea back through pagan and Christian writers as
          far as Democritus.

<u>43</u>   <u>in simple terms</u>] Copt. has <u>haplôs</u>. A normal procedure
          in introductory treatments.

everything . . . about coming-into-being] All the
essential points (15).

coming-into-being] The realm of physis, cf. 27-28 ('law
of the natural order . . . death') and 44. For the
idea cf. Clem. Stro. III. 44.3:

> οὐ γὰρ λόγον ψιλὸν εἶναι τὴν γνῶσίν φαμεν, ἀλλά
> τινα ἐπιστήμην θείαν καὶ φῶς . . . τὸ πάντα
> κατάδηλα ποιοῦν τὰ [τε] ἐν γενέσει αὐτόν τε τὸν
> ἄνθρωπον ἑαυτόν τε γινώσκειν παρασκευάζον καὶ
> τοῦ θεοῦ ἐπήβολον καθίστασθαι διδάσκον ('to become
> possessed of God', Chadwick, Alexandr. Chr. 60).

With ἑαυτὸν γινώσκειν compare 44 and 167ff.

44   undoing] Probably a compound of *-λύσις.

manifestation] 'The revealing', with the implication of
its having been hidden before. Cf. 133.

superior] Or 'choice' in the sense of what is highly
preferred, hence the best. It does not, I think, mean
'elect' in a predestinarian sense. Clem. Stro. IV.
164.3 κρεῖττον μὲν . . . ἡ ψυχή, ἧττον δὲ τὸ σῶμα.
Cf. Clem. Paed. I. 32.1 sq.

undoing . . . manifestation] The former comes about by
means of the latter; this line recapitulates 32-33.
The Savior's career is essentially pedagogical.

spirit] Copt. has pneuma. The term is nowhere explained
in the Treatise. I think this passage has nothing to do
with Valentinian aeons (of which Pneuma is not one in
any case), pace Peel.

45   grace] Copt. has kharis.

truth] Clem. Stro. VI. 167.5: Christian didascalia

(opp. to Gk. philosophia) is a δωρεά θεοῦ.

46   swallowed] *καταπίνειν. The self-conscious way in
      which the author glosses this word (47-50) and then
      returns to it (52) shows that it is for him a mere
      metaphor; this is explicitly stated at 161. There is,
      I suppose, a deliberate evocation of the striking
      Pauline metaphor of 1 Cor.15.54, although the parallel
      is far from exact.

47   Pedagogical language as in 2 Tim.2.7 νόει ὅ λέγω.

48   laying aside] *ἀποτίθεσθαι τὸν βίον can mean 'die'
      (Euseb. V. Const. 1.21; 2.21), while ἀποτ. τὸ σῶμα can
      mean merely 'renounce the body' (John Chrys. Reg. fem.
      cohab., MPG 47.258, cf. Lampe, s.v.). In gnostic
      psychic agôgê the νοῦς finally ascends above the body:
      Clem. Stro. VII. 57.1 sq.

50   exchanged] The same construction as in Rom.1.26 (Sahidic
      version of this passage has almost the same construction
      as our text). Cf. Clem. Stro. IV. 167.4, the soul that
      chooses the best life γῆς οὐρανὸν ἀνταλλάσσεται. The
      other possible rendering of the Coptic words, 'changed
      himself into . . .', seems to me odd because I under-
      stand aiôn to mean 'eternal realm'.

      eternal realm] Copt. has aiôn. This is not a Valentin-
      ian hypostasis, but the timelessness of the realm of
      being where he dwelt 'before this structure came into
      being' (35). There is of course only one eternity; to
      speak of it as an eternal realm is merely a figure.
      The event is paradigmatic: cf. Clem. Paed. I. 102.2
      τοῦ δὲ αἰῶνός ἐστιν ἀρχὴ τὸ ἡμέτερον τέλος.

51   raised Himself] So too, the believer will raise himself

through his newly acquired 'acquaintance' (γνῶσις) with
his true self, imparted by the Savior's teaching. Paul
by contrast has God raising Jesus; but the first principle of our author's theology is too far removed from
the mundane realm for such aggressive intervention.
For self-resurrection cf. Ign. Sm. 2.1: ταῦτα γὰρ
πάντα . . . ἀληθῶς ἔπαθεν, ὡς καὶ ἀληθῶς ἀνέστησεν
ἑαυτόν.

52   having swallowed] I.e., having overcome. 'Death . . .
       coming-into-being . . . evil . . . the perishable world
       . . . the visible . . .' are equatable. The principle
       was classically stated by Plato (Ti. 31 B): σωματοειδὲς
       δὲ δὴ καὶ ὁρατὸν ἁπτόν τε δεῖ τὸ γενόμενον εἶναι, with
       the important difference that for him matter is not
       evil, simply intractable.

       by means of] *ἐκ.

53   way] The metaphor (*ὁδός) commonly implies some systema-
       tic practice of life, and is used by Greek and Jewish
       wisdom alike. Porphyry calls philosophy τῆς σωτηρίας ἡ
       ὁδός (Ad Marc. 8).

       immortality] *ἀθανασία. Presumably the νοῦς is inher-
       ently eternal (cf. on 84-90); the question here is its
       separation from the realm of mortality. The idea that
       'immortality' was a gift of god through the Savior, was
       a commonplace in Christianity from early times (Didache
       10.2; cf. Lampe, Lex. s.v.). But in a context where
       νοῦς already has preexisted and then became incarnate,
       immortality means not a change from mortality to its
       opposite, but departure from the realm of mortality and
       flesh.

54   So then] This use of τότε is unclassical, for it
       introduces 'a subsequent event but not one taking place

at a definite time ("thereupon", not "at that time")':
the usage is well attested in koine, however (Bl.-D.-F.
459.2).

55-58   What follows is meant as a literary reference to
        Pauline sacramental metaphor, but not as a citation of
        specific passages.

55   Apostle] Copt. has apostolos. Obviously Paul is meant,
        though various apostolic writings are referred to in
        this way in second-century gnosticism: Paul, cf. Clem.
        Exc. Theod. 22.1, 35.1 etc., 23.2 ('apostle of resurrec-
        tion'); Luke, ibid. 74.1; John, Ptol. Ad Floram (Epiph.
        Pan. haer. 33.3.6); Peter, Exc. Theod. 12.3.

56   we have suffered] The 'way' spoken of in 53. Resistance
        to the flesh (164), if not incarnation as such, is
        meant.

        with Him] From Sahidic version of Eph.2.6, we see that
        the Greek model may have merely used συμπαθεῖν without
        any accompanying prepositional phrase. So also in 57
        and 58.

57   arisen] By spiritual resurrection, as the author will
        explain in the next paragraph: he has in mind his own
        terms, not Paul's.

58   ascended into heaven (or possibly just ascended)] The
        ascent of the mind 'up' the staircase of abstractions
        may be meant: Pla. Smp. 210 C, Clem. Stro. VII. 57.1
        sq. When an overriding cosmic dualism makes definitive
        escape from the world of flesh a possibility, 'up' is
        the natural direction of that escape. Within a contin-
        uous monistic universe, the escape can only be 'to
        within' (Marcus Aurelius IV.3 εἰς ἑαυτὸν ἀναχωρεῖν).

This kind of diluted use of Pauline 'mysticism'
(i.e., sacramental metaphor) is also found in 2 Tim.
2.11, a work probably contemporary with our Treatise.
2 Tim. combats precisely the major thesis of our work
(2 Tim.2.18), and also shows numerous minor similari-
ties. Cf. esp. 2 Tim.1.9-11 with the foll. lines of
our text: 34 88 43 45 32 44 41. So 2 Tim.2.14 μὴ
λογομαχεῖν (cf. 69-74, 1 sq.), contrasting ὀρθοτομεῖν
τὸν λόγον τῆς ἀληθείας (cf. 9 40); 2.23 ζητήσεις
παραιτοῦ; 2.24 ἤπιον (15); 2.25 ἐπίγνωσιν ἀληθείας (13).
2 Timothy differs from the Treatise in its reference to
god, its emphasis upon the scriptural basis of theology,
and its insistence that resurrection is only a future
and universal event. On the other hand both works
emanated from circles where it was fashionable, or
dogmatically necessary, to sound Pauline, even if Paul's
essential points were in fact glossed over by both.

59-60   since we are manifestly] I.e., 'given the clear fact
        that . . .' With δῆλος, φανερός, φαίνεσθαι, Greek
        normally uses the personal construction (Kühner-Gerth[3],
        482.2 Anm. 2), which is reproduced in the Coptic of this
        passage.

60   world] Copt. has kosmos.

61   is our garment that we wear] Text has simply 'we wear
        (φορεῖν) it'. Incarnation is the donning of an unwanted
        garment, the world of visible, perishable matter. The
        goal is to take it off, just as the Savior 'laid aside
        the perishing world' (48): this is an aspect of spiri-
        tual resurrection.
            The image of salvation as an act of offstripping
        is an old one in Greek thought. It might mean on the
        one hand the λύσις καὶ χωρισμὸς ψυχῆς ἀπὸ σώματος at
        death (Pla. Phd. 67 D, cf. Pla. Crt. 403 B, Emped. fr.
        126 Diels, PPF; Cumont, Or. Relig. 269 n. 54). As such,
        the image is common, e.g., in epitaphs of our author's

(61)   period: Kaibel, Epigr. 403,5 (Sebastopol, late);
         651,6 (Sabine countryside) σῶ[μα] χ[ι]τὼν ψυχῆς, fully
         quoted at 106; Anth. Pal. VII. 337,8.

              Equally, though, it might mean the offstripping of
         the senses and passions while still incarnate. Philo's
         use of it thus has been discussed by Dodds (Pagan and
         Christian 95) in connection with a metaphor in Plotinos
         (I. 6.7.4ff.). Clement Stro. V. 67.4 (ransacking
         Philo's De sacr. Ab. et Cain) speaks similarly of the
         gnostic soul's offstripping of 'bodily φλυαρία',
         'passions', 'vain and false ὑπολήψεις', and 'fleshly
         desires'. Such, I think, would be our author's meaning.
         So Maximus of Tyre 11.11 E (with Zeph Stewart, JTS N.S.
         17 [1966] 164).

              But when Clement (Stro. IV. 160.1) speaks of
         putting off sins (exegeting Job 1.21) he goes beyond
         our author's expressed concerns; it is on this issue
         that our author later departs e silentio from Paul and
         Clement. Needless to say, the classic references in the
         Pauline corpus, Col.3.9, Eph.4.22f., may influence our
         author's choice of diction.

              The correlate image, 'putting on' and 'wearing'
         something (or 'someone') new in place of the body or
         passions is harder to parallel outside of Jewish and
         Christian sources (Rom.13.12-14, Eph.4.22-24, Col.3.8-
         12, 1 Cor.15.49): perhaps cf. Epict. II. 8.12 θεὸν
         περιφέρεις. Thus Clem. Stro. VII. 82.2: θεῖος ἄρα ὁ
         γνωστικὸς καὶ ἤδη ἅγιος, θεοφορῶν καὶ θεοφορούμενος.

62   Him] Text has *ἐκεῖνος, literally 'that one', but often
         merely the equivalent of an emphatic personal pronoun:
         Smyth, Gram. 1258, cf. Bl.-D.-F. 291.3; John 5.35,
         Greek and Sahidic).

         rays] *ἀκτῖνες. The author slides into a new metaphor;
         perhaps a 'garment of light' is momentarily spoken of;
         for this see, e.g., Clem. Paed. II. 113.4 (on Ps.
         103.1f. LXX).

62-66 rays . . . the sun . . .] The usual Platonic context of
this image is apprehension of the Good or the Ideas by
the soul (intellectual illumination), not the soul's
preservation. But knowledge or 'acquaintance' with the
divine could save (Christian baptism, e.g., was called
φώτισμα).

In this passage the solar metaphor is expanded with
unusual literalness, anticipating as the edd. note a
later, Neo-Platonic way of speaking. But our author's
kind of language is already well attested in the Odes of
Solomon, probably contemporary with his text, and not
yet Neo-Platonic. I quote from Harris-Mingana, vol. II:

> He became like me that I might receive Him. / In
> similitude was He reckoned like me, that I might
> put Him on. (7.4)

> And I forsook the folly cast away over the earth; /
> And I stripped it off and cast it from me. And
> the Lord renewed me in His raiment, / And possessed
> me by His light; And from above He gave me rest
> without corruption / . . . And the Lord (was) like
> the sun (shining) upon the face of the land; My
> eyes were enlightened. (11.10-14)

> Because (the Lord) is my Sun, and His rays have
> lifted me up; / And His light hath dispelled all
> darkness from my face. . . . And I have received
> Salvation from Him abundantly. . . . I have put on
> incorruption through His name, / And I have put off
> corruption by His grace. Death hath been destroyed
> before my face. (15.1b-9a)

> And I put off darkness, / And clothed myself with
> light: And my soul acquired members / Free from
> sorrow, / Or affliction or pain. . . . And I was
> lifted up in the light, / And I passed before Him.
> (21.3,6)

> Love is of the elect! / And who shall put it on,
> but those who have possessed it from the beginning?
> (23.3)

> And I was covered with the covering of thy spirit;
> / And I removed from me the raiment of skins.
> (25.8)

> And they who have put me on [says Wisdom] shall
> not be injured: / But they shall possess incorrup-
> tion in the new world. (33.12)

63   sunset] A very commonplace metaphor. τὸ γῆρας δυσμαί
βίου: Arist. Po. 1457^{b}24, D. Hal. 4.79, Philo Som.

II.147, Sext. Emp. Adv. Math. IX.90 (quoting Cleanthes);
Diog. Oen. fr. 2 (Chil.) ii,7, Ign. Ro. 2.2, Cyril Alex.
In. Rom. 5.14 (184,10 Pu.), Iambl. Myst. V.22, p. 231,
1 Parthey.

64   the present life] Copt. has 'this bios'. Viz., the
      career of the flesh, cf. 164 'this flesh'. This quali-
      fication is crucial: there is no death for the
      believing νοῦς, only for its σάρξ.

65   drawn] A synonym of 'held fast' 63: drawn up and then
      'pulled' continually; not as in a single, decisive act,
      for that will occur only at 'setting'. However, spiri-
      tual resurrection begins now. Julian (Or. IV 152 B)
      speaks of τὸ λεπτὸν καὶ εὔτονον τῆς θείας αὐγῆς οἷον
      ὄχημα τῆς εἰς τὴν γένεσιν ἀσφαλοῦς διδόμενον καθόδου
      ταῖς ψυχαῖς. The idea of spiritual τόνος, the basis of
      materialist Stoic physics, provided a background against
      which this way of speaking would not seem strange. The
      theory was still being discussed by second-century
      writers (S. Sambursky, Phys. Stoics). As Peel notes,
      the image is already present (in a weaker form) in John
      12.32 πάντας ἑλκύσω πρὸς ἐμαυτόν; 6.44. This, though,
      is slightly different: cf. Clem. Stro. VII. 10.3, on
      the power of τὸ ἐραστόν to draw to contemplation of
      itself everyone who devotes himself to theoria (using
      Pla. R. 525 B, Smp. 204 B).

66   restrained by nothing] Viz., not restrained by flesh.
      (So of death itself, Acts 2.24.) Lack of restraint
      upon the soul was an ideal even of materialist philoso-
      phies: Zeno fr. 216 Arn. SVF οὔτε ἀναγκάζεται . . .
      οὔτε κωλύεται (ὁ σοφός). Thus too Marcus Aurelius V.
      34: it is common to the souls of god and man and every
      rational creature μὴ ἐμποδίζεσθαι ὑπ' ἄλλου.

67   this] The process of being drawn up and 'held fast'
          'stretched' by the Savior, unrestrained by flesh and
          its associated evils. Use of a metaphor like that of
          the uprising solar rays makes it possible for the
          author to still call this an anastasis, 'rising-up'.

          resurrection of the spirit] Copt. has anastasis
          pneumatikê.

68   resurrection of the soul] The hope that the soul (but
          not specifically νοῦς) would survive, get loose, and
          ascend at the moment of death (but not before). Copt.
          has psukhikê (scil., anastasis).

          swallows] Viz., 'makes irrelevant'.

          resurrection of the flesh] A doctrine such as that
          defended by Athenagoras, Res. Copt. has sarkikê (scil.,
          anastasis).

          A tripartite anthropology seems to be presupposed: the
question is, which part or parts will arise? The author has a
definite answer in mind, but his terminology fluctuates. The
highest faculty of man in the most limited sense he calls
'mind'--nous--or 'the superior element' (cf. on 84-90). This
contrasts with flesh or the inferior element (cf. on 101).
Yet the author can speak of the superior also as a vivifying
principle: this function is proper to soul (which probably
includes nous as a constituent part) rather than nous as such
(cf. on 106). When the discussion concerns soul rather than
nous, the contrasting term becomes sôma, body, following in a
simple way the Platonic model (112).
          Such a tripartite division is common in our period.
Justin, e.g., speaks of σῶμα, ψυχή, and νοῦς. But the terminology varies from author to author. Marcus, following the
Pneumatist physicians, uses 'pneumatic' of the second component
or anima (pneumation) rather than the third; for nous he will
often have hêgêmonikon (Farquharson on II.2).

It is not clear why our author uses 'pneumatic' at <u>67</u>
('<u>spiritual</u>' <u>resurrection</u>). Elsewhere there does not seem to
be any suggestion that the highest faculty (<u>nous</u>) should be
called <u>pneuma</u>. Perhaps the adjective <u>pneumatikē</u> characterizes
the force by which proleptic resurrection comes about: cf. <u>44</u>,
'offshoot of . . . spirit', and Bauer, <u>Lex</u>., s.v. πνεῦμα (2).

(69-83) <u>Resurrection depends upon faith (pistis)</u>.
<u>Philosophical argument alone cannot produce it. Through faith</u>
<u>comes acquaintance with the Savior and His destruction of death</u>.

     Thus far the author has relied on traditional Christian
imagery to explain <u>anastasis</u> as he understands it. But far
from providing a resolution to his disciple's problem, this is
merely the beginning of the author's proper explanation. He
now returns to his opening theme (problem-oriented philosophy
<u>versus</u> gnosis), almost as a signal that the discussion is to
begin again. From here on the treatise increasingly relies
upon an essentially philosophical and Platonizing conception
of salvation, expounded through the discussion of a series of
<u>aporiae</u> or special problems. It eventually becomes clear that
the author has rejected the Pauline notion that the body must
share in the resurrection state. So too the notion of resurrection as a concrete future event is substantially devalued
(<u>163</u>ff.) in favor of an eschatology in which ipso facto the
<u>nous</u> is an entity that is, or can be, undying. Within this
framework resurrection cannot be said to occur after death or
even at death, except insofar as it is the imperishable mind's
physical offshucking of a body.

<u>69-73</u> By 'argumentation' (*τὸ πείθεσθαι) is meant rigorous
     demonstration and propositional knowledge. For the
     idea cf., e.g., Julian <u>Or</u>. IV 152 B: 'as for the sun's
     gifts, which free our souls from the body and draw them
     up by his sunshine as it were in an ὄχημα [<u>Phaedrus</u>],
     ὑμνείσθω τε ἄλλοις ἀξίως καὶ ὑφ' ἡμῶν πιστευέσθω μᾶλλον
     ἢ δεικνύσθω'. The edd. aptly note a parallel in Italian
     Valentinianism (Heracleon <u>apud</u> Orig. <u>In</u>. <u>Jo</u>. XIII. 60.
     419): the <u>psykhikoi</u> desire persuasion by <u>aisthêsis</u>, the
     <u>pneumatikoi</u> are content λόγῳ πιστεύειν.
          <u>Pistis</u> was of course an important traditional
     Christian virtue. But within the Platonic tradition it
     had a much lower status, meaning something like
     'unreasoned belief' or 'mere faith': <u>pistis</u> is to
     <u>alêtheia</u> 'as becoming is to being' (Pla. <u>Ti</u>. 29 C).

Thus even Justin will say (Apol. I. 17.4) πιστεύοντες,
μᾶλλον δὲ καὶ πεπεισμένοι, where peithesthai has a
higher status than pisteuein. Our Platonizing author,
then, is here exerting himself to use traditional
Christian language in a non-Platonic way. In fact he
seems to use pistis as a kind of equivalent of gnosis
(cf. on 19). At 84-90 he will finally explain that
'belief' means contemplation by the nous of an undying
object.

71   cannot be] *οὐκ *ἔχει.

72   domain] Copt. has topos. This word has a broad meta-
        phorical extension: 'occasion' or 'appropriate moment',
        Orig. In. Jo. II. 15.110 τόπος ἀπολογίας; 'subject' for
        a debate, Orig. Dial. c. Heracl. 1.17, 4.24; 'domain' of
        philosophy (like meros), Marcus Aurelius XI.37.

74   dead (plural) will arise] Again the diction is deceptive:
        the author makes maximum concession to traditional modes
        of speaking (1 Thess.4.16) before further elaboration of
        spiritual resurrection (which 'devours', e.g., resurrec-
        tion of the flesh). Cf. 82f. What counts is belief in,
        i.e., gnosis of the truth (84 sq.).

75   scholars here] 'Worldly philosophers', those who devote
        themselves to mundane questions; cf. above on 2. An
        essential thrust of second-century Christian apologetic
        was the claim to be engaged in philosophia rather than
        fanaticism. Justin wore the philosopher's beard,
        Athenagoras finds it useful to speak of philosophers
        who believe in resurrection (Suppl. 36). On the
        shallowness and decline of philosophy in the later
        second century and following, cf. Nock, Sallustius xxi-
        xxiv. Our author has only scorn for this: despite
        their profession, they too can be saved if only they

'believe'.   Remarkably similar is Clem. Stro. V. 87.1:
δεῖ τοίνυν διὰ Χριστοῦ τὴν ἀλήθειαν μεμαθηκότας σῴζεσθαι,
κἂν φιλοσοφήσαντες τὴν Ἑλληνικὴν φιλοσοφίαν τύχωσιν.

here] Probably *ἐνταῦθα or the like, literally 'here'.
In Platonic context the word reminds us of the existence
of some other world beyond (ἐκεῖ: Arist. Metaph.
990^b34).

77   in one who has caused his own conversion] The enterprise
        of philosophy, following the Platonic model, was often
        thought to be a turning of the soul (Albinos Did. I,
        p. 152,2ff. Herm.) away from unworthy objects to truth.
        On this see Nock, art. 'Bekehrung', RAC (1954). Our
        author only means to emphasize the crucial role played
        by the Savior's teaching--and example--in the conversion
        of nous from flesh to truth.
              Clement, in Stro. VI. 123.2f., summarizes the
        principal differences between 'philosophy' (i.e.,
        Platonism) and gnostic Christianity, and the principal
        similarities: philosophy teaches providence, reward of
        good and punishment of evil, one God, speaks of Christ--
        but omits that he is son of god and the details of pro-
        vidential economy, because it does not know ἡ κατὰ τὸν
        θεὸν θρησκεία, worship. Philosophy as opposed to gnosis
        teaches κατὰ περίληψιν, οὐ πρὸς ἀλήθειαν.

79   For] Through faith the philosopher, like us, must gain
        acquaintance with the Savior and hence the truth.
              Some Valentinians, known to Clement (Stro. II.
        10.2), distinguished the faith of the ἁπλοῖ from their
        own gnosis, claiming to be φύσει σῳζόμενοι. This
        Clement rejects, along with a mechanistic Basilidean
        view (II. 10.1), defending the element of free choice
        in πίστις.

son of man] The Savior qua artificer of the return
(apokatastasis) of minds into the Fulness (33).

81   <u>He</u> <u>arose</u>] As at <u>74</u>, but now the author explains.

        <u>from</u> <u>the</u> <u>dead</u> (plural).

83   <u>became</u> <u>death's</u> <u>undoing</u>] Or 'became a release from
        death', i.e., 'released us from death'. The figure is
        poetic (activity for actor), as at 1 Cor.1.30, Christ
        ἐγενήθη ἡμῖν . . . ἀπολύτρωσις.

(84-90) <u>The cognitive object of the believer's mind is</u>
<u>great and imperishable; so, too, that mind and its thoughts</u>
<u>are great. This is how the mind can be said to have been pre-</u>
<u>ordained for salvation (that is, for knowledge of the truth.)</u>

Only that which is divine can know the divine--this
thought is by no means rare. Sen. <u>NQ</u> I praef. 12: [<u>homo</u>] <u>hoc</u>
<u>habet argumentum diuinitatis suae</u>, <u>quod illum diuina delectant</u>;
Lact. <u>Inst</u>. <u>diu</u>. II. 8.68; Sallustius VIII p. 14,32 sq. Nock:

ἀθάνατον δὲ αὐτὴν [λογικὴν ψυχὴν] εἶναι ἀνάγκη ὅτι
τε γινώσκει θεούς (θνητὸν δὲ οὐδὲν ἀθάνατον οἶδε) τῶν
τε ἀνθρωπίνων πραγμάτων ὡς ἀλλοτρίων καταφρονεῖ καὶ
τοῖς σώμασιν ὡς ἀσώματος ἀντιπέπονθε.

So also <u>C</u>. <u>H</u>. XIII.22, νοερῶς ἔγνως σεαυτόν. As such, this
view <u>presupposes</u> the divinity of the cognitive faculty, of
<u>nous</u>, and is something quite different from the concept of
'assimilation (of soul) to the divine', taught by Plato. The
latter concept is extremely common; it is found, e.g., in
Clement <u>Stro</u>. V. 96.2 (quoting Pla. <u>Ti</u>. 90 D), II. 52.3, etc.,
and in occidental Valentinianism (Hipp. <u>Ref</u>. VI. 32.8-9: soul
in itself is mortal and becomes immortal when ἐξομοιωθῇ τοῖς
ἄνω or conversely perishes if τῇ ὕλῃ). But in the present
passage our author does not seem to teach a causal relationship
between cogitation of divine objects and (thence) imperish-
ability, rather the opposite: <u>nous</u>, like its cognitive object,
<u>is</u> 'great' and imperishable, <u>hence</u> (88) it can be said to be
preordained for salvation. Knowledge is its telos. The pre-
supposition throughout, is that 'the believer' <u>is</u> the <u>nous</u>; it
is the cognitive faculty which amounts to the essential man.
This identification is already present in Aristotle, though
without the suggestion that <u>nous</u> carries any personal traits
which give to a specific person his identity: <u>EN</u> 1178^{a}2
δόξειε δ' ἂν καὶ εἶναι ἕκαστος τοῦτο (viz., νοῦς); 1178^{a}6 τῷ
ἀνθρώπῳ δὴ (κράτιστον καὶ ἥδιστον) ὁ κατὰ τὸν νοῦν βίος, εἴπερ
τοῦτο μάλιστα ἄνθρωπος.

The Aristotelian theory of <u>nous</u> is clearly one of the
elements which informs the philosophical background of our
author's thought: within man, Aristotle's <u>nous</u> is the purely

cognitive faculty. Existent from eternity, it enters man at
his creation 'from without' (θύραθεν, GA 736^{b}28) and here continues its independent existence as the divine element (GA
736^{b}28; EN 1179^{a}26), the ruling element (τὸ κύριον, EN 1178^{a}3).
Though called a 'part' of soul (De an. 429^{a}10 sq.), its
independence and its unaffected survival of bodily disintegration distinguish it from soul as a whole. At death it simply
ὑπομένει (Metaph. 1070^{a}25-26). It is, accordingly, unimpaired
by old age (De an. 408^{b}18 sq.). For cognitive objects it is
said to have τὰ ἀληθῆ καὶ πρῶτα καὶ ἄμεσα καὶ γνωριμώτερα καὶ
πρότερα καὶ αἴτια τοῦ συμπεράσματος (An. post. 71^{b}21-22). Cf.
Rohde, Psyche^8 XIV.i.2 (tr. Hillis, 493ff.).

        Two important questions naturally arise in the context
of our author's use of this idea. First, might there be men or
souls without nous, so that immortality was denied to them?
The view that there are both mortal and immortal souls, only
the latter being endowed with νοῦς upon birth, was common,
e.g., in Hermetism (though not held unanimously), as also it
was held by Iamblichus; furthermore, the idea begins to emerge
well before the supposed time of our text (cf. Nock, Sallustius
lxv with notes). Second, will a nous necessarily survive
bodily disintegration, no matter what kind of moral βίος it
may have attended (Aristotle's view)?

        (1) For the first of these questions, the evidence of
the text is ambiguous. (a) The opposition of the ignorant (*οἱ
*ἀγνοοῦντες) to those who are personally acquainted with the
truth, 89-90, probably refers to choices open to the nous.
The terms are a commonplace of wisdom literature and need not
imply the predetermined existence of two classes of men,
although this remains a possibility. (b) 'Those who are saved'
is a term by which the author repeatedly characterizes himself
and his readers (86 122 127 123): however, it is never contrasted to an opposite term. Hence the predestinarianism of
88-90 may simply refer to the telos of the nous as such, and
it remains an open question whether it dwells in all men or
only in some.

        (2) To the second question the answer is presumably
affirmative, cf. 88-91, despite the exhortation with which the
work closes. But in this treatise the author is not primarily

concerned with the salvation which begins <u>after</u> death, rather
with the recovery of bodilessness, one's 'former state of
being' (<u>183</u>), while he is still incarnate: this is spiritual
resurrection, an <u>anapausis</u> which begins now. For this an act
of volition is apparently required. The concept of spiritual
resurrection, like the doctrine of Pleromatic Deficiency, puts
the author's idea of the <u>nous</u> into a perspective utterly
different from Aristotle's.

84   the <u>object</u> of <u>belief</u>] Literally 'he who (or that which)
        is believed in' (Coptic does not make a distinction
        between personal and impersonal pronouns).

        <u>great</u>] Copt. means 'great, large, old (as, an <u>old</u> man)'.
        This is not an especially philosophical word because of
        its vagueness; the tone is that of <u>acclamatio</u>.

86   <u>thought</u>] Copt. (<u>meue</u>) means either the process of think-
        ing, or that which is thought (a 'thought').

87   <u>mind</u>] Copt. has <u>nous</u>.

        <u>such an object</u>] Text has simply 'it' (or 'him').

88   <u>Thus</u>] *διὰ *τοῦτο. I.e., 'On this basis we can under-
        stand the sense in which . . .'. Clement explains
        election similarly, starting from the doctrine of
        <u>exhomoiôsis</u> (<u>Stro</u>. IV. 168.2): ὁ δ' ἐν γνώσει καθεστώς
        ἐξομοιούμενος θεῷ εἰς ὅσον δύναται, ἤδη πνευματικὸς καὶ
        <u>διὰ τοῦτο</u> ἐκλεκτός.

        <u>salvation</u>] *σωτηρία, which has a wide range of meanings
        in the Imperial age. Perhaps 'preservation', as opposed
        to 'dissolution'.

        <u>we are chosen</u> . . . <u>set apart</u>] We are members of the
        Fulness.

ransom] A traditional (Pauline) way of speaking, but
here the word is taken out of its Pauline context of sin
and expiation. Escape from the body back to the Fulness
is meant; it is thus an empty metaphor.

90   the truth] This (and not 'the son of man', 79) is the
        cognitive object spoken of at 84.

(91-100) <u>Truth and the whole structure of the Fulness
are mighty, being indissoluble. In contrast, the material
universe is insignificant. The Entirety, however, was held
fast. It did not come into being; it was.</u>

The Platonic distinction between the realms of being
and becoming is now made explicit.

91   <u>are</u> <u>wakeful</u>] *γρηγορεῖν *πρός (for the construction, cf.
        Clem. <u>Paed</u>. II. 79.3). As Clement says (<u>Stro</u>. VI.
        98.3) ἐν ἀδιαλείπτῳ θεωρίᾳ ἡμᾶς εἶναι. Ign. <u>Pol</u>. 1.3
        γρηγόρει ἀκοίμητον πνεῦμα κεκτημένος.

        <u>brought</u> <u>to</u> <u>naught</u>] The alternate translation, '. . .
        cannot be let go of', would refer to the hypnotic
        nature of truth, its power to draw the mind to itself
        (cf. on <u>65</u> and Plotinus I.6).

94   <u>mighty</u>] 'Strong', 'enduring'. Clem. <u>Stro</u>. I. 54.3
        μόνη γὰρ ἡ ἀλήθεια δυνατή.

        <u>structure</u>] Copt. has <u>sustêma</u>, and for 'Fulness' <u>plêrôma</u>.
        'Structure' goes unexplained; either its compositeness
        out of all the saved minds is meant, or possibly some
        more complex hierarchical structure of aeons. The word
        often means simply a 'congregation' or 'community', cf.
        Lampe, <u>Lex</u>., s.v.

96   <u>trifling</u>] *μικρόν, a word with a wide range of meanings.
        Perhaps merely 'insignificant', cf. Pla. <u>Smp</u>. 210 C;
        Plot. VI. 4.2.27: ἡμεῖς δὲ τὸ ὂν ἐν αἰσθητῷ θέμενοι
        . . . καὶ μέγα νομίζοντες τὸ αἰσθητόν . . . τὸ δέ ἐστι
        τοῦτο τὸ λεγόμενον μέγα μικρόν. V. 8.9.30 σώματος
        δύναμις μικρά.

97   <u>held</u> <u>fast</u>] Copt. (<u>emahte</u>) either means 'held fast' (as

at 63, *κατέχειν), or 'encompassed' (*περιέχειν), as by
the envelope of the Fulness.

Entirety] *τὸ *ὅλον. The totality of minds; cf. 121,
where the Entirety is specifically identified with 'us'.
It is held as the sun's rays are by the sun (63-66).
Apparently all minds of the Entirety are so held without
regard to their mental disposition (cf. on 84-90). Edd.
give references for use of the technical term elsewhere
in gnosticism.

98-99 did not come into being . . . was] Neatly reversing
popular pessimism about the afterlife, as attested on
numerous funerary inscriptions: IG XIV 1201 (Rome)
οὐκ ἤμην· γενόμην· ἤμην· οὐκ εἰμί· τοσαῦτα· εἰ δέ
τις ἄλλο ἐρέει, ψεύσεται· οὐκ ἔσομαι. Cf. MAMA VIII
353 (Kara Ağaç), etc.; L. Robert in Hellenica 13 (1965)
95; Bull. ép., REG 63 (1950) no. 204; R. Lattimore,
Themes 84f.; Cumont, Mus. Belge 32 (1928) 73-85.

99   was] Like the Savior (34).

100   So] (Copt. has hôste.) Because survival of nous is
inevitable.

(101-114) (<u>Someone might ask</u>): "Even though you became
incarnate only when you entered this world, why will you not
take your flesh with you when you go to eternity? After all,
it is the superior part which is sole cause of life for the
flesh. Indeed, if the flesh came into being for the sake of
the superior, for 'your' sake, it might properly belong to the
superior, and what is the property of the superior surely will
continue to coexist with it for all time". No: to impute
flesh to mind as though it were its property entails the mind's
existing in a corrupt state, which is surely wrong.

It is clear by now that the believer is mind, that he
belongs to an eternal realm of perpetual, timeless, pure
existence, and that this realm contrasts to all that 'has come
into being'. By implication, flesh has been seen to be excluded from such an eternal realm. Now the author must openly
attack the traditional belief in resurrection of flesh.

101-   The dialogue between the author and an imaginary inter-
114   locutor imparts a lively, conversational tone after the
       preceding dogmatic exposition. This is classroom style,
       in which the lecturer himself adduces possible objec-
       tions and then answers them. It is common, e.g., in
       Epictetus.

101   flesh] Copt. has <u>sarks</u> here and in the following discus-
       sion. This term occurs, e.g., in Marcus Aurelius, who
       presupposes a commonplace trichotomous division of man,
       <u>sarkion</u> (or <u>sarkia</u>), <u>pneumation</u> (soul, pneumatic system),
       and <u>hêgêmonikon</u> (i.e., mind). Farquharson on II.2 (Vol.
       II, p. 496) notes that <u>sarks</u>, rather than <u>sôma</u>, is the
       appropriate term to contrast with 'mind'; this contrast
       is also found outside the philosophical literature
       (Aesch. <u>Sept</u>. 622): "σάρξ is ἀρχὴ καὶ σῶμα καθ' αὐτὸ
       τῶν ζῴων and the seat of sensibility, Arist. <u>P</u>. <u>An</u>.
       653^{b}21. Marcus elsewhere uses σάρξ . . . for the body
       as the origin of sensations, esp. of κινήσεις which

cause πάθη and ὁρμαί. This is derived from Epicurean
usage, where σάρξ is employed because σῶμα includes the
bodily ψυχή, anima, as in this chapter it includes
πνεῦμα, D.L. X.140, 144-5. The word has a slightly
depreciatory sense, perhaps originating in the criticism
of athleticism: Pla. R. 556 D, Lg. 959 C, Galen i.32
[add Smp. 211 E]". Such considerations probably weigh
as heavily for our author as does traditional Christian
usage. Nothing is said, or implied, about a special
kind of 'resurrection flesh' as in Paul: the author
speaks of the flesh of our present life.

104   take with you] Text has simply 'take' (or 'receive',
       'get').

105   realm of eternity] Copt. has aiôn, cf. 50. The time-
       lessness of the realm of being.

106   The terms of the objection now become more traditionally
       Platonic. Soul (the vivifying principle) and body are
       contrasted, rather than mind and body-cum-soul.

       imparts vitality to it] Copt. has 'exists for it as
       aitios of *ζωή (or *τὸ *ζῆν)'. It is not a function of
       mind but of soul to be the vital principle. The imagi-
       nary objector, then, is failing to distinguish nous from
       the other psychic faculties vis-a-vis its survival; he
       does the same at 130 when he speaks of 'the living
       interior members'.
             This is an idea which naturally occurs in associa-
       tion with the soul's heavenly origin, immortality, and
       independence from body. The verse epitaph of Aelianus,
       found in the Sabine countryside, aptly illustrates this
       (Kaibel, Epigr. 651):
             Αἰλιανῶι τόδε [σῆμα] πατὴρ ἀγαθῶι πι[νυτῶι τε,]
                   θ[νη]τὸν κηδ[εύσα]ς σῶμα· τὸ δ' ἀθάνατ[ον]
             ἐς μακά[ρ]ων ἀνόρο[υσ]ε κέαρ· ψυχὴ γὰρ ἀείζ[ως,]

ἢ τὸ ζῆν παρέχει [κ]αὶ θεόφιν κατέβη.
ἴσχεο [σὺ] στοναχῶν, πά[τε]ρ, ἴσχε δέ, μῆτερ,
ἀδελφούς·
σῶ[μα] χ[ι]τὼν ψυχῆς· τ[ὸ]ν δὲ θεὸν σέβε μου.

('The good and discreet Aelianus was given this tomb by
his father in concern for his mortal body; but his
heart, which is immortal, has leapt up among the
blessed; for the soul lives forever, it is what gives
life, and it has come down from God. Stay your tears,
my father, and you, mother, stay my brothers from weep-
ing. The body is the soul's tunic: but you must
respect the god [or θεῖον] in me', R. Lattimore, Themes,
34.)

That ψυχή can be defined as the vivifying principle
is a Platonic commonplace. Ps.-Pla. Def. 411 C ψυχὴ τὸ
αὐτὸ κινοῦν [Pla. Lg. 895]· αἰτία κινήσεως ζωτικῆς
ζώων. It appears for example in John 6.63 [τὸ] πνεῦμά
ἐστιν τὸ ζωοποιοῦν, ἡ σὰρξ οὐκ ὠφελεῖ οὐδέν. Pla. Cra.
399 D: ψυχὴν . . . ὅταν παρῇ τῷ σώματι, αἴτιόν ἐστι τοῦ
ζῆν. Albinus Did. XXV, p. 177,16ff. Herm., using Phaedo.
This meaning of ψυχή, is of course already suggested by
Homeric usage (ψ.='life').

The superiority of soul is a function of its
priority (Pla. Lg. 892 A) and mastery of body (Phd.
79 E - 80 A). Nothing can be greater than soul nor
rule over it: Arist. De an. 410^{b}13, Marcus (cited above
on 66), Albinos Did. XXV, p. 177,28 Herm. Conversely,
what is superior should rule (Pla. R. 590 D, Lg. 690 B,
Clem. Stro. VII. 8.3: the political sphere).

107   What exists for something else is necessarily inferior
(Pla. Lg. 870 B; Marcus Aurelius VII.55 τὰ χείρω τῶν
κρειττόνων ἕνεκεν). The principle is similarly applied
in the Coptic Gospel of Thomas, Log.29: 'if it is for
the sake of spirit that the flesh came into being, this
is remarkable: but if spirit for the sake of flesh, it
is incredible'.

The thrust of this objection, however, is that if

(<u>107</u>)   body is providentially created and with the telos of
being alive, it would be offensive to the notion of a
providential and all-powerful god to suppose it might
not continue to do so; and for this it must continue to
coexist with it. The extremely abbreviated form in
which this argument appears in the text seems to pre-
suppose its currency, or at least familiarity, on the
part of the readers. A full statement of the argument
is given by Athenagoras <u>Res</u>. 12, p. 62,21-63,1 Schw.,
as he tries to establish the necessity of a fleshly
resurrection:

> ὁπόσα μὲν γὰρ ἄλλου του χάριν γέγονεν, παυσαμένων
> ἐκείνων ὧν ἕνεκεν γέγονεν, παύσεται εἰκότως καὶ
> αὐτὰ [τὰ γενόμενα] τοῦ εἶναι καὶ οὐκ ἂν διαμένοι
> μάτην, ὡς ἂν μηδεμίαν ἐν τοῖς ὑπὸ θεοῦ γενομένοις
> τοῦ ματαίου χώραν ἔχοντος· τά γε μὴν δι' αὐτὸ τὸ
> εἶναι καὶ ζῆν καθὼς πέφυκεν γενόμενα, ὡς αὐτῆς τῆς
> αἰτίας τῇ φύσει συνειλημμένης καὶ κατ' αὐτὸ μόνον
> τὸ εἶναι θεωρουμένης, οὐδεμίαν οὐδέποτε δέξαιτ'
> ἂν τὴν τὸ εἶναι παντελῶς ἀφανίζουσαν αἰτίαν.
> ταύτης δὲ ἐν τῷ εἶναι πάντοτε θεωρουμένης, δεῖ
> σώζεσθαι πάντως καὶ τὸ γενόμενον ζῷον, ἐνεργοῦν
> τε καὶ πάσχον ἃ πέφυκεν, ἑκατέρου τούτων ἐξ ὧν
> γέγονεν (scil. body and soul) τὰ παρ' ἑαυτοῦ (scil.
> μέλη?) συνεισφέροντος κτλ.

The converse argument, that soul is purposeless unless
it has a body to direct (that being <u>its</u> τέλος), is
adduced later, in the reign of Julian, by Sallustius
(XX p. 36,3 sq. Nock). It is the second of three arguments he gives for the transmigration of souls:
(1) congenital defects of soul (blindness etc.) indicate punishment for former misdeeds; (2) καὶ ἐκ τοῦ
φύσει ἐχούσας ἐν σώματι πολιτεύεσθαι τὰς ψυχὰς μὴ δεῖν
ἅπαξ ἐξελθούσας τὸν πάντα αἰῶνα μένειν ἐν ἀργίᾳ ('the
fact that souls which are naturally qualified to act in
the body must not, once they have left it, remain
inactive throughout time', Nock); (3) all things in the
universe, souls included, are limited in number, hence
transmigration is needed to restock new bodies.

108   yours] I.e., 'what you (the <u>nous</u>) have and care for'.

      coexist] I.e., eternally.
         As stated here, the imaginary objection is already
an absurdity. Cf. Pla. <u>Alc</u>. I 128 D: Ἄλλῃ μὲν ἄρα
τέχνῃ αὐτοῦ ἑκάστου ἐπιμελούμεθα, ἄλλῃ δὲ τῶν αὐτοῦ.--
Φαίνεται.--Οὐκ ἄρα ὅταν τῶν σαυτοῦ ἐπιμελῇ, σαυτοῦ
ἐπιμελῇ.--Οὐδαμῶς. So Marcus Aurelius XII.3: you have
σωμάτιον, πνευμάτιον, νοῦς. τούτων τἆλλα μέχρι τοῦ
ἐπιμελεῖσθαι δεῖν σά ἐστι· τὸ δὲ τρίτον μόνον κυρίως
σόν. V.33: 'What lies within mere flesh and spirit
[as opposed to <u>nous</u>] is neither yours nor in your power'.

109   <u>Nay</u> <u>rather</u>] Coptic has <u>alla</u>.
         The author's answer is from experience: the flesh
is obviously in constant decay, constantly becoming a
corpse. It will be a blessing to depart from such a
condition. Neither of the two objections raised by the
imaginary objector warrants serious consideration.

110   <u>are</u> <u>alienated</u> <u>from</u>] Or 'lack' (*ὑστερεῖν?).

112   <u>have</u> <u>endeavored</u>] This may be <u>ad</u> <u>hominem</u>; if so it is
the only personal touch in the author's exposition, and
would indicate that he and Rheginus had some prior discussion of the topic.

      <u>bodily</u> <u>envelope</u>] The Coptic has   ΧΟΡΙΟΝ, <u>khorion</u>,
i.e., χόριον: 'the χόριον of the body'. This word is
well attested, primarily in biological writings, where
it refers to the <u>membrane</u> enclosing the foetus in the
womb (Hippoc. <u>Nat</u>. <u>puer</u>. 16, Arist. <u>H</u>. <u>an</u>. 562^a6, Diosc.
<u>De</u> <u>mat</u>. <u>med</u>. III.150, Galen <u>De</u> <u>usu</u> <u>part</u>. XV.4, Rufus
<u>Onom</u>. 230) or to the <u>membrane</u> of a chicken's egg (Arist.
<u>GA</u> 754^a1); so also (χόρια) it is attested by Comic
writers (Cratinus, Aristoph., Alexander) and Theocritus
as the name of a dish prepared by stuffing <u>intestine</u>

(112)   with honey and milk (cf. LSJ). Besides this it figures
in a proverb cited by Theoc. X.11, χαλεπὸν χορίω κύνα
γεῦσαι.

If χόριον is the correct reading, it is a harsh
and unprepared (also undeveloped) metaphor for 'body'.
The following genitive, 'of the sōma', will be a genitive of constituency or 'content': 'the membrane which
consists in body' enclosing mind until its 'birth'
(bodily death), at which time the mind will burst forth
into life. Bodily death is for mind a birth; mind
leaves behind the corrupt and lifeless corpse as a new-
born child its χόριον.

The abruptness of the image is easily paralleled:
Pla. Phdr. 250 C: before incarnation we were καθαροὶ
ὄντες καὶ ἀσήμαντοι τούτου ὃ νῦν δὴ σῶμα περιφέροντες
ὀνομάζομεν, ὀστρέου τρόπον δεδεσμευμένοι ('imprisoned
in the manner of an oyster'). For medical imagery, see,
e.g., 1 Cor.15.8 ἔσχατον δὲ πάντων ὡσπερεὶ τῷ ἐκτρώματι
ὤφθη (ὁ Χριστός) κἀμοί. The infelicitous lack of a
particle of comparison casts some doubt upon our text,
but for the textual critic this is offset by occurrence
of the same image within a very similar context in
Porph. Ad Marc. 32 (noted by van Unnik, JEH 15 [1964]
166):

> εἰ μὴ τὸ σῶμα οὕτω σοι συνηρτῆσθαι φυλάξεις ὡς
> τοῖς ἐμβρύοις κυοφορουμένοις τὸ χόριον καὶ τῷ σίτῳ
> βλαστάνοντι τὴν καλάμην, οὐ γνώσῃ σεαυτήν . . .
> ὥσπερ οὖν τὸ χόριον συγγενόμενον καὶ ἡ καλάμη τοῦ
> σίτου, τελεωθέντα δὲ ῥίπτεται ἑκάτερα, οὕτω καὶ τὸ
> συναρτώμενον τῇ ψυχῇ σπαρείσῃ σῶμα οὐ μέρος
> ἀνθρώπου· ἀλλ' ἵνα μὲν ἐν γαστρὶ γένηται,
> προσυφάνθη τὸ χόριον, ἵνα δὲ ἐπὶ γῆς γένηται,
> συνεζύγη τὸ σῶμα, κτλ.

Now Porphyry turned to medical problems elsewhere (Ad
Gaurum), so his use of such a metaphor is not entirely
surprising. And in defending the idea that soul must
enter the child only at the moment of parturition, he
joins a philosophical discussion that extends back into

(112) the second century and even before (Ad Gaurum II.1,
       translated in Festugière, Révélation d'Hermès III, 267).
       This takes us to the probable time of our author's work,
       an age otherwise characterized by modish public interest
       in anatomy, the age of the ἰατροσοφισταί (G. W. Bower-
       sock, Greek Sophists ch. 5). The text, then, even
       though odd, can be defended as a mode of expression
       understandable in our author's time.

            But the metaphor occurs in other, and earlier,
       sources than Porphyry. Origen's use of it, though to
       a different point (soul puts off its precarnate state
       upon its entry into this world, as a child its khorion),
       attests to its currency. Half a century before, Marcus
       Aurelius (IX. 3.2) could urge placid acceptance of
       Death as one of the natural functions, καὶ ὡς νῦν
       περιμένεις πότε ἔμβρυον ἐκ τῆς γαστρὸς τῆς γυναικός
       σου ἐξέλθῃ, οὕτως ἐκδέχεσθαι τὴν ὥραν ἐν ᾗ τὸ ψυχάριόν
       σου τοῦ ἐλύτρου τούτου ἐκπεσεῖται. Here the word
       khorion is not used, but the image is clearly implied
       by the more general word ἔλυτρον ('container'). Now
       ἔλυτρον is a Platonic metaphor, occurring in an impor-
       tant passage of the Republic (588 D-E): the soul has
       three parts,

            περίπλασον δὴ αὐτοῖς ἔξωθεν ἑνὸς εἰκόνα, τὴν τοῦ
            ἀνθρώπου, ὥστε τῷ μὴ δυναμένῳ τὰ ἐντὸς ὁρᾶν, ἀλλὰ
            τὸ ἔξω μόνον ἔλυτρον ὁρῶντι, ἓν ζῷον φαίνεσθαι,
            ἄνθρωπον.

The image was not forgotten: Lucian (Demon. 44) ridi-
cules the epitaph of a certain Admetus: γαῖα λάβ'
Ἀδμήτου ἔλυτρον· βῆ δ' εἰς θεὸν αὐτός.
     In the imagery which our author has adopted, the
notion of a 'container' of the inner man has been
colored by another idea found in Plato, that senectitude
is for the soul a time of preparation for birth. This
idea, which provides the context for the khorion image,
is found in Platonic passages cited below on 115. Cf.
Seneca Ep. 102.23: quemadmodum decem mensibus tenet nos
maternus uterus . . . sic per hoc spatium, quod ab

infantia patet in senectutem, in alium maturescimus
partum. Strabo (713) considers this idea to be
'Brahman': τὸν μὲν ἐνθάδε βίον ὡς ἄν ἀκμὴν κυομένων
εἶναι· τὸν δὲ θάνατον γένεσιν εἰς τὸν ὄντως βίον.

113   i.e., old age] Here the true difficulty with the manuscript reading χόριον emerges. In 112 the phrase 'of
the body' must be a genitive of constituency, for only
in a very strained sense is old age itself 'the envelope
of the body', i.e., what encloses the body. Furthermore,
if the remarks here are ad hominem, it is likely that
the addressee inquired about old age (a topic of discussion found elsewhere in Imperial philosophy) and not
body as such. Thus the author apparently equates old
age with body itself, perhaps meaning '(you inquire
about) the bodily envelope such as it is in old age'.
    I have translated the text of 112 as it is trans-
mitted, but an emendation is possible: ὅριον, terminus;
for old age marks the boundary of bodily life. We
should then have a recurrence of the thematic statement
found in 27f., '(the Savior spoke about) the law of the
natural order . . . death'. I cannot off hand cite an
ancient parallel to this metaphorical use of ὅριον, but
something similar occurs in literary Modern Greek,
though not perhaps in the vulgar language, cf. D.
Démétrakou, Mega Lexikon tés Ellénikés Glossés, v.6,
s.v. ὅριον ἡλικίας.

114   mere corruption] Literally, 'do you (qua mind) exist as
corruption (*φθορά)?'. This is a reductio ad absurdum,
since the deteriorating body merely contains soul as an
envelope. φθορά is an abstract term for the process of
passing out of existence (γενομένῳ παντὶ φθορά ἐστιν
Pla. R. 546 A). By extension it sometimes means 'that
which is wont to perish', though this usage is figura-
tive (Clem. Exc. Theod. 80.2, ἵνα . . . λυθῇ ἀναστάσει
. . . ἡ φθορά, 'might be destroyed by resurrection').
Peel's translation 'you exist in [i.e. 'within']

(114)   corruption' is attractive, but I doubt the Coptic will
support this: an indefinite article would be needed
from the Coptic point of view (otherwise, N̄ for ϨN̄
'in' is well attested). φθορά is also a medical term,
the process whereby the foetus is aborted or miscarries;
this seems to me irrelevant, though perhaps a pun is
intended (as in 115). For the figure, cf. 83 'he
became . . . undoing'.

     Clement rejects our author's idea, because of the
Incarnation (Paed. III. 2.3): ὁ δὲ συμπαθὴς θεὸς αὐτὸς
ἠλευθέρωσεν τὴν σάρκα τῆς φθορᾶς.

(115-125) <u>In fact, absence from the flesh can be thought</u>
<u>of as a benefit, for only the inferior part will be forfeited</u>
<u>when the superior part is separated from it. There is no sal-</u>
<u>vation for the inferior part. It is the Entirety, the totality</u>
<u>of minds, which constitutes 'the saved'; it has been always</u>
<u>'saved'. This is how we must understand the concept of</u>
<u>resurrection</u>.

<u>115</u>   <u>can count</u>] Literally 'have'.

         <u>absence</u>] Copt. has <u>apousia</u>. This is a pun:
         (1) 'absence' (from mind's point of view) of body,
         once the mind has gone back to the Fulness (cf. Bauer,
         <u>Lex</u>. s.v.); (2) 'shortage', 'deficit', a technical term
         from the accounting system of mints, Latin <u>intertrimen-</u>
         <u>tum</u> (Livy XXXII.2). When worn-out coins are reminted,
         there is a discrepancy between their bullion value and
         the value--as computed by tale--of the old coins to be
         reminted. This discrepancy, called in antiquity the
         ἀπουσία, results from poor condition of the old coins
         due to circulation, errors in manufacture, wastage at
         the mint, etc. For this meaning of ἀπουσία there is
         continual papyrological and literary evidence (Arist.
         <u>Meteor</u>. 383^{b}3, Agatharcides fr. 28 Mü.) as well as
         inscriptions (<u>F</u>. <u>Delphes</u> nos. 49, 67, 68; <u>IG</u> II^2 839).
         Cf. Stephanus-Dindorff, <u>Thesaurus</u> I/2 1764 D-1765 A,
         quoting Suicerus; E. J. P. Raven, <u>Numism</u>. <u>Chron</u>., 6th
         ser. 10 (1950) 1-22 (Delphic inscriptions); L. Robert,
         Bull. ép., <u>REG</u> 65 (1952) no. 63 (<u>IG</u> II^2 839); Ch.
         Dunant-J. Pouilloux, <u>BCH</u> 76 (1952) 32-60; A. M. Wood-
         ward, <u>Numism</u>. <u>Chron</u>., 6th ser. 11 (1951) 109-11, with
         Robert, Bull. ép., <u>REG</u> 66 (1953) no. 86.
              While the mind is still incarnate in an aging body,
         the body's decay--its failure to meet the standard--is
         for the mind a profit. The fiscal imagery continues
         below.

         <u>profit</u>] *κέρδος. Phil. 1.21 ἀποθανεῖν κέρδος. Pla.
         <u>Apol</u>. 40 D: θαυμάσιον κέρδος ἂν εἴη ὁ θάνατος.

For the idea that intellectual vision begins to
see clearly only when that of the eyes is beyond its
prime, cf. Pla. Smp. 219 A (on the text cf. Renehan in
Cl. Rev. N.S. 19 [1969] 270); Lg. 715 DE; Alc. I 131 E;
Clem. Stro. III. 18.4 quoting Pla. R. 328 D.

116   pay back] Or 'give back'. Text has either a compound of
       διδόναι or the simple form: e.g., ἀποδιδόναι, cf. Matt.
       5.26 (Sahidic Coptic and Gk.) et al. m.
            The sentiment in 116-118 expressly contradicts a
       popular and widely-used figure for death in Greek and
       Latin epitaphs and the closely related consolatio litera-
       ture, that life is on loan, a debt that must be paid up,
       surrendered (ἀποδιδόναι, reddere) to the creditor at its
       close. In the epitaphs it is usually pessimistic,
       referring to total annihilation (cf. R. Lattimore,
       Themes 171 n. 111):
            Cumont, Stud. Pont. III no. 143 (Gazacene)
                 ἀλλ' ἀποδοὺς τὸ δάνιον πεπόρευμε· ταῦτα
                 πάντα κόνις.
       (On the tauta formula, see now L. Robert, Hellenica
       13 (1965) 185.)
            Kaibel, Epigr. 613, 6-7 (Rome, a poet):
                 πνεῦμα λαβὼν δάνος οὐρανόθεν τελέσας χρόνον
                 ἀνταπέδωκα / καὶ μετὰ τὸν θάνατον Μοῦσαί μου
                 τὸ σῶμα κρατοῦσιν.
            IG 12 vii 119 (Amorgos):
                 τὸ τέλος ἀπέδωκα.
       (With a pun: telos = end/tax.)
       So IG 12 vii 120 (Amorgos); Kaibel 509 (Doliche, aet.
       rom.); 772a (Rome); Keil-Premerstein I 90 (near Phila-
       delphia); REG 28 (1915) 55, 1-2 (Thebes, aet. rom.), the
       latter consolatory.
       In Latin, from 10 A.D.:
            CIL VI 25617   debitum reddidit.
            Buecheler, Carmina 1327.13 (Cirta)   quot dedit, it
            repetit natura.
            CIL VI 3580 (Rome)   debitum naturae soluit.

ibid. VI 11693 (Rome)   debitum persoluit.
Similarly: CIL VI 37317 (Rome): VIII 16374, 16410
(Abuzza); RArch., 6 sér., 2 (1933) 389 no. 74 (Salonae);
Buecheler, Carmina 1120.2 (Vicetia), 2156.1 (Aquileia),
and as consolatio 1001.3-4 (Rome) quod quaeritis, id
repetitum apstulit iniustus creditor ante diem. The
figure rarely occurs as a consolatory sentiment in
inscriptions, but abundantly so in the literature,
apparently deriving from Simonides (in Anth. Pal. X.105)
and Crantor's lost peri penthous (Eurip. Alc. 782,
Palladas Anth. Pal. XI.62); cf. B. Lier, Philologus 62
(1903) 578ff.
        So in Clem. Stro. IV. 75.4.

118   takes a loss] Or 'is diminished'. Possibly the fiscal
        imagery does not continue here. Copt. literally 'has
        the [envisaged] diminishing' (*ἐλάττωσις etc.), as per-
        haps Hierocl. Stoicus BKT iv 49 (LSJ s.v.) ἐλαττώσεις
        σωματικαί. For ἔχειν with bodily states cf. LSJ s.v.
        A.I.8.

119   owes . . . gratitude] *χάριν *ὀφείλει. It is only thanks
        to the soul's presence (106) that it has lived at all.

120   buys us back] This traditional theological metaphor
        ('ransom') is heightened by the fiscal imagery of the
        context.
                The only true ransom is abandonment of the flesh.
        Yet we--qua superior element--are saved because we are
        inherently undying. The author now directs his thoughts
        away from proleptic resurrection to the aftermath of
        bodily death: cf. below.

121   we] Perhaps a wider audience is already addressed; cf.
        180 185.

123   salvation] *σωτηρία, here 'preservation', a common
        meaning. The inherent σωτηρία of mind makes 'ransom'
        a useless concept.

        start to finish] The exact meaning of the Coptic idiom
        can only be guessed at, cf. the Coptic commentary.
        Presumably it must be understood spatially, because the
        existence of the Fulness antedates time.

125   accept] Scil., νῳ, as often in Greek (λαμβάνειν plus
        adverb of manner: Hdt. VII.142, Thuc. IV. 17.3, Pla.
        Hipparch. 227 C, Arist. SE 174[b]27, Plut. Alc. 18, etc.).

(126-133) <u>Soteria ('salvation' or 'preservation') of</u>
<u>mind is immediate when mind is separated from the body. Will</u>
<u>the dead visible members (body) be preserved, then, when the</u>
<u>interior members (mind) within them arise? No, for resurrec-</u>
<u>tion is the uncovering of that which, as it were, has arisen</u>.

The <u>aporiae</u> or special problems now continue.
Again the doctrine of fleshly resurrection is attacked.
If, as in the traditional view, there is to be a general
resurrection, then the dead corpses must <u>wait</u> until the day
of judgment and their salvation (as flesh) will not be 'immediate'. Our author argues that this problem is beside the point
since mind inherently has the property of σωτηρία, and flesh
will not share in its fate.

126   <u>investigation</u> <u>of</u> <u>their</u> <u>investigations</u>] Ironic: the
        <u>figura</u> <u>etymologica</u> makes the research sound very scien-
        tific (Arist. <u>An</u>. <u>post</u>. 90^{a}5-6 συμβαίνει ἄρα ἐν ἀπάσαις
        ταῖς ζητήσεσι ζητεῖν ἢ εἰ ἔστι . . . etc.) and difficult
        (cf. <u>1</u> sq): while in fact the matter is 'simple' (<u>43</u>
        <u>sq</u>.).

127   <u>saved</u>] For the author this means 'inherently preserved';
        for the imaginary objector, 'saved' seems only to mean
        'destined to be preserved'.

        <u>taking</u> <u>off</u>] Putting off the flesh at death; the same
        metaphor is presupposed at <u>61</u>.

129   I.e., 'the answer is yes'.

130-   The final statement of objections raised at <u>101</u>-<u>108</u>.
131

130   <u>surely</u>] Literally, 'How, then, will the . . . members
        not be preserved?', using *πῶς of disbelief. See the

Grammatical Notes in loc. and Kühner-Gerth[3], 588.5 Anm.
9: πῶς . . . οὐ = affirmative statement.

members] Copt. has the plural of melos, 'limbs': i.e.,
one's body qua flesh.

131   members] Again the plural of melos, 'limbs', but here
       probably meaning the psychic faculties (no doubt includ-
       ing the nous). ὥσπερ τὰ μέλη τοῦ σώματος πολλὰ ὄντα εἷς
       ἄνθρωπος λέγεται, οὕτως καὶ μέλη ψυχῆς εἰσι πολλά, νοῦς,
       συνείδησις, θέλημα, λογισμοὶ κατηγοροῦντες καὶ
       ἀπολογούμενοι, ἀλλὰ ταῦτα πάντα εἰς ἕνα λογισμόν εἰσιν
       ἀποδεδεμένα· μέλη δέ ἐστι ψυχῆς, μία δέ ἐστι ψυχὴ ὁ ἔσω
       ἄνθρωπος, Ps.-Macarius Hom. 7.8; sim. Act. Thom. 27
       (Lips.-Bon. II/2 142,19); Odes of Solomon 21.3 ('my soul
       acquired members free from sorrow or affliction or
       pain'); cf. also Lampe s.v. 3. The implied comparison
       is of soul, perhaps even merely nous, to an interior
       man. The metaphor is Plato's (R. 589 A) and was ini-
       tially facilitated by his view that soul has μέρη, parts
       (μέλος and μέρος are close in meaning; μέλη καὶ μέρη
       occurs often in Plato, e.g., Phlb. 14 E, Lg. 795 E;
       though Arist. H. an. 486[a]9 distinguishes μέλη as neces-
       sarily ὅλα and comprising other μέρη in themselves).
       Thus by the time of Philo, the nous itself is called
       ὁ ἐν ἡμῖν πρὸς ἀλήθειαν ἄνθρωπος Plant. 42; ὁ ἄνθρωπος
       ἐν ἀνθρώπῳ Congr. 97; cf. ὁ ἔννους ἄνθρωπος C. H. I.18
       and 21 and Marcus's τὸ κυρίως σόν: here the metaphor
       has lost any necessary reference to a plurality of
       psychic parts, intending rather to distinguish the self
       from the organism. The Valentinian distinction between
       an indwelling man and the psyché (e.g., Iren. Haer. II.
       19.2 sq. [II. 28 sq. H.]) would seem to rest upon usage
       like that of Philo. The parallel gnostic usage is
       emphasized by edd. and Peel for exegesis of this passage,
       but this is unnecessary in light of the metaphor's
       earlier history.
           The plural in this passage may indicate that soul
       and its parts rather than nous alone is spoken of; or

the usage may be loose (cf. Bauer, Lex. μέλος s.v. [2];
cf. 2 Cor.4.16, Eph.3.16). In any case, our author
never really clarifies whether soul or, less inclusive-
ly, mind is the faculty to be saved. His metaphor is no
doubt suggested by the idea that though there is no
bodily resurrection, the spiritual resurrection can be
spoken of in a parallel way.

are supposed to] Literally 'would', scil. 'given the
assertions made above'.

132   Again the author answers a question with a question:
       cf. 109-114.

133   uncovering] *τὸ *ἀποκαλύπτειν or *ἡ *ἀποκάλυψις. Just
       as the rational part can be said to be 'hidden within'
       the flesh (Marcus Aurelius X.38 τὸ ἔνδον ἐγκεκρυμμένον),
       so it is natural to speak of its 'uncovering' or, in a
       literal sense, 'disclosure' when flesh disintegrates.
       The Coptic word (côlp) very often means 'revelation',
       but e.g., Shenute (C 73:14,25) can speak of the côlp
       ebol 'uncovering' of a sword out of its sheath.

       any given time] I.e., for each nous at its resurrection.
       Now the author's meaning is deliberately made ambiguous:
       on the one hand, spiritual 'uncovering' begins before
       the body's death, when we as it were strip off the body
       and wear the Savior instead (61); and on the other hand,
       the death of body also marks a definitive and final
       stage in the earthly career of the nous. A passage on
       resurrection in Clem. Paed. (I. 28.1 sq.) expresses this
       ambiguity in similar terms (though Clement, who is
       speaking of baptism, places less emphasis upon proleptic
       resurrection than does our author) and ends with a simi-
       lar use of the word ἀποκάλυψις:

              . . . οὐρανόθεν ἐπεισρέοντος ἡμῖν τοῦ ἀγίου
              πνεύματος. This is the eternal adjustment of
              the vision, which is able to see the eternal

(133)   light, since like loves like: and that which is
               holy, loves that from which holiness proceeds,
               which has appropriately been termed light . . .
               But [man] has not yet received, say they, the
               perfect gift. I also assent to this; but he is
               in the light, and the darkness comprehendeth him
               not . . . But the end is reserved till the resur-
               rection of those who believe . . . For we do not
               say that both take place together at the same
               time--both the arrival at the end, and the anti-
               cipation of that arrival . . . Faith, so to speak,
               is the attempt generated in time; the final result
               is the attainment of the promise, secured for
               eternity . . . If, then, those who have believed
               have life, what remains beyond the possession of
               eternal life? Nothing is wanting to faith, as it
               is perfect and complete in itself . . . having in
               anticipation grasped by faith that which is future,
               after the resurrection we receive it as present
               . . . And where faith is, there is the promise;
               and the consummation of the promise is rest. So
               that in illumination what we receive is knowledge,
               and the end of knowledge is rest . . . by illumina-
               tion must darkness disappear. The darkness is
               ignorance, through which we fall into sins,
               purblind as to the truth . . . . (ANL translation)
               [I 29.5:] ἀλλὰ καὶ ἡ τῶν χειρόνων ἀποβολὴ τῶν
               κρειττόνων ἐστὶν ἀποκάλυψις. ἃ γὰρ ἡ ἄγνοια
               συνέδησεν κακῶς, ταῦτα διὰ τῆς ἐπιγνώσεως
               ἀναλύεται καλῶς. τὰ δὲ δεσμὰ ταῦτα, ἢ τάχος,
               ἀνίεται πίστει μὲν ἀνθρωπίνῃ, θεΐκῇ δὲ τῇ χάριτι,
               ἀφιεμένων τῶν πλημμελημάτων ἑνὶ παιωνίῳ φαρμάκῳ,
               λογικῷ βαπτίσματι.

the elements that have arisen] I.e., 'each thing as it
"arises"': once a mind has 'arisen', it can be said to
'be uncovered'.

(134-162) <u>The Transfiguration of Jesus did not indicate</u>
<u>that resurrection is a phenomenon perceptible to the illusory</u>
<u>sensory faculties. Resurrection pertains to the domain of the</u>
<u>real and the incorruptible, not to what is visible and in flux</u>.

A possible counterexample from scripture is now
disposed of.

134   <u>if</u> <u>you</u> <u>should</u> <u>recall</u>] Schenke is bothered by the present
        perfect (Coptic Perf. I), but this is still meant <u>ad</u>
        <u>hominem</u> to the imaginary objector in <u>130</u>-<u>131</u>.

135   <u>in</u> <u>the</u> <u>Gospel</u>] Copt. has <u>euaggelion</u>. Besides the
        canonical gospels which contain this pericope there
        were a number of gospel harmonies circulating in the
        second century, cf. <u>HTR</u> 61 (1968) 350 n. 24, adding
        Clem. <u>Stro</u>. IV. 41.2 with Stählin's bibliog. in loc.
        Any of these, too, might be meant by the words found
        here.

136   Vis-à-vis the canonical gospel texts, this is not a
        quotation, but an extreme condensation (cf. <u>18</u>-<u>19</u>). It
        is meant as a <u>reference</u> to the entire pericope. The
        words 'with him' presumably refer to Jesus: ὤφθη αὐτοῖς
        Μωϋσῆς καὶ 'Ηλίας συλλαλοῦντες μετ' αὐτοῦ (Matt.17.3 or
        sim. parallel texts, Mark 9.4, Luke 9.30). Nothing can
        be concluded as to which gospel text is used here:
        perhaps all three. Peel (p. 19f., 89f.) would eliminate
        Matt. and Luke from question on the grounds that 'the
        order of appearance of Elijah and Moses corresponds to
        Mark's account instead of to Luke's or Matthew's'. Yet
        does not Mark's 'Ηλίας σὺν Μωϋσεῖ, 'Elias in the company
        of Moses', imply the same order of precedence as Matt.
        and Luke Μωϋσῆς καὶ 'Ηλίας? Matt. and Luke have simply
        corrected Mark's Greek stylistically, but keeping his
        intent: Moses and, accompanying him, Elijah, where the
        order of precedence is historical. Our text <u>136</u> has

something different: Elijah is singled out as the most
important figure and for this reason is mentioned first:
'that Elias appeared--and Moses--with Him'. By consult-
ing the remainder of the canonical text, we can see that
Elijah is there said to be the one who ἀποκαταστήσει
πάντα (using Mal.3.23), 'will bring about the return of
all things': Matt.17.12, Mark 9.12 (not in Luke 9.28
sq.). And this seems to resonate with our text's use of
apokatastasis, the 'return' to the Fulness.

137   suppose] I.e., 'conclude from this'.

       resurrection] The resurrection--i.e., spiritual
       resurrection--of every believing nous is meant, not
       specifically that of Jesus.

138   an apparition] Copt. is ambiguous, implying either
       *φαντασία or *φανταστική. So in the following line and
       at 140, 'real' is either *ἀληθής or *ἀλήθεια.
          The objection here entertained is still that of
       130-131: if Elijah and Moses, though dead, could be
       seen in their resurrection state, will not the body,
       vivified by the superior part, continue to exist at
       least as a kind of shade, visible but insubstantial--a
       φάντασμα? To answer this the author makes reference to
       the basic distinction between the visible world of flux
       and inevitable decay, and the invisible realm of eternal
       being, to which mind inherently belongs.
          The word *phantasia or *phantastikê, which I trans-
       late an apparition, has the basic meaning of 'unreal'
       throughout this passage: it contrasts with 'real' (139-
       140). This use of φαντασία is more pejorative than its
       usual meaning, 'impression' or 'first impression', a
       usage whose intent is to be noncommittal as to the
       reality of what seems to be the case (thus Alexander of
       Aphrodisias can say, addressing Severus and Caracalla:
       οὐδεμίαν γοῦν πρᾶξιν ὑμῶν ἐστιν εὑρεῖν ἢ τὴν φαντασίαν
       πρὸ τῆς ἀληθείας σκοπὸν πεποίηται, De fato I, p. 165,8

(<u>138</u>)   Bruns). Cf. Clem. <u>Stro</u>. I. 39.1 (using Pla. <u>Soph</u>. 239
C, 236 C, 240 D, 226 A):

ἡ δὲ σοφιστικὴ τέχνη, ἣν ἐζηλώκασιν ῞Ελληνες,
δύναμίς ἐστι φανταστική, διὰ λόγων δοξῶν
ἐμποιητικὴ ψευδῶν ὡς ἀληθῶν· παρέχει γὰρ πρὸς
μὲν πειθὼ τὴν ῥητορικήν, πρὸς τὸ ἀγωνιστικὸν
δὲ τὴν ἐριστικήν.

Behind this usage lies a long history of technical discussion in the field of epistemology. <u>Phantasia</u> is both
the psychic <u>image</u> implying the reception of sense-data,
and the faculty of reconjuring such an image (i.e., the
<u>imagination</u>). As such it is contrastible with both
sense-data and things in themselves. Sceptic and
Empiricist attacks upon the reliability of <u>phantasiae</u>,
as well as interference from the word <u>phantasma</u>
('ghost'), help to account for ordinary usage like
that of our author.

Both <u>phantasia</u> and <u>phantasma</u> are terms which occur
in the Docetist debate, but there the issues are quite
different--whether Jesus suffered in real or imaginary
flesh, and the nature of his resurrection appearance
(e.g., Hipp. <u>Ref</u>. VII. 38.4 αὐτὸς εἴη, καὶ οὐ φάντασμα
ἀλλὰ ἔνσαρκος ἦν). For our author there is no doubt,
first that the Savior (and like him, all saved minds)
had preexisted discarnate and became incarnate in real
flesh; and second, that resurrection involves the complete laying aside of flesh, first by anticipation, then
literally.

142   <u>world</u> <u>is</u> <u>an</u> <u>apparition</u>] Hyperbolic. (The technical
meaning is of course true; the visible world is 'produc-
tive of <u>phantasiae</u>': to an Epicurean these constituted
perceptible reality as such, without qualification,
φαντασίας ἀληθεῖς ἁπάσας, Epic. fr. 254 Us.) This
hyperbolic inversion of terms is used with similar
apologetic intent in the context of Docetist controversy,
for example, by Ignatius (<u>Sm</u>. 2.1):

ἀληθῶς ἔπαθεν, ὡς καὶ ἀληθῶς ἀνέστησεν ἑαυτόν, οὐχ
ὥσπερ ἄπιστοί τινες λέγουσιν, τὸ δοκεῖν αὐτὸν
πεπονθέναι, αὐτοὶ τὸ δοκεῖν ὄντες ('while it is
they who are unreal'). καὶ καθὼς φρονοῦσιν, καὶ
συμβήσεται αὐτοῖς, οὖσιν ἀσωμάτοις καὶ δαιμονικοῖς.

143   Savior . . . Excellent] Copt. has sôtêr . . . khrêstos,
      as at 11.

144- The changeability of the visible world is evident in the
150   ethical as well as the physical domain. Social insta-
      bility was for Stoics 'a matter of indifference'
      (ἀδιάφορον), so that life in this world could be tolera-
      ted calmly, whatever fate might bring. Here it is not:
      our author totally deprecates life in this world. This,
      as much as a priori considerations of ontology or
      physics (cf. 27 etc.), makes the kosmos only a place
      from which one must escape. This short harangue ends
      (149) with a reference to an appropriate dictum of
      Heraclitus and gently turns the discussion back to
      ontological distinctions.

145   suddenly] The untimeliness of physical death is an
      exceedingly common lament in ancient Greek and Latin
      epitaphs: cf. B. Lier, Philologus 62 (1903) 453ff.
      (much Greek material); more briefly, R. Lattimore,
      Themes 184ff. So too it is a stock topos recommended
      by the rhetorician Menander for an epitaphios (περὶ
      ἐπιδεικτικῶν p. 435, 1 Spengel, Rh. Gr. III; 435,39;
      413,15; 419,30, cf. Lier 455f.), an occasion to
      σχετλιάζειν . . . πρὸς δαιμόνας καὶ πρὸς μοῖραν ἄδικον,
      πρὸς πεπρωμένην νόμον (Men. p. 435,10 Spengel, Lier 461).

      'living'] Ironic: what is commonly said to be 'alive',
      i.e., physically alive, must die. Cf. 167 sq.

146   Literally, 'How [pôs] can they be alive in a . . .'.

The 'living' of 145 are not really alive at all: the
body is meant.

147-   Commonplace paradigmatic examples, wealth and power.
148   Such a reference to 'rulers' is not strange in the
       Imperial period. It is normal, for example, as a con-
       solation in Imperial Latin epitaphs and the related
       literature to compare the ultimate fate of the common
       man to that of 'kings': haec eadem et magnis regibus
       acciderunt (Buecheler, Carmina 970 etc.); Ps.-Plut.
       Cons. ad Apoll. 15,110 D; Lucret. III.1025; Sen. Cons.
       ad Pol. XI.4 etc.; Cons. ad Marc. XV.1 ('Caesar', Lier,
       l.c. 575-578). The perfect tense is used because the
       author is arguing from past experience.

149   Heraclitus, cf. D. L. IX.8 = Diels, Fr. Vorsokr. I.69
       etc. The dictum was frequently used to describe
       ontological flux: Pla. Cra. 411 C: αὐτὰ τὰ πράγματα
       οὕτω πεφυκέναι, οὐδὲν αὐτῶν μόνιμον εἶναι οὐδὲ βέβαιον,
       ἀλλὰ ῥεῖν καὶ φέρεσθαι καὶ μεστὰ εἶναι πάσης φορᾶς καὶ
       γενέσεως ἀεί: Tht. 182 C ('changing'), etc. The idea
       remained a commonplace (Sallustius IV, p. 8,11 Nock).
       It might of course be either more, or less, negative in
       tone; Marcus Aurelius uses it both ways (τοῦ ἀνθρωπίνου
       βίου, ὁ μὲν χρόνος στιγμή, ἡ δὲ οὐσία ῥέουσα, ἡ δὲ
       αἴσθησις ἀμυδρὰ κτλ. II.17, cf. IV.43: less negatively,
       VI.15, VII.19, IX.29). For the social implications, cf.
       ἀπάνθ' ὁρῶ ἅμα τῇ τύχῃ ῥέοντα μεταπίπτοντά τε, Com.
       adesp. 200; Kock CAF iii. Cf. Democrates Gnom. 85
       (Democritus fr. 115 Diels Fr. Vorsokr., Marcus Aurelius
       IV.3): ὁ κόσμος ἀλλοίωσις, ὁ βίος ὑπόληψις.

151   For the rhetorical figure of epidiorthosis (where the
       author catches himself conveniently too late), cf.
       Pauline examples noted by Bl.-D.-F. 495.3. Cf. C. H.
       XIII.13 ἵνα μὴ ὦμεν διάβολοι τοῦ παντός, XIII.22, etc.

153   real] *ἀληθής.

154   It is what is constant] Or simply 'It is constant'
       (*μόνιμος). This is a stock attribute of the realm of
       being, cf. Pla. Cra. 411 C, above with 149; Ti. 29 B;
       Clem. Stro. VII. 57.5 (φῶς ἑστὸς καὶ μένον ἀϊδίως,
       παντῇ πάντως ἄτρεπτον); II. 51.6; cf. Herm. Tris. fr.
       IIa apud Stob. (C. H. vol. III pp. 4-8 Festugière), etc.

155-   In what follows the author summarizes his earlier
162   description of the Savior's efforts to turn the believ-
       ing minds towards higher objects.

155   revealing . . . what truly exists] Cf. 44 'manifestation
       of the superior part', 133 'uncovering . . . of the
       elements that have arisen'.

156   what one receives in exchange] Or 'a change', i.e., a
       change of location and not of inherent attribute.

       circumstances of this world] Text has simply *πράγματα,
       circumstances of this world as at 21. Just as the
       Savior 'laid aside the perishable world and exchanged
       it for an unperishing eternal realm' 48-50, so do all
       believers in spiritual resurrection.

       migration] (Copt. has metabolê as in Arist. H. an.
       597ᵃ3.) As a metaphor for the soul's transition at
       physical death, this word is attested also in the
       Hermetic literature (C. H. XI.15, XII.6 with Nock in
       loc.); also in Philost. VA VIII.31; often with preposi-
       tional phrase Clem. Stro. VII. 56.7, 57.5 ἐπὶ τὸ
       κρεῖττον, IV. 28.2 ἐπὶ τὰ ἀμείνω . . . ἐκ νυκτερινῆς
       τινος ἡμέρας (using Pla. R. 521 C); τῶν κατ᾽ ἐκεῖνον
       τὸν χρόνον περιόντων ἔτι πρὸς τὸ κρεῖττον Athenag. Res.
       12, p. 63,9f. Schw. [of anastasis]; εἰς τὴν ἀφθαρσίαν

Method. Symp. IV.2; εἰς τὸ κρεῖττον . . . ἀπὸ ταύτης τῆς καταστάσεως τοῦ κόσμου Method. De res. I. 48.1; etc.

newness] *καινότης, but without the pejorative classical nuance of novelty. Here the metaphor is probably taken, not entirely aptly, from traditional Christian ways of speaking (Paul; Odes of Solomon 36.5 'like his own new-ness he renewed me', etc.), since in fact neither bodi-lessness nor location in the Fulness will be new to the superior part. The change is new only if compared solely to incarnate existence.

157-162   These concluding words of summary are written in a self-consciously emotional prose style. The terms themselves have already been used. This is the climax; we need not suppose that an external source is drawn upon simply because of the author's change in style. The stylistic model for this procedure is already found in Plato (Symposium, Phaedrus). Plato is followed in this, e.g., by Plotinus, who will resort to long periods in a meta-phorical, 'poetic' style when speaking of the Beautiful, the vision of the supernatural home of the soul, etc., but otherwise will write as an academician or teacher. Cf. Norden, Kunstprosa 400.

157   incorruption . . . corruption] Both of these terms and the image of 'swallowing' are found in 1 Cor.15.53-54; perhaps a literary allusion is intended.

158   light . . . darkness] A restatement of the same idea: saving knowledge was brought down by the Savior; it is intellectual 'illumination' (a commonplace Greek image since Plato). For the Savior as sun, cf. 62. Darkness is the obvious image for ignorance; cf. Athenag. Res. 19, p. 71,30f. Schw.: ζόφος δέ τις βαθὺς κατακέχυται τῆς γῆς ἀγνοίᾳ καὶ σιγῇ κρύπτων αὐτούς τε τοὺς ἀνθρώπους καὶ τὰς τούτων πράξεις.

is streaming down] Later this became a Neo-Platonic
mode of speech (the dogma of the inexhaustible outpour-
ing of sunlight). But it is already anticipated, e.g.,
by Marcus Aurelius VIII.57, who speaks of light
'pouring forth' (κατακεχύσθαι) and never 'running out',
and of its being stretched as above at 65. So too he
says, of the guardianship of providence for this world,
πάντα ἐκεῖθεν ῥεῖ II.3 (perhaps the thread of fortune
is meant; yet XII.2 the nous has flowed into the fleshly
envelope from God); the image is partly encouraged by
his Pneumatist materialism.

159   swallowing] Cf. 46 the Savior swallowed death; 52 he
      swallowed the visible by means of the invisible; 68
      spiritual resurrection swallows other kinds.

160   lack] This doctrine is discussed below in
      chapter III.

161   symbols] Copt. has sumbola.

      likenesses] The Coptic word does not suggest *εἰκόνες
      (as Ptol. Ad Floram, Epiph. Pan. haer. 33.5.9, 6.5
      εἰκόνες καὶ σύμβολα) but rather some other word, e.g.,
      *ὁμοιώματα.
          Presumably the author does not include 'Fulness'
      and 'lack' among what he calls metaphors. Insertion of
      this parenthetical remark allows a transition back to
      an ad hominem pedagogical style.

162   this] Or 'he' (the Copt. is ambiguous). The pronoun
      (which is grammatically masculine or neuter) cannot
      refer to 'the resurrection' (which is grammatically
      feminine). It must refer either to the Savior (above
      spoken of as light and incorruption: *αὐτός, ipse), or
      to the Fulness, or to light, or to all the facts

(162)   narrated in 157-160 (*αὐτό): probably the latter. Cf.
        Pla. Ep. II 312 E: περὶ τὸν πάντων βασιλέα πάντ' ἐστὶ
        καὶ ἐκείνου ἕνεκα πάντα, καὶ ἐκεῖνο αἴτιον ἁπάντων τῶν
        καλῶν. Clem. Protr. I. 6.4f. makes the latter passage
        personal, however, referring to Christ the Reason, and
        thus supporting the other possible interpretation of
        our passage.

(163-178) <u>Strive to escape from conformity to life in</u>
<u>the flesh, escape from its bondage and the state of dispersion</u>,
<u>and you already have spiritual resurrection. Do this for the</u>
<u>sake of oneness. 'Know thyself'. The flesh knows that it is</u>
<u>inevitably dying: can you not see that the real 'you' has</u>
<u>arisen and is headed for a different end? Indeed the flesh is</u>
<u>already dead.</u>

There is much of convention in what follows. Yet here
the author also comes to his most explicit explanation of
proleptic or spiritual resurrection: the escape from fleshly
bondage, which comes at death (an event towards which philosophy could only 'practice', Pla. <u>Phd</u>. 67 A)--can <u>begin</u> as soon
as one ceases to νοεῖν μερικῶς and ceases to live for the body.
It is this state of spiritual and physical asceticism which is
'resurrection'. Close behind the author's exposition lies the
gnostic doctrine of Pleromatic Deficiency (discussed below in
chapter III). Through spiritual resurrection the believing
mind can 'recover its former state' (<u>183</u>) of bodilessness, a
state of repose in the Fulness; and correspondingly the Fulness
can regain its oneness (<u>164</u>) through recovery of its lacking
members, cf. <u>160</u>.

163   <u>concentrate</u> <u>on</u> <u>particulars</u>] Copt. has <u>noei(n)</u> <u>merikôs</u>.
       Presumably this means νοεῖν κατὰ μέρος, referring to the
       kind of questions which the author has so brusquely dis-
       posed of in the preceding sections: κατὰ μέρος is used
       of the detailed treatment of a subject, cf. Pla. <u>Tht</u>.
       157 B, <u>Soph</u>. 246 C; much later evidence is given in ·
       Bauer <u>Lex</u>. s.v. For μερικῶς, e.g., Sophronius of Jerus.
       <u>Ep</u>. <u>syn</u>., <u>MPG</u> 87.3196 B: τὰ δόγματα ἅπερ μερικῶς ὑμῖν
       καὶ διὰ βραχέων ἐκτέθειμαι. Clement uses the word in
       opposition to τελείως, contrasting the 'Greek' claims to
       full knowledge of truth with their view of Christianity
       (<u>Stro</u>. VI. 55.4): but he has in mind Paul's γινώσκειν
       ἐκ μέρους (1 Cor.13.9 sq.), as does Orig. <u>In</u> <u>Jo</u>. XIII
       10.58, cited by edd. So at <u>Stro</u>. VI. 160.1, where he
       turns the table on Greek philosophy with the same term

(ἐπιτευτικὸν τῆς ἀληθείας κἂν μερικὸν τυγχάνῃ).

Our author, however, speaks not of the acquisition
of knowledge or of gaining acquaintance but of the constant and natural activity of <u>nous</u>. νοεῖν is the only
activity proper to the believing mind. If the mind is
deflected from its hypnotic 'alertness' to truth (<u>84</u>
sq.), spiritual resurrection is not possible. This,
then, is why detailed investigations like those attacked
in <u>1</u> sq., must be avoided; academic speculation is not
merely fruitless but positively harmful. This, too, is
why the author is reluctant to give more than a mere
<u>logos</u>, an 'account', and why his replies to the <u>aporiae</u>
or imaginary objections are so dogmatic and abrupt.

164   live] Copt. has <u>politeuesthai</u>, a normal Hellenistic and
       Imperial metaphor, having lost its original political
       overtones. This is hardly a 'Pauline and Valentinian
       term', <u>pace</u> edd. Cf. Bauer <u>Lex</u>. for documentation (πολ.
       κατά . . . from 188 B.C., <u>SIG</u>³ 618,12).

       <u>do</u> <u>not</u>] I add these words for the sake of clarity.

       <u>oneness</u>] The exact meaning is unclear. The Coptic word
       (<u>mnt-oueei</u>, 'one-ness': -<u>oueei</u> = 'one-', <u>mnt</u>- = '-ness')
       is poorly attested. It may be a translation of ὁμόνοια,
       thus 'for the sake of harmony'; ἑνότης is also a possi-
       bility, 'for the sake of unity'.
              The idea that all minds are cognate is commonplace,
       e.g., in Stoic monism: Marcus Aurelius XII.30 μία ψυχὴ
       κἂν φύσεσι διείργηται μυρίαις καὶ ἰδίαις περιγραφαῖς.
       μία νοερὰ ψυχή, κἂν διακεκρίσθαι δοκῇ. Such a view is
       not limited to Stoics, cf. Sext. Emp. <u>Adv</u>. <u>math</u>. IX.127
       (Pythagoreans). 'We live in parts' (Emerson). πάντα
       ἄρα ἐσμὲν ἕν Plot. VI. 5.7.8. So, too, Pythagorean
       dualism might describe its first principle as Unity
       (<u>Plac</u>. <u>philos</u>. I. 7.18, Diels, <u>Doxogr</u>. <u>Gr</u>. p. 302):

              Πυθαγόρας τῶν ἀρχῶν τὴν μονάδα θεὸν καὶ τἀγαθόν,
              ἥτις ἐστὶν ἡ τοῦ ἑνὸς φύσις, αὐτὸς ὁ νοῦς· τὴν

δ' ἀόριστον δυάδα δαίμονα καὶ τὸ κακόν, περὶ ἥν
ἐστι τὸ ὑλικὸν πλῆθος.

But the context (160 'the Fulness is filling up its
lack') suggests something different--a unity that is
contingent upon abnegation of particularity, both men-
tally and physically. This kind of unity is in effect
the reunification of the Fulness.

Such a view is found in Valentinian sources of the
second century. These are assembled and cited by the
edd.: e.g., Irenaeus Haer. II. 12.3 (13.3 H.) quemadmodum autem et ipsi ad unitatem recurrere dicunt, et
omnes unum esse; I. 13.3 'go up with Him into τὸ ἕν';
21.3 (14.2 H.) 'into henôsis' (so Clem. Exc. Theod.
22.3); II. 17.4 (21.4 H.) in principalem unitionem
recurrunt. Several passages in Gosp. Tr. are quite
close: CG I 25:10-19 'it is within the Unity (mnt-
oueei) that each will recover himself' (cf. 181). So
in 24:26-28, 'the place of the Unity is fulness (sic)'.

This view, which is found in our text, must be
finally distinguished from two others, adduced by
Clement: first, that the Church is the unity to which
all Christians belong (Stro. VII. 14.1 ἐκφωτιζόμενος
εἰς ἕνωσιν), mirrored by unity of belief (Stro. VII.
107). This is in Clement a bowdlerizing of Valentinian
gnosticism with the aid of Eph.4.3. Second, there is
Clement's opinion that discarnate souls are neither male
nor female, but rather that the soul upon leaving body
μετατίθεται εἰς ἕνωσιν, οὐθέτερον οὖσα Stro. III. 93.2f.
This view is widely held and is typically though not
exclusively encratitic (III. 92).

165   dispersion] This is the natural pendant idea to 'unity'
above. An odd parallel is formed by the closing exhortation of Aristophanes' speech in the Symposium (192 E
sq.):

τοῦτο γάρ ἐστι τὸ αἴτιον, ὅτι ἡ ἀρχαία φύσις
ἡμῶν ἦν αὕτη καὶ ἦμεν ὅλοι· τοῦ ὅλου οὖν τῇ
ἐπιθυμίᾳ καὶ διώξει ἔρως ὄνομα. καὶ πρὸ τοῦ,

(165)   ὥσπερ λέγω, ἓν ἦμεν, νυνὶ δὲ διὰ τὴν ἀδικίαν
διῳκίσθημεν ὑπὸ τοῦ θεοῦ, καθάπερ ᾿Αρκάδες ὑπὸ
Λακεδαιμονίων . . . (If we disobey the gods we
shall be further sundered.) ἀλλὰ τούτων ἕνεκα
πάντ᾿ ἄνδρα χρὴ ἅπαντα παρακελεύεσθαι εὐσεβεῖν
περὶ θεούς, ἵνα τὰ μὲν ἐκφύγωμεν, τῶν δὲ
τύχωμεν . . . .

This term figures also in Valentinianism: Clem.
Exc. Theod. 36.2 ἡμεῖς ἦμεν οἱ μεμερισμένοι. Jesus was
baptized to divide the indissoluble (death) μέχρις ἡμᾶς
ἐνώσῃ αὐτοῖς εἰς τὸ πλήρωμα. ἵνα ἡμεῖς οἱ πολλοί ἓν
γενόμενοι κτλ.

bondage] The body is a prison, the flesh a chain bind-
ing the soul to lower things. A commonplace image
deriving from Plato, Phd. 62 B (ἔν τινι φρουρᾷ ἐσμεν);
82 E; 84 A; 81 D: evil souls ἀναγκάζονται πλανᾶσθαι
. . . ἕως ἂν τῇ τοῦ συνεπακολουθοῦντος τοῦ σωματοειδοῦς
ἐπιθυμίᾳ . . . ἐνδεθῶσιν εἰς σῶμα. Cra. 400 C. In
Plato the image appears in association with that of 'the
body a tomb' (σῶμα σῆμα), which Plato calls Orphic (Cra.
400 C) and Clement (Stro. III. 17.1) attributes to
Philolaus (fr. 14 Diels, Fr. Vorsokr.). So too the
passage which follows in our text speaks of body simply
as 'the dying part' (167) or that which 'has died' (178).
This chain of associations is Platonic.
     Taken alone, the image of the body as a prison is
widespread and well-known. It is popular on epitaphs:
Kaibel, Epigr. 463 λειποῦσα δεσμόν, ᾧ φύσις συνεῖχέ με,
Buecheler, Carmina 679 corporis exutus uinclis; 743; 783
corporeo laetae (scil. animae) gaudent se carcere solui;
91 [a schoolmaster of ?Capua] dum haberet clausum in
castello ani[mu]lam mortalem. So in consolationes:
Sen. Ad Pol. IX.3 (ex diutino carcere emissus), IX.8;
Ad Marc. XXIV.5. Cf. Cic. Tusc. I.31; I.49; De rep.
VI.14; De diuin. I. 49.110; Ps.-Pla. Ax. 370 D; Ps.-
Dionys. Rhet. VI.5; Clem. Stro. VII. 40.1.
     So, too, in the most read passage of the Symposium
(210 C) there is the image of slavery associated with

attention to <u>particulars</u> (τὸ παρ' ἑνί) instead of genus;
with this, cf. the author's remarks in <u>163</u>.

166   <u>and then</u>] Text has simply 'and', but this is the verna-
cular equivalent of a conditional sentence, Bl.-D.-F.
471.3.

<u>already</u>] Copt. has êdê (ἤδη), the key-word in realized
eschatology (frequent in Clement). This was the view of
Hymenaeus and Philetus, who are opposed in 2 Timothy.
Hippolytus attributes the view to a mysterious, and perhaps entirely fictitious, Nikolaus (<u>De</u> <u>res</u>. fr. I, p.
251,10-17 Ach.: his proleptic resurrection is said to
be the baptismal uprising, without any doctrine of
fleshly resurrection). Using Platonic terms, Clement
(<u>Stro</u>. VII. 71.3 [cf. <u>Phd</u>. 67 D]) paraphrases our
author's idea as follows:

ἡ γνῶσις οἷον ὁ λογικὸς θάνατος, ἀπὸ τῶν παθῶν
ἀπάγων καὶ χωρίζων τὴν ψυχὴν καὶ προάγων εἰς τὴν
τῆς εὐποιΐας ζωήν.

<u>have</u> <u>resurrection</u>] I.e., 'are arisen'. For ἔχειν with
a bodily or mental state, cf. LSJ s.v. A.I.8, and cf.
<u>118</u> 'the inferior has (the) diminution', i.e., takes a
loss.

167-   The arrangement of clauses is explained in Gramm.
175   Appendix 7.
      The harangue continues on another commonplace of
Greek thought, the Delphic maxim 'know thyself'. A
close parallel is provided, e.g., by Epict. III. 1.18
and 25 sq., where a young man is urged to give up care
for his body, to know that ἄνθρωπος εἶ, comprising a
mortal body (θνητόν) and a superior element (ἐξαιρετόν).
In our text this kind of dualism is so strongly presupposed that the body is completely apostrophized: <u>it</u>
can know itself--and so too <u>nous</u> should know <u>itself</u>.

(167-   'Know' in this idiom means 'become acquainted with',
175)   ginôskein.

        The offhand manner in which the maxim appears in
our text is not unusual because it was so widely known.
For this we have rich literary documentation, partly
assembled by E. G. Wilkins in two monographs (Delph.
Maxims in Lit. [1929], 'Know thyself' in Gk. and Lat.
Lit. [1917]; cf. also J. E. B. Mayor, commentary on
Juv. XI.27). As Plutarch notes, the meaning of this
adage was both uncertain (Sept. sap. 21, 164 B) and the
object of much discussion (De E 2, 385 D, ὅσας ζητήσεις
κεκίνηκε φιλοσόφους . . .). It was attributed to
various of the Seven Wise Men (Thales, Solon, given by
Pythian Apollo to Chilon: Corp. Paroem. Graec. II.750)
and along with two other sayings was inscribed at the
great temple of Delphi (Xen. Mem. IV. 2.24-30; Plut. De
garr. 17, 511 B). Thus its dissemination was at least
partly due to Delphic propaganda (J. Defradas, Thèmes
propag. delph. 268ff.) and tourism to Delphi. There was
also the literary transmission mentioned above (attested
in belles lettres from the time of Aeschylus), as well
as constant citation in ethical investigations, with
interpretations that vary according to the philosophical
context.

        At least one Greek gymnasium has yielded a stela on
which the three great Delphic maxims were transcribed,
IG XII 1020 (4th ct. B.C.); in a Bactrian heroön other
Delphic paraggelmata are inscribed (L. Robert, CRAIBL
1968, 421 sq.), as at Mysian Miletopolis (SIG[3] 1268).
So too our maxim figures in the popular pessimism of
funerary inscriptions: Buecheler carm. 241, cogitato
te hominem esse et scito moriendust uale; 389; 71; 808;
1544; Kaibel, Epigr. 533 γνῶθι βίου τὸ τέλος, etc.
Closely related is the Greek βλέπε formula on epitaphs,
cf. L. Robert, Rev. Phil., 3 sér., 18 (1944) 53-56, and
now Hellenica 13 (1965) 271-73. A mosaic floor from the
Via Appia and now at the Museo dei Termi in Rome depicts
a skeleton with the motto ΓΝΩΘΙ ΣΑΥΤΟΝ (R. Paribeni, Le
terme di Diocleziano, 2nd ed., 64 no. 57 [inv. no. 1025]).

The connotation of the maxim is usually pessimis-
tic, as in our text (thus the Byzantine paroemiographers,
probably using Theophrastus, have it concern 'those who
boast beyond their abilities', Corp. Paroem. Graec.
I.391, II.19 and 349; for Theophr., cf. II.750). But
in a context of anthropological dualism there is always
another side to the coin: if the body is limited, so
too is human knowledge (Pla. Phdr. 229 E), but self-
examination reveals that the soul is divine (τὸ θεῖον
γνοῦς) Pla. Alc. I 133 C. This interpretation of the
maxim in the Platonizing tradition (it is as old as
Plato himself) has been recently discussed by H. D. Betz
in HTR 63 (1970) 465-484, and it is this double aspect
upon which our author plays.

167   knows itself, and knows that] Gk. construction probably
       like Xen. Cyr. II. 1.11 τοὺς . . . Πέρσας γιγνώσκειν
       ὅτι . . ., cf. Kühner-Gerth[3], 600.4 (subject of subord.
       clause anticipated as object in main clause).

169   the present life] Copt. has 'this bios'.

170   it is rushing] Text has *φέρεται which often means 'is
       carried or borne inexorably' (cf. LSJ s.v.). For this
       use of φ. cf. Marcus Aurelius V.16:

           οὗπερ ἕνεκεν ἕκαστον κατασκεύασται, <πρὸς τοῦτο
           κατεσκεύασται (Gat.)> , πρὸς ὃ δὲ κατεσκεύασται,
           πρὸς τοῦτο φέρεται ('tends')· πρὸς ὃ φέρεται δὲ,
           ἐν τούτῳ τὸ τέλος αὐτοῦ.

       With the idea, cf. the popular funerary tag, ταῦτα
       or τοῦτο τὸ τέλος, now discussed by Robert, Hellenica 13
       (1965) 185 (with bibliogr.). So on a Syrian epitaph
       (Mél. fac. or. Univ. St.-Jos. Beyrouth I, 149, no. 18)
       εἰς αὐτὸ ἐγεννήθης.

171   you] Emphasized by a pronoun, *σύ. The 'real you',

the <u>nous</u>.

<u>examine</u>] Copt. 'look at', but this Coptic verb trans-
lates many Greek models. Cf. Pla. <u>Apol</u>. 38 A ὁ . . .
ἀνεξέταστος βίος is not worth living; Marcus Aurelius
III.5, do not act ἀνεξέταστος etc.; another commonplace.

176   <u>even though</u>] Copt. has <u>hōs</u>, 'on the belief that'.

177   <u>the former</u>] Text has *ἐκεῖνος. The dying body is meant.

178   <u>has died</u>] The body is never of itself alive, cf. <u>106</u>.
       Spiritual resurrection is both the discarnation of the
       <u>nous</u> and the de-vivification of the body. Body is mere
       *φθορά (<u>114</u>). Marcus Aurelius IV.41 ψυχάριον εἶ
       βαστάζον νεκρόν, ὡς ᾿Επίκτητος ἔλεγεν. Philo <u>LA</u> III.69:

            μὴ γὰρ ἄλλο τι νοήσῃς ἕκαστον ἡμῶν ποιεῖν, ἢ
            νεκροφορεῖν, τὸ νεκρὸν . . . σῶμα ἐγειρούσης
            καὶ ἀμοχθὶ φερούσης τῆς ψυχῆς.

(179-end) I shall be lenient with you because of your
lack of training. Strive and practice to obtain release from
the body, so that you might recover your former state of being.
These are the basic teachings of the Savior: if they are too
profound as I have presented them, I shall offer further
elaboration. Share them with your brethren, for they can be
of benefit. I greet all of you.

179   inadequate training] Coptic 'non-gymnazei(n)-ness',
        i.e., ἀγυμνασία. This was a usual athletic metaphor
        for the training of mind or soul, and was popularized
        by Stoic-Cynic preaching.

180   practice] Copt. askei(n). Another athletic metaphor,
        and as such practically synonymous with gymnazein.

        in many ways] Pla. Smp. 212 B (Socrates), καὶ αὐτὸς
        τιμῶ τὰ ἐρωτικὰ καὶ διαφερόντως ἀσκῶ κτλ. Clem. Stro.
        VII. 71.1 ὡς ἔνι μάλιστα προγυμναστέον ποικίλως τὴν
        ψυχὴν ἵνα εὐεργὸς γένηται πρὸς τὴν τῆς γνώσεως
        παραδοχήν.
            Most unfortunately, it is impossible to know
        exactly what the author means by this phrase: at the
        very least, he must refer to practices which will allow
        mental application and concentration upon what is
        thought to be the truth. The author of 1 Timothy
        (4.7-8) admonishes γύμναζε σεαυτὸν πρὸς εὐσέβειαν· ἡ
        γὰρ σωματικὴ γυμνασία πρὸς ὀλίγον ἐστὶν ὠφέλιμος,
        further elaborated at 4.16 ἔπεχε σεαυτῷ καὶ τῇ
        διδασκαλίᾳ· ἐπίμενε αὐτοῖς, probably in reaction to
        certain people who urge encratitic practices. Cf.
        Symposium (supra) where much more than doctrinal adher-
        ence is meant. Marcus Aurelius X 11: διηνεκῶς πρόσεχε
        καὶ συγγυμνάσθητι περὶ τοῦτο τὸ μέρος (reason) . . .
        (Such a one) ἐξεδύσατο τὸ σῶμα . . . ἀνῆκεν ὅλον ἑαυτὸν
        δικαιοσύνῃ. Clem. Stro. VI. 74.1 ἡ μὲν γὰρ γνῶσις
        συνάσκησιν, ἡ συνάσκησις δὲ ἕξιν ἢ διάθεσιν, ἡ
        κατάστασις δὲ ἡ τοιάδε ἀπάθειαν ἐργάζεται.

this element] Copt. has 'this stoikheion'. Only two
components of man are supposed here, flesh and mind,
'inferior' and 'superior'. This simple scheme does not
preclude at the same time a more complex anthropology,
cf. Epict. III. 1.25 quoted at 167-175 and Marcus
Aurelius IV.41 quoted at 178. The use of stoikheion
is unusual; much more commonly it refers to the
Empedoclean ῥιζώματα, or for Epicureans, to the ἄτομα
στοιχεῖα or 'atoms'. Perhaps, however, Marcus Aurelius
II.17 offers a parallel: 'death is nothing more than
λύσις τῶν στοιχείων of which each creature is composed'.
His phrase in itself is Epicurean, but for Marcus it
probably resonates with the Platonic λύσις καὶ
ἀποχωρισμός of soul from body.

182   wander aimlessly] Or 'err'. Copt. has plana, for
πλανᾶσθαι. The word may be deliberately chosen for
its association with the well-known idea that souls
that were morally unsuccessful would be forced to
'wander' and finally become reincarnate, cf. Pla. Phd.
81 E, quoted at 165; Sallustius XIX, p. 34,21 Nock.
For the popular belief in this idea, Nock, Sallustius
xcii n. 217.
       However, the release from the fleshly component is
at first proleptic; hence the 'error' spoken of here is
primarily a moral or epistemological 'error'; Dio Chrys.
IV.115 πλανῶνται. . . δεδουλωμέναι ἡδοναῖς. The same
play upon the word is made by Clem. Protr. II. 27.1:
'I shall show the true nature of idols ἵν' ἤδη ποτὲ τῆς
πλάνης λήξητε, αὖθις δὲ παλινδρομήσητε εἰς οὐρανόν--but
some lines later we see that planê is meant to contrast
with alêtheia. So in Stro. III. 94.2f. on possible
interpretations of Matt.18.11 (the Lord came to save
those who had 'gone astray') the impiously literal
exegesis of Tatian is explicitly rejected so that the
text means πεπλανωμένοι τὰ νοήματα.

183   recover his former state of being] This is not ἡ γνῶσις

τίνες ἦμεν, as the edd. suggest, but the actual discarnate state of the mind's prior existence in the
Fulness. The cyclic personal recurrence of earlier
states of being is known from Stoic apokatastasis, in
which there will recur all the figures of the past and
present. Cf. on 33. Clem. Stro. V. 9.4 takes this
theory as a veiled reference to anastasis (or the other
way around): καθ᾽ ὃν καὶ τὸν ἰδίως ποιὸν ἀναστήσεσθαι
δογματίζουσι (scil. Stoics), τοῦτ᾽ ἐκεῖνο τὴν ἀνάστασιν
περιέποντες.

It is this 'recovery' towards which mind is rushing, and this which constitutes the goal of the
Pleromatic drive for reintegration. Just as such
considerations motivated the Savior in his career of
teaching, so they are the sole reason for the author's
having given instruction. By implication this forms
the paradigm for the social relationship of all minds
dispersed in an alien kosmos; it is essentially one of
pedagogy and discipleship.

The rest is peroration.

184   What] Literally, 'these which . . .'. The abrupt
       asyndeton perhaps stood in the Greek model as well,
       marking sectional articulation (as probably at 21).

       received] Possibly, but not necessarily, *παρέλαβον,
       the usual word for reception of a school tradition.
       Direct revelation by the Savior need not be meant.

       generosity] Copt. 'not-aphthonei(n)-ness', i.e.,
       ἀφθονία. It is a commonplace of Platonism and of
       Christian Platonism that the divine has no φθόνος
       towards man (reversing the story of Prometheus). This
       is a necessary implication of its goodness: Phdr 247 A,
       Ti. 29 E (with the precautionary remarks of Cornford,
       Plato's Cosmology, in loc.), Clem. Stro. VII 7.2, V.
       63.7 (Resch, Agr. no. 84), Iren. Haer. V. 24.4, Celsus
       apud Orig. C. Cels. VIII.21, Athanas. C. gentes 41 (MPG

25.81 D). It was on such a Platonic basis that Marcion
criticized and rejected the Jewish god for withholding
the fruit of knowledge (Theoph. Autol. II.25).

185   have taught] Viz., in the present treatise.

you and your brethren] The metaphor of spiritual sonship
(1) is extended. Cf. C. H. I.32, a prayer of illumination of μοῦ ἀδελφούς, υἱοὺς σοῦ. Clem. Stro. V. 98.1,
ἀδελφοὺς δὲ εἶναι ἡμᾶς, ὡς ἂν τοῦ ἑνὸς θεοῦ <ὄντας>
καὶ ἑνὸς διδασκάλου. The letter is addressed to a
single recipient down to the last (e.g., 194 'this--
which I have written for you [sing.]'). But eventual
publication of the letter's doctrinal contents is
envisaged. It is far from certain, however, that a
definite conventicle or church is being addressed: all
minds belong to the Fulness, all are brothers. Yet the
reference to 'any that belong to you' (191) may suggest
the existence of some coterie, or at least a potential
circle of listeners, as does 190 'if you (plur.)
inquire'. Reference to co-disciples is a normal
literary convention to promote publication (Festugière,
Révélation d'Hermès I.309-354), but in any single case
this does not disprove that an organized circle actually
existed.

186   without omitting any of the points necessary] This is
just what was promised at 15-20. The author's own
aphthonia is an imitation of the Savior's. This is a
commonplace of Hellenistic wisdom (Wisd. Sol. 7.13, Ps.-
Arist. De mundo 391^{a}17, PGM XII 28, Clem. Stro. I. 14.3,
etc.), possibly related to the 'generosity' of the
divine and all that is Good. It is also the essence
of wise pedagogy. Pla. Smp. 210 A (Diotima) ἐρῶ μὲν
οὖν, ἔφη, ἐγὼ καὶ προθυμίας οὐδὲν ἀπολείψω. Substantially the same claim is made by Athenagoras Res. 23,
p. 77,6-9 Schw. (a captatio benevolentiae, well needed):

οὐ γὰρ τὸ μηδὲν παραλιπεῖν τῶν ἐνόντων εἰπεῖν
πεποιήμεθα σκοπόν, ἀλλὰ τὸ κεφαλαιωδῶς ὑποδεῖξαι
τοῖς συνελθοῦσιν ἃ χρὴ περὶ τῆς ἀναστάσεως φρονεῖν.

188   my exposition] Copt. literally 'the statement
        (apaggelia) of the discussion (logos)'. An ἀπαγγελία
        is either the act of giving a continuous narrative
        account concerning events, persons, things, concepts,
        etc. (Arist. Po. 1449^{b}26, contrasted with 'action') or
        as here the substance of such an account (ambassador's
        report, Demos. 19.5, Lycurg. 14; metaphorically of the
        senses, Plot. IV. 6.3.42), Thuc. III. 67.6.

190   Further communication is invited.

191   Since this is so] *νυνὶ δέ. The envoi commences.

        hesitate to share with] Copt. has phthonei(n). The
        same topos as above at 184. Cf. Clem. fr. 5 (To the
        Newly Baptized), vol. III, p. 222,6 sq. Stä.:

            μάνθανε δὲ ἀσμένως, καὶ ἀφθόνως δίδασκε, μηδὲ
            ὑπὸ φθόνου ποτὲ σοφίαν ἀποκρύπτου πρὸς τοὺς
            ἑτέρους, μηδὲ μαθήσεως ἀφίστασο δι' αἰδῶ.

        A similar explicit is found in 1 Thess.5.26ff.:

            Ἀσπάσασθε τοὺς ἀδελφοὺς πάντας ἐν φιλήματι
            ἁγίῳ. Ἐνορκίζω ὑμᾶς τὸν κύριον ἀναγνωσθῆναι
            τὴν ἐπιστολὴν πᾶσιν τοῖς ἀδελφοῖς. Ἡ χάρις
            τοῦ κυρίου ἡμῶν Ἰησοῦ Χριστοῦ μεθ' ὑμῶν.

192   benefit] Copt. has ōphelei(n). The understood subject
        is 'the logos'.

193   many people] All minds can be, indeed ought to be,
        benefitted by this logos.

195   to them I address] The author finally confesses to have
        written for all humanity, another conventional point of
        view.

        peace . . . and grace] Copt. (e)irênê . . . kharis.
        Since the author knows Paul (54), it is tempting to
        take this as a mock-Pauline closing. By peace is
        meant anapausis, as in the opening of the work. Kharis
        is said at 45 sq. to be the work of the Savior, with
        reference to the apokatastasis.

196   greet] *ἀσπάζομαι. A closing formula in letters; to
        'hail' upon leaving. (It is also, and more commonly,
        the first greeting: Pla. Euthd. 273 C.) The treatise
        ends as a letter. But there is no need to suppose that
        it began as one and was subsequently abridged, as does
        Peel, for the author himself never calls it a letter.

197   with fraternal love] Literally 'being brother-loving',
        i.e., *φιλαδελφούς. On this note of peace and
        benevolence, the author closes his discourse.

title   'The logos about anastasis'. This, of course, is the
        transmission title and not necessarily the author's.
        It refers to line 20, 'so let this be the topic of our
        logos', namely, resurrection.

III

THE CONTENT AND ARRANGEMENT
OF THE TREATISE

III

THE CONTENT AND ARRANGEMENT OF THE TREATISE

i. The avowed purpose of the treatise is to give a
statement of 'the essential points' (peteśśe, 'whatever it is
necessary', scil., 'to believe') about the doctrine of resurrection, specifically 'spiritual resurrection'.[1] Such at
least was the request that occasioned the work.[2] It is
directed to a single recipient (mentioned by name in line 1);
but wider publication is definitely envisaged, as are further
communications on the same topic.[3]

The concluding salutation, epistolary in style,[4] has led
various critics to consider the work a letter.[5] Against such
a view may be cited the lack of any epistolary greeting and the
author's own reference to the piece as a logos (the Greek word
is kept in the Coptic version), 'treatise' or 'discussion'. He
speaks of it thus both in the introduction and in the concluding offer of further elaboration ('the contents of the logos').[6]
The transmissional title ('The Treatise [Logos] on Resurrection') has adopted the same term. Indeed, even the conclusion
of the work (except for the final sentence) is written in terms
conventionally found in esoteric treatises and dialogues.[7]

---

[1]20; from 67 onwards primarily spiritual resurrection is
meant.

[2]15-16.   [3]190.

[4]196 'I greet you (*aspazomai) and whoever love you'.

[5]Peel, 5ff., cites the literature.

[6]20 and 188.   [7]184, 191, and the commentary.

An occasional work of this sort would be communicated through the same channels as a personal letter, hence the distinction between treatise and letter primarily concerns the author's own arrangement and execution of his literary product. Letters, of course, might be utilized to transmit philosophical doctrine as well as other matters; certain of the epistles attributed to Plato, the dogmatic epistle of Epicurus to Menoeceus,[1] and the moral epistles of Seneca are the classic examples. But even though an author might write and collect his own personal epistles for publication (Pliny, Gregory of Nazianzus, etc.) they would still remain, at least in their literary guise, personal communications directed to specific individuals and couched in the conventions of a certain kind of occasional communication.[2] A scientific treatise, despite its possible dedication to a particular person, would follow a different set of conventions.

To some extent our document does not fit well into either of these categories. Apart from its concluding formula, there are two features that distinguish it from the usual scientific treatise of the period: first, its extreme brevity; and second, the kind of argumentative style in which it is written. In many ways the body of our treatise resembles a class-room lecture, and it may be supposed that the author has deliberately adopted such a tone and procedure because of the pedagogical and elementary nature of the work. It is especially significant in this regard that he concludes with a personal exhortation to the reader, and indeed to 'everyone'[3] as though addressing a larger audience.

Though other more specific literary terms could be applied to such a discourse, the Greek term logos refers quite aptly to a public oration or indeed to a discussion or deliberation of a less than formal nature, in which counter-objections or alternative points of view might be entertained and criticized. So, too, it can even mean a dialogue. The latter two uses are well attested in, for example, Plato, Aristotle, and later writers

---

[1] D.L. X. 122-135, Us. pp. 59-66.

[2] J. Schneider, art. 'Brief', RAC s.v. (1954).

[3] 180.

(see LSJ, s.v. VI. 3).

ii. It suffices merely to read through the treatise with its elementary pedagogical aim in mind in order to note how the author leads his audience on through what he feels is difficult material. The teaching is compressed, its simplicity is emphasized, and it is sometimes given in the form of summary followed by exposition, or conclusion followed by premise. On the other hand there is emphasis upon accepting what is taught without logical compulsion. In place of logical argument, the author depends upon the force of his own personality and upon his claim to have direct access to the truth. Accordingly his tone is patronizing and ad hominem throughout, the recipient being called 'my child'. But he indulges in more than mere pedagogical authoritarianism, for he constantly assumes the worst about the recipient's capacity to understand or practice what is recommended. This scolding tone is well known from contemporary philosophical harangue; it was popularized by Cynic-Stoic preachers, and ultimately derives from a certain picture of Socrates. Familiar terms are used to introduce non-familiar ideas (this partly accounts for the Pauline tone of certain sections). There are frequent internal summaries or points of conclusion. Punning, rhetorical questions, and asides, as well as the sporadic use of self-consciously rhapsodic prose help to maintain the reader's interest.[1] Special questions (aporiae) and objections by an imaginary interlocutor help the author to sharpen his own point;[2] but these are dealt with summarily (note the frequent use of alla to mean 'despite all this . . .', escaping from possible objections).[3] Right and wrong methodology are touched upon.[4] Finally, the railing condemnation of worldly affairs and the

---

[1]Puns: 10 *anapausis, 14 'rest upon', 115 apousia, 119 'owes thanks', and correspondingly 120 'ransoms'. Rhetorical questions: 21, 109, 111, 114 (red. ad absurd.), 132, 144, 172, 179. Asides: 26 ('the place where you dwell'), 38-40, 47-50, 52, 151. Rhapsodic: 153-162.

[2]Imaginary interloc.: 75, 101-108.

[3]Grammatical Appendix 2, s.v.

[4]1-10, 69-74.

edifying explanation of <u>gnôthi</u> <u>sauton</u>, 'Know Thyself', cannot
but call to mind philosophical harangue of the same period.[1]

The disadvantages of such a style are obvious: uninter-
rupted systematic presentation becomes impossible, and the
compressed reference to a stock argument tends to replace a
careful exposition of it.[2]

iii. Only a small portion of this brief work is devoted
to doctrinal exposition: lines <u>21</u>-<u>37</u>, <u>44</u>-<u>68</u>, <u>79</u>-<u>99</u>, <u>163</u>-<u>166</u>
and a few other individual sentences. The remainder is proto-
col or deals summarily with questions of method or with
special problems (<u>aporiae</u>) in relation to certain important
points. This gives us, as it must to the recipient, only a
sketchy idea of the author's own philosophical views. He
clearly knows much more than he is telling, and the very
brevity of his presentation is a great hindrance to the reader
at almost all points. Furthermore, the author makes oblique
reference to certain quite technical concepts known from other
Christian gnostic literature of the time, without definition
and without any but the slightest explanation.[3] These must be
the matters that he suspects (<u>187</u>-<u>190</u>) are 'too profound' for
the reader and of which he suggests the possibility of a subsequent elaboration. The alternative explanation, that he uses
terms already familiar to his readers but uses them in a new
way, seems unlikely from the apologetic statement (<u>38</u>ff.) that
immediately follows the opening of his doctrinal exposition
('I know I am phrasing this explanation in difficult terms').
Subsequent instruction of a more advanced nature might for
example be provided by scientific monographs. The <u>Apocryphon</u>
<u>of</u> <u>John</u>, which is a complex uranographical treatise, begins
precisely from <u>aporiae</u> such as might trouble a student not yet
advanced in the kind of mythological system which seems somehow
presupposed by our work: 'And I was deeply grieved in my

_____

[1] <u>141</u>-<u>149</u>, <u>167</u>-<u>178</u>.

[2] <u>101</u>ff. (which is just barely intelligible).

[3] 'The <u>apokatastasis</u>', 'the Entirety', 'the Fulness' and
its 'lack', 'the oneness', 'seed of the truth' and 'offshoot
of the truth', 'the spirit' and finally as well 'the truth'.

heart, saying, "How indeed did it happen that the Savior was
put to death? And why was he sent into the world by his Father
who sent him? And who is his Father? And of what sort is that
eternity towards which we are proceeding? He said to us that
the present realm is modelled upon that eternal realm, and he
did not instruct us about it, as to what sort it is'" (BG
20:6ff. ed. Till, in TU 60). Naturally this illustration is not
meant to suggest that the Apocryphon of John and the present
treatise are in any way directly related.

iv. Some acquaintance with writings of the New Testament
is presupposed. There is a reference to 'the Apostle',
followed by a passage reminiscent of Paul, and also a reference
to the Transfiguration of Jesus as something the reader will
remember from 'the Gospel'.[1] Just as the introductory section
contains a literary allusion to the gospel of Matthew (18-19),
so it closes (195) with a self-consciously Pauline cliche,
'peace and grace' (that this does not exactly parallel any
formula used by Paul is of no matter; the same loose imitation
may be observed in closing salutations of the letters of
Ignatius of Antioch).[2] In addition, there are various other
approximations to Pauline language throughout (without the
author's theological position being any way substantially
Pauline, however). In contrast to this, the absence of
Johannine influence is striking.[3] Perhaps more important,
there are many points at which the language and substance of
the text, in its explanation of spiritual resurrection,
approach closely to the Odes of Solomon.[4] It is far from
certain, however, that the latter text was directly known to
the author.

v. It remains, then, to comment upon the treatise's plan
and doctrinal contents.

It is important to note that whenever our author addresses
his reader, he addresses only a soul, or rather a mind. A

---

[1] The Apostle: 54ff.; the Gospel: 134ff.

[2] Ign. Sm. 12.2.

[3] The Savior is not, for example, the truth but rather its
'seed', 34.

[4] See commentary.

rigid dualism of mental faculty versus material body is implied
and finally stated in an open and self-conscious way. The
terms used are νοῦς and σάρξ, mind and flesh, rather than the
more traditionally Platonic ψυχή and σῶμα, soul and body.
Since Aristotle it was often asserted that specifically the
cognitive faculty, nous, was the part that would survive disintegration of the body. Its survival was held to be intima-
tely related to its ability, indeed its innate tendency,
towards cogitation of undying and immortal conceptual objects.
All of this is found, if briefly, in our text. As for 'flesh',
this term is frequent in Paul and subsequent Christian authors,
a fact that may partly explain our author's penchant for this
term rather than 'body'. But 'flesh' is also a way of refer-
ring to the body specifically as the origin of sensation but
apart from nous or the bodily psychê (sôma might mean carnis
cum anima).[1] These two components, mind and flesh, are also
referred to as the superior (i.e., nous) and the inferior (i.e.,
sarks), scil. 'part' (meros), a usage attested in Clement of
Alexandria and in any case one whose meaning in the context is
obvious.[2]

   Not surprisingly, this rigidly dualist conception of man
is but a reflection of an overriding cosmic dualism between
what comes-into-being and is subject to change (Greek τὸ
γενόμενον) and what simply 'is', or perpetually exists uncon-
ditioned by time (τὸ ὄν). The usual Platonic contrast is made:
imperishable versus perishable, invisible versus visible,
stable versus changing.[3] Some of these characterizations are
found in writings of the New Testament, but the clean dualistic
contrast is not. On the other hand the radical degree of this
dualism goes beyond Plato, the upper world being as completely

---

[1]Farquharson thus explains the use of sarkia in Marcus
Aurelius II. 2 (Comm. in loc.) and passim, using Aristotle and
Epicurus. This point is discussed more fully above in the
commentary. Sôma occurs only at 112 127.

[2]44 106 116 118; for Clement see the commentary.

[3]Imperish.: 50 86f. 157, perish.: 49 114 157; invisib.
52, visib. 52; stable 154f., changing 149.

transcendant from this one as visible matter is different from nous.[1]

vi. Salvation of the nous, the essential 'You', is escape from the world of change, an exchange of the bodily garment for the condition of primeval nakedness.[2] The nous existed before its incarnation; the goal is not merely 'preservation' (σωτηρία) of nous, but its return to the specific place whence it came and to which it belongs.[3] This point of origin is described in spatial terms: it is the πλήρωμα, the 'Fulness', and it is located apart from the present world.[4] Central to the author's psychology is the notion that all minds inherently and always belong to the Fulness, because they once had existed there in primeval unity. No word is said about how minds came to enter the visible world where they now sojourn; but their present state of 'bondage' and 'dispersion' contrasts with the primordial state of 'Entirety' which obtained in the 'Fulness' before they entered the world. Until there comes to pass the return (apokatastasis) of all minds to the Fulness whence they came, the term πλήρωμα is not in fact descriptive of the place towards which they are headed; for the πλήρωμα is not yet full, but suffers a 'lack' (šta, *ὑστέρημα), which can be 'filled' only by that return.[5] Hence the soul can be exhorted to escape from bodily bondage 'for the sake of the oneness', i.e., so that the original unity of the full plêrôma, its

---

[1] Speaking to Rheginos qua nous, the author can refer to the flesh simply as Greek *ekeinos (177). Emphasis upon the mutuality and hence interdependence of these two opposites, totally evil or alien matter and a totally transcendant principle of goodness has been recently emphasized by S. Pétrement; cf. Dodds, Pagan and Christian 13, using her Le dualisme dans l'histoire de la philosophie et des religions 105. The principle itself, of the necessary interdependence of opposites, is Plato's, and was developed by Aristotle.

[2] The bodily garment is alluded to by implication at 59.

[3] Preexistence 101, 89 ('since the first'), 183 ('former state'), 97-99; sōtēria clearest at 130, cf. 86f. ('will not perish'); return 33; belongs cf. 121f.

[4] 33-34.

[5] 160 describing the work of the Savior (the probolê).

'Entirety', may once again obtain.[1] For the individual soul,
this means 'recovering one's former state of being'.[2]

Obviously the precondition for definitive escape from
flesh is separation from it at the moment of death. As Plato
had taught, so our author: the preparing for this separation
must begin now in the present lifetime; that is our task, to
'practice' and 'exercise'.[3] This imperative presumably means
something like what it does in some other dualist philosophies,
achievement of passionlessness and cogitation of divine cognitive objects: but ascesis might be thought to entail also
abstinences or taboos of one sort or another. Of any such
specifics we hear absolutely nothing in our text. They are
presupposed, and clearly the readers already know what proce-
dures are meant.[4]

However, complete escape can in some proleptic way be
realized even during the present incarnate life. This is what
the author writes to emphasize; this is his point.[5] 'Leave the
state of dispersion and bondage, and then you already have
resurrection', i.e., spiritual resurrection (165f.). By spiritual resurrection the author means a kind of bodilessness
achieved through faith in the Savior.[6] Again at this point
the reader must already understand what is meant by 'faith',
presumably some kind of definitive conversion, possibly accompanied by rites such as baptism, leading to gnosis.

The author's exposition of spiritual resurrection, i.e.,
proleptic separation from the body, depends in part upon a
Platonic metaphor of the body and its influences as a garment
(Cra. 403 B, so Emped. fr. 126 Diels, PPF). Upon the attain-
ment of faith, we as it were shuck off the encumbrance of the

---

[1] 164. [2] 183. [3] 179f.

[4] 179 'inadequate training' is unexplained.

[5] The author knows three senses of anastasis, of which he
feels only one worth discussing (67f.); this is presumably the
meaning of 'the essential points on resurrection', for he never
discusses any but spiritual resurrection. Discussion of the
non-essential or even wrong senses of anastasis would fall
under polymathy (1-9).

[6] 126-128 'take off the body' could easily be taken in a
'spiritual', i.e., proleptic sense.

body, i.e., ignore it altogether, and perhaps 'wear' instead
the luminous body of the Savior (62). In Christianity this
imagery is earliest attested in the writings of Paul (where
however the luminosity of the new body is not mentioned).
There the context is baptism: but that fact does not necessarily indicate the same context here. Indeed the image of a
garment of light that can be donned by the religiously qualified has been pointed out in sources which do not depend upon
Paul.[1] In any case in our text the image is no more than
hinted at, for it is blended into a solar metaphor in which
the Savior is the sun (Pla. R. 507E sq., etc.; Odes of Solomon
11.10-14 Harris-Mingana), holding the believer fast as the sun
does its rays. The point is simply this: that the believing
mind can, through faith or gnosis, surrender itself entirely
into the power of the Savior while still incarnate, no longer
restrained by the fetters of the body in which it dwells.[2] Its
newly gained independence is possible precisely because the
sole function of mind, nous, is cogitation. By an act of
faith, the nous can direct its thought totally away from body
and totally towards the truth. This amounts to total separation from body already. Physical death is thereupon no more
than the physical expression of what will already have
happened.[3] Thus questions about bodily resurrection or ascent
of the soul[4] after death become irrelevant. 'This is resurrection of the spirit, which "swallows" resurrection of the soul
along with resurrection of the flesh', i.e., does away with the
need for them.[5]

vii. As for 'the Savior', he both is one who teaches--
about the nature of death and coming-into-being, i.e., the
contrast between the metaphysical and the physical realms,

---

[1]Od. Sol. 21.3 sq. Harris-Mingana, 11.10-14, cf. 25.8.

[2]66 'restrained by nothing', 165 'leave . . . bondage'.

[3]Explicit in 59-67.

[4]I understand thus 'fleshly and psychic resurrection'
68.

[5]The fundamental sense of 'swallow' in the text is 'make
irrelevant': 46, 52, 68, 159.

between mind and flesh[1]--and is in a sense coextensive with truth itself, i.e., is the cognitive object of the believing nous.[2] He preexisted before His incarnation, and exists again discarnate now that He has departed.[3] He is a 'seed of the truth (34)' i.e., it is He whom truth has sown in this world. This is a somewhat different use of the Philonic image of seeds that we find in Justin Martyr, where the Savior is a cosmic rational principle that has sown innate ideas of Himself (especially as concerns morality) into all generations of man, even before His incarnation. In Justin the 'seeds' sown by the Savior into each human mind provide knowledge of Himself, the universal reason.[4] While in the metaphor of our text, truth sows the Savior into this world, and He imparts to minds a knowledge of their capacity to free themselves from the incarnate state and to return into the Fulness through knowledge of that truth.

Now sperma and probolê, 'seed' and 'offshoot', are metaphors (perhaps even technical terms) regularly used in second-century Valentinianism to describe the generation of the various abstractions (aeons) of the metaphysical hierarchy.[5] Though the application of these terms within our text is quite different, we may take this clue from the Valentinian sources

---

[1]Death 28, 'coming-into-being' 43. His destruction of death (32, 46, 83) presumably results from teaching by instruction and by example. This is the author's purpose as well.

[2]A delicate point. The nous 'knows' the son of man (the Savior qua artificer of the apokatastasis) only according to 79; otherwise its cognitive object is said to be truth: 12 and 87 interpreted by 90-91. The gnostic knows both the Savior and the truth just as a pupil knows both the teacher and his teaching. The Savior is not truth but only its 'seed'.

[3]34f. 'before there came into being this cosmic structure'; 48 'laying aside the perishable world', cf. 127 for similar words 'if one who is saved, upon taking off his body . . . .'.

[4]J. H. Waszink, 'Bemerkungen zu Justins Lehre vom Logos Spermatikos', Mullus (Fest. Klauser, 1964) 380-390.

[5]Usage is illustrated by Lampe, Lex. s.vv., Tert. Adv. Prax. VIII. For proballô of fruit cf. Josephus Ant. 4.226; of a flower cf. LSJ s.v. IV (Aetius) and Stephanus-Dindorff s.v. 1649 (Dioscorides). Behind Valentinian usage lies the Stoic spermatic cosmic generation.

and treat sperma (34) and probolê (44) as parts of the same
metaphor. Just as the Savior is the seed, so His accomplish-
ments are termed its offshoots or progeny (probolê). 'The
undoing of evil and the manifestation of the superior part,
these are the offshoot of the truth and the spirit' (44).
These two aspects of the Savior's career are referred to at
several points in the text.[1] He was 'a son of god' and 'a son
of man',[2] which seems to mean no more than 'He was of divine
origin but became incarnate', thus having the same admixture
of metaphysical and physical components as any man. Through
His divinity, i.e., because He (like every nous) belongs to
the metaphysical world and pre-existed there, He 'conquered
death'. Since death is merely a 'law of the natural order',
(27f.), to depart from that natural order, to belong inherently
to another order, is to overcome, indeed to have already overcome, the threat of death. The Savior's conquest of death, we
are told, means that 'laying aside the perishable world, He
exchanged it for an unperishing eternal realm' (50). In so
doing He 'devoured' or overcame 'the visible' (52), the world
of deceptive sensory perception (phantasia) and change and
bodily death, and 'raised Himself up', that is, returned to
the metaphysical realm.[3] It is through 'the son of man',
through the Savior's human aspect, or through the fact of His
incarnation and teaching career, that there can be 'the return
into the Fulness' (33), the return of the other minds back to
their place of origin. In teaching us to give up all interest
in the natural order in which we have no proper membership,[4]
'He gave us the way to our immortality' (53). This 'way' begins
with proleptic 'spiritual resurrection' and continues without

---

[1] 46 sq. 'swallowed death' etc. and 53 'gave us the way to
our immortality'; (in the opposite order) 155 'the revealing of
what truly exists' and 156 'what one receives in exchange for
the circumstances of this world'.

[2] 24-29.

[3] phantasia 138-142; change and phantasia 149f.; death and
the natural order (physis) 27f.; 'raised himself' 51, returned
50.

[4] The point at 114 ('are you mere corruption?'), a reductio
ad absurdum.

interruption beyond death of the body.[1]

    viii. Among the disputed questions (aporiai) disposed of towards the end of the treatise is one concerning the Transfiguration of Jesus. It was the moment when--according to 'the Gospel'--Jesus changed himself into a body of light, when the signs appeared for the 'return of all things.'[2] This pericope might seem to imply that the fleshly body can be transformed into a kind of Homeric shade or phantasma: the transformation of Jesus, Elias, and Moses would then be a paradigm for the mysterious resurrection flesh to which Paul seems to refer. This exegesis of the pericope is attractive indeed; but our author rejects it out of hand;[3] or at most, he refuses to commit himself on the possibility of a phantasmagoric resurrection flesh. The only flesh of which he speaks is the flesh of this world: it is an inferior element totally alien to the real self and is rushing towards perdition. Phantasia is not an attribute of the resurrection state, for the soteria of the Superior Element is an unqualified reality. Rather, and here the author quotes a stock phrase from Heraclitus, 'all changes'--the material world is in flux. 'One ought to maintain that the world, not resurrection, is phantasia' (141-142).[4]

    It is striking how poorly these simple ideas are expounded in the treatise. This partly results from the author's tone and the stylistic conventions that he has adopted for the occasion. It may also reflect his disdain for philosophical exposition and 'persuasion', which are explicitly condemned in the treatise. One can hope that the further exposition of his

---

[1]'Without interruption', cf. 63f. (like a ray of the sun 'until our sunset'), yet the definitiveness of the withdrawal upon separation is important (156 'a migration into newness') since backsliding under the influence of the flesh (for which the author admonishes his pupil, 163-179) will then be no longer possible. The notion of predestination in 88-90 is probably mechanistic, but it describes the innate telos of the nous to cogitate the truth: this does not rule out malevolent influence of the sarks during the period of incarnation.

[2]Matt. 17.11 parr. using Mal. 3.23, Êlias . . . apokatastêsei panta. Cf. 134-150.

[3]Against A. Orbe, Gregorianum 46 (1965) 172-174.

[4]'Rushing', cf. 170. Heraclitus, Diels Fr. Vorsokr. I. 69.

ideas, which he offers at the end of the treatise, would have
elaborated the philosophical system with somewhat more clarity.

ix. In a brief work of this sort one cannot expect to
find all the seeds of a systematic philosophy, even if they
existed in the author's mind. Nonetheless the absence of certain points is striking when other texts of the second century
are compared. There is, for example, no concern at all for the
problems raised by use of the Old Testament in early Christianity. These bulk large in the works of, say, Justin Martyr and
Clement; they would seem to reflect social as well as theoreti-
cal conflicts which were taking place at the time. Behind them
lies the great exegetical tradition of Hellenistic Judaism.
But these problems are ignored by our author. Indeed there is
no explicit mention made of 'god', except in the phrase 'son of
god'. Yet there is a principle that is higher than the Savior,
hence the author cannot properly be said to have no theology
(pace Peel). This principle is 'the truth', which may be
surmised to function systematically in a way analogous to 'god'
in other Christian systems of the period. The Savior was
eternally 'seed of the truth' before His incarnation: this
amounts to saying He was the progeny of the truth. His saving
work is described as 'the offshoot of the truth and the spirit'
(44), as being given by the truth (45). Absolutely nothing can
be known about the author's meaning of 'spirit' since he makes
no further mention of it. It may be worth noting that the reference to spirit gives us a triad, Truth - Seed of the Truth
(Savior) - Spirit, which is just possibly related to trinitar-
ian speculation. But against such an interpretation is the
fact that, at least in the metaphor, the Savior is not as it
were the plant, but only its seed. The offshoot (probolê) of
truth is ultimately not the Savior but His saving work.

When we compare this text to the writings of Clement of
Alexandria, which have so much in common with it, another
striking difference becomes immediately apparent. There is no
emphasis upon divine providence vis-à-vis the cooperation of
created matter in the soul's return to eternity. For Clement
(as for Plato) the body, e.g., is created upright so that it
might be led to contemplate the order of the heavens and thence

132

be led to higher and more abstract conceptions.[1] In our text
the body and all creation are a purely negative factor in the
mind's drive towards the return. There is in fact no reference
at all to the creation of the universe except to note that
unlike the metaphysical world it came into being: there was a
time when it was not.[2] Instead, we find the doctrine of
Pleromatic Deficiency. Unlike the idea of universal providence, the main thrust of this doctrine is the necessity of a
decisive divine intervention into a world totally alien to the
nous--'the darkness'. And while the return of the individual
mind may appear to result from divine humanitarianism ('this',
viz., the filling of the pleromatic deficiency, 'is what
brings about goodness' 62), the pleroma's motivation in send-
ing forth a Savior to recall minds is ultimately selfish. It
represents as it were the pleroma's own drive towards self-
reintegration and entirety.

     x. It would be misleading to say that the treatise
adheres to a lucid overall plan. Nevertheless the flow of the
prose seems to cadence regularly, dividing the work into a
number of small sections each with some obvious coherence.

     It opens on a note commonplace to introductory treatises
of antiquity, the demand for proper mental orientation towards
the task at hand (1-14),[3] followed by programmatic remarks on
the importance and difficulty of the topic, and the occasion
for the work's composition, 15-20, 38-43. The author concludes
the treatise by consideration of various special problems,
aporiae (these were typically treated at the end of such a
work),[4] 101-140; but these provide the opportunity for further
elaboration of the author's fundamental views, so they hardly
form an appendix in the strict sense of the word. They are
followed, a bit unexpectedly, by a harangue combining some
typical elements from Cynic-Stoic diatribe style (141-150, 163-
183) and a lyrical recapitulation of some earlier doctrinal

_____

[1]Stro. IV. 163.1 (Ti. 90 A).

[2]35; 95f.

[3]Nock, Sallustius xl n. 2 gives the necessary references.

[4]Ibid. cxiv n. 28, using Praechter in Woch. Klass. Phil.
17 (1900) 182-86 and Norden, Kunstprosa 90 n. 2.

material, composed in self-consciously high style, 154-162.
Then there are more programmatic remarks and the envoi (184-end).

For the central section of doctrinal exposition the author
follows a plan vaguely dictated by its contents: first a
description of the nature and work of the Savior; next an
exposition of the spiritual (proleptic) resurrection of the
believer; and finally, a reference to the mechanism of salvation through belief (a nous cogitating imperishable objects,
which will not perish, etc.). This leads naturally into the
first aporia (a hypothetical objection raised by the addressee)
on the possibility of co-survival of the flesh after death,
which takes the author in effect into a brief treatment of the
dualistic nature of man (100-123). There is a closing formula
(124-125), and thereupon the subsequent aporiae commence,
126ff. The overall plan might be summarized in tabular form
as follows:

I.   Proper orientation for success: polymathy vs. direct
        acquaintance with truth (1-14).
II.   Program: importance and difficulty of the topic (15-20).
III.   Nature and work of the Savior (21-53).
        (Interrupted at 38-43 by more programmatic remarks.)
IV.   Spiritual resurrection of the believer (54-68).
V.   Nature and mechanics of belief: the object of belief
        (69-99).
VI.   Special problems:
        (1) Dualism of the imperishable mind versus the perish-
            able flesh: will the flesh continue to exist?
            (100-125).
        (2) Is salvation immediate? (126-129).
        (3) Will flesh be preserved by the nous? (130-133).
        (4) Is spiritual resurrection phantasmagoric?
            (134-140).
VII.   Harangue:
        Against the visible world (141-153).
        Lyric recapitulation on salvation (154-162).
        Exhortation (163-183).
VIII.   Programmatic remarks and envoi (184-end).

IV

GRAMMATICAL NOTES

Transliteration: a b g d e z ê th i k l m n
ks o p r s t u ph kh ps ð. Demotic letters:
ś (ⱳ), f (ϥ), h (ϩ), j (ϫ), c (ϭ), ti (ϯ).

1   pašêre rêginos] Coptic vocative. The proper name occurs
     first in the nominative case; subsequent instances
     retain the Gk. form of the vocative (29 100 163).

2   euôše] Crasis. The correct spelling is euouôše. For
     similar errors cf. John 7.10 hn (ou)ouônh (Beatty B with
     77 91 92), John 19.33 mpou(ou)ecp (B with 13 93 95 110
     m^1), John 19.23 (ou)ouôn mpoua poua (AB with 75 110 m^1),
     Acts 4.36 ešau(ou)ahmef (Budge = Horner's papyrus a);
     Achmimic: marou(ou)ônh 1 Clem. XXI.7 (30,19 Schm.),
     ḫn (ou)ouôḫe 1 Clem. XXI.7 (30,26); Subachmimic: see
     Thompson preface to John p. XIX.

3   pi-] 'This'. See Grammatical Appendix 1.

4   euemahte] Circumstantial.

     hn-] Sa. hen-. The short form of the plural indefinite
     article is used throughout.

5   eušaat] Adnominal circumstantial, the antecedent being
     hnzêtêma. The following m-(ꙡ) marks not a recipient of
     action (cf. edd.s' ambiguous translation lack their
     solution) but that in which or from which something is
     'cut short', hence from which it 'falls short'. To
     šôôt/šaat n- the manuscripts often show the variant
     šôôt/šaat e- 'fall short with respect to'. This meta-
     phorical usage of šôôt is already established in
     Demotic.

     peubôl] Coptic infin. as nn., often equivalent to a Gk.
     nomen actionis (e.g., *λύσις). Preceding this form,
     the Copt. possessive article very often expresses an
     objective genitive (recipient of action, with the actor
     unspecified). Hence bôl 'solve', pbôl 'the (act of
     someone's solving', peubôl 'the (act of someone's)

solving them'. Thus in Luke 1.13-14 snajpo nak nouŝêre
. . . and many will rejoice in pefjpo (where Gk. has ἡ
γένεσις αὐτοῦ). An especially instructive parallel is
2 Pet.1.20: prophêteia nim ngraphê, mere pesbôl ŝôpe
haros mauaas, which the Vulgate renders omnis prophetia
Scripturae propria interpretatione non fit. Hence our
text = 'which fall short of being solved' or simply
'unsolved'.

<u>6f.</u>   euŝan- . . . ŝau- . . .] 'whenever . . .', a present
       general condition.

<u>8</u>   n- . . . en] Unlike Thompson's Subachm. John, this text
       does not omit negative n- with the bipartite pattern
       except before the imperfect (<u>101</u>).

<u>9</u>   auahe] I perfect. Schenke would read as II present
       (dialect mixing from <u>ABF</u>), but the tense is here present
       perfect, a backwards glance at the past efforts of
       philosophy and rhetoric.

<u>10</u>   eu-] II present, with emphasis upon <u>apeumtan</u>. The
       emphasis is reinforced by <u>nhouo</u>, probably *μάλιστα.
       Schenke takes <u>nhouo</u> a- as introducing a direct object
       ('more than'), but this interpretation is probably
       impossible, since <u>ŝine</u> n- takes as its object the per-
       son asked; a topic of inquiry is introduced by <u>e</u>-. Cf.
       Crum 569<u>a</u> (Ryl 339 belongs elsewhere).

       apeumtan] Cf. on <u>5</u>, <u>peubôl</u>. Like εἰς of purpose with a
       <u>nomen actionis</u>, Bl.-D.-F. 402.2; e.g., Rom.15.4, εἰς τὴν
       ἡμετέραν διδασκαλίαν ἐγράφη, <u>etensbô</u>.

<u>11</u>   peei ntahn-] The non-restrictive relative, Gk. ὅ(ς)
       (cf. Sa. 1 Cor.1.2, 1.4, 1.8, 1.9) or ὅστις (Sa. Rom.
       16.4, 16.7, 16.12). Contrast restrictive relatives,

without pai: Rom.16.1, 16.2, 16.5, 16.14). The II
perfect and relative I perfect are formally identical
in this text (except at 143, relative in initial e). The
substantivized relative also shows e, but this is con-
ditioned by the preceding article (cf. pemto, perpe).

hitm] 'From' (etymologically 'from the hand of') after
a verb of receipt or acceptance. For agential expressions, abâl hitm-/hitoot= is used, cf. on 32.

pn-] So tn- at 53 79, pn- 63. The text fluctuates
between the short form (as in Achm.) and the full
class. Sa. spelling pen- (64 143). Otherwise the
possessive articles which occur are the class. Sa.
forms: pa- (1), pef- (127), peu- (5), tek- (179), na-
(185), nek- (185).

12   ntahn-] II perfect, with emphasis upon the two following
      clauses.

13   souôn-] The status absolutus of this vb. is commonly
      used as a status nominalis (all dialects); so at 90,
      yet soun- 79. Before a pronoun the text uses souôôn-
      87, cf. ôônh 106, aanh 131 145.

14   auô anmtan] Continuing the temporal clause begun in 13;
      cf. in Sa., Rev.22.8 (Gk. ὅτε ἤκουσα καὶ ἔβλεψα), Luke
      24.37 (πτοηθέντες δὲ καὶ ἔμφοβοι γενόμενοι).

15   alla] Use of sentence-connective particles is discussed
      in Grammatical Appendix 2.

      ekśine] II present, emphasizing apeteśśe, i.e., 'only
      the bare essentials'. Note the typical interlace of
      peteśśe etbe tanastasis with hn ouhlac.

peteśśe Substantivized relative clauses, while formed with the definite article, usually function semantically like a nn. with zero article: they are unspecified as to particular identity (i.e., not cross-referential [anaphoric], not generic). Compare Gk. ὁ with participle, or ὅστις . . ., ὅτι . . ., 'whoever . . .'. On the one hand, this semantic feature makes possible constructions like oun-petsôtm 'Is there anyone who hears . . .', cf. 75; on the other hand, it necessitates the generic definite article before words like pethau 'whatever is evil', petnanouf 'whatever is good', petouaab 'whatever is holy', when spoken of generically or cross-referentially.

17   te] and not pe, hence ouanagkaion is a qualifying (classifying) predicate, i.e., adjective, rather than an identifying predicate, i.e., predicate noun. The distinction is elaborated by Polotsky, 'Nominalsatz . . .', following Praetorius.

18   oei] (Sa. oᵗ). This, rather than śoop, is used because there is no emphasis upon permanent or inherent existence: oei is the non-marked counterpart of śoop and shifts all logical interest onto the expression which completes it. o or oei with such a predicative expression is often equivalent to a Gk. denominative vb.

19   netcine] Cleft Sentence = ne etcine. Cf. 82 106 110 162.

21   ntaha] II perfect with emphasis upon neś nhe. The position of neś nhe is optional in Sa. when a second tense is used, cf. 1 Cor.7.32-34 Tho.: πῶς ἀρέσῃ τῷ κυρίῳ; . . . πῶς ἀρέσῃ τῇ γυναικί; . . . πῶς ἀρέσῃ τῷ ἀνδρί; efnaareske mpjoeis naś nhe . . . efnaareske ntefshime naś nhe . . . naś nhe esnaareske mpeshai.

r-khrô There seems good reason to doubt that this, like
the other Gk. vbs. used in Sa. and the related dialects,
is imperative in form, pace A. Böhlig, Lehnwörter.
Adoption of the middle voice imperative is rare, but
even so (r)khrô itself is the usual Sa. form even if
formally eccentric.

22   šoop] Cf. on oei 18. šoop could stand alone here (without hn sarks), while oei would necessarily be a vb. of
incomplete predication.

hn sarks], presumably *ἐν σαρκί as again at 101
(omission of the article is common in the Gk. NT).
The Sa. NT, in contrast, regularly translates this
phrase by using the generic definite article, hn tsarks
(cf. Rom.2.28, 8.9, 2 Cor.10.3, Gal.2.20, 6.12, Eph.
2.11 bis, Phil.1.22, 1 Tim.3.16, Phlm. 16).

23   ntaref-] Contrasts with efšoop (circumstantial) as
punctual to stative. The underlying statement is 'he
exists incarnate and has revealed himself'. For
ntaref-, cf. Grammatical Appendix 5.

24   eušêre etc.] (Circumstantial) predicative, complementing
-f of ouanhf.

nnoute] See Grammatical Appendix 4.

25   afhmahe] Sa. afmooše. Two paradigms of the I perfect
occur in our text, (1) base a= and (2) base ah=:

[aei] or [ahi] 185		[ahi] or [aei] 185	
ak	102 etc.	--	
af	46 etc.	--	
an	14 etc.	ahn 79 80 123	
au	9 etc.	ahou 89	
a before nn. 36 136		--	

mahe 'to walk' is attested in Subachm. in the Manichaean
corpus, as well as in Achm. and certain other texts
(Kasser, Compléments): Jo and AP have maahe. afhmahe
is a misspelling either of ahf-mahe (as Barns suggests)
or of af-mahe (erroneously written hmahe, perhaps by
prospective influence of hmast in the following line,
44:18f.), but in any case an error. The scribe is
falling asleep as we know from his original error
afhm[e]he, which has been corrected by him in the manuscript.

25   pi-] On this and subsequent occurrences of pi-, ti-,
ni-, see Grammatical Appendix 1. Note peei in the
following line, and cf. 35 ti-. . . hn teei . . .

26   peei etk-] Again a non-restrictive relative; this construction is always expressed thus in our text; cf. 143
(teei entas-), 194 (apeei, peei ntaei- *τοῦτο, *ὅ
. . . .; contrast sentence-initial neei ntahi- at 184).
For 183 cf. the commentary below. The restrictive
relative assumes the form of simple et: 75 77 91
(cross-referential) 130 131 191. In the latter cate-
gory fall instances of the relative clause with self-
contained antecedent 185 ≠neei ntahi- (*ὅ . . .) and
the substantivized relative clause (e.g., 52 et pass.).
(e)t- of the Cleft Sentence (19 etc.) resists logical
analysis. Strict distinction of the restrictive from
the non-restrictive relative is often difficult from
the context alone; the usage of class. Sa. has not been
worked out and so cannot serve as a guide.

27   ef-] Circumstantial. Schenke's rendering of a- as
'against' is quite possible. śeje only occurs here,
so no other passages in our text offer a clue.

28   eeijou nde] must be a II present because of the

connective particle. [de introduces a circumstantial
only when it stands in parallel to an earlier circumstantial clause of the same sentence: Shenute MIF
23:113,55 sq. 'Is it not in him (Pharaoh) that he (God)
revealed his power,

> eftre oulaos jioor nteruthra thalassa,
> efôms de mmof ntof nhêts

> ('making a nation cross the Red Sea,
> and [de] personally submerging it in it')?'

So 120,15 sq., connected by alla pantôs]. The emphasis
rests upon je pmou, not upon the speaker as Peel claims:
nde sets off the remarks as a parenthesis, it does not
emphasize 'I'. (For the latter, e.g., Matt.5.22: ἐγὼ
δὲ λέγω ὑμῖν ὅτι, anok de tijô mmos nêtn je . . .)
The Greek equivalent is λέγω δὲ τὸ δεῖνα, literally
'I am talking about so-and-so', a completely neutral
idiom like i.e. (id est). The phrase occurs constantly
throughout the Greek literature, cf. LSJ (e.g.,
Demosthenes XIX.152). The exact equivalent is missing
in the NT, yet Gal.3.17: τοῦτο δὲ λέγω· διαθήκην κτλ.
('I mean this: that as for a covenant . . .'): pai de
eijô mmof je oudiathêkê . . . nfnatstos ebol an.
Without the influence of a Greek model, Shenute will
say (more naturally) eišaje e- . . ., e.g., MIF 23:110,
20.

29ff.   pšêre . . . (o)ušêre etc.] See Grammatical Appendix 4.

30   emahte arau mpesneu] mpesneu 'together' (of two things),
        or when resuming or anticipating a pronoun simply
        αμφοτερα, 'both (of two things)' (cf. the Concordance).
        Its state of determination is definite since it antici-
        pates a listing of known items. In Gk. ἀμφότερα
        typically precedes its referents when emphasis is
        desired (Kühner-Gerth[3], 406 Anm. 10).

        emahte] This is not the normal transitive use of the

verb (for which see 4 63 66 97). An intransitive construction with e- is meagerly attested in Coptic legal
texts (S), probably meaning 'hold title to' (real
estate or commodity, rather than 'possess' chattels),
or a similar legal concept. To Crum's few examples,
s.v. (I, end), I can add only ST 324 (ostracon), quoted
Dict. s.v. soi 318a,4: mmeros hn tsoi (wood) etenamahte
eros 'have title to' (?). Such a usage belongs to the
domain of Coptic jurisprudence; it is late and lacks any
literary evidence at all. But amahte transitive without
any direct object is quite common (κρατεῖν abs., etc.)
and from the context (cf. 21) the meaning of the present
construction is clear enough: 'held sway' or 'was
master of the situation in two respects' or even 'for
two purposes'. Hence the following vb. of possession
euntef is not redundant.

31 e-] Circumstantial.

  t-] Definite article used with abstract concepts.

32 abal hitm-] Agential preposition, 'by' his being . . .
  abal serves both this and the following hitootf (33);
  repetition is avoided for stylistic reasons. By their
  combination with abal, expressions of agent or means
  are distinguished from simple hitn- 'from' (11). Cf.
  52 63 65-66 143.

  trf] Short form as 89 trn; elsewhere the vowel is
  written (tref 43 77 180).

  ptrfšôpe] Either τὸ εἶναι or τὸ γίνεσθαι; contrast of
  the two is possible only within the present system
  (including its conversions and the second tense).

33 hitootf . . . m-] Substitution of this for its equivalent hitm- is optional. Here it allows earlier

intervention of <u>nde</u>.

<u>tapokatastasis</u> . . . <u>pplêrôma</u>] Definite article, the author refers to well-known topics.

<u>ahoun</u> <u>a-</u>] Goes with <u>apokatastasis</u>.

34 <u>abal</u> <u>hm</u> <u>psa</u> <u>n-</u>] The usual class. Sa. equivalent is simply <u>ebol</u> <u>hn</u>, though <u>psa</u> <u>n-</u>/<u>pisa</u> <u>n-</u> occurs in various other compound prepositions in the Sa. bible, rendering simply Gk. prepositions where simpler Sa. expressions could be used (cf. Crum, <u>Dict</u>.). Compounds of <u>sa</u> are especially frequent in PS and Gosp. Phil., but without exact parallel to our text. In the Sa. NT both οὐρανόθεν and ἄνωθεν can be rendered by <u>ebol</u> <u>hn</u> <u>tpe</u> (Acts 14.17, 26.13; John 19.11); otherwise the latter is usually <u>jin</u> <u>tpe</u> (Matt.27.51, etc.). (For the other meanings of ἄνωθεν other translations are used: 'again' <u>nkesop</u> John 3.3, etc.; 'from the beginning' <u>jinnšorp</u> Luke 1.3.)

35 <u>šôpe</u>] Means both 'began to exist' and 'existed' in this conjugation.

35f. <u>ti-</u> . . . <u>hn</u> <u>teei</u>] Probably translating a non-restrictive relative, like <u>pi-</u> . . . <u>peei</u> at <u>25f</u>.: 'in which'.

36f. <u>šôpe</u> <u>enašôou</u>] The periphrastic conjugation of <u>naše</u>, I perfect corresponding to the English present perfect. Apart from the periphrastic conjugation, adjective verbs occur only where a qualitative could be used; their circumstantial alternates freely with all other circumstantials (especially with qualitative) and also with the attributive noun:

   Mt.9.37 <u>pôhs</u> <u>men</u> <u>našôf</u>, <u>nergatês</u> <u>de</u> <u>sobk</u>.
   Jo.12.3 <u>oulitra</u> <u>nsocn</u> <u>nnardos</u> <u>mpistikê</u> <u>enaše</u> <u>sounts</u>.

146

Deut.4.6 Ci. <u>eis</u> <u>oulaos</u> <u>nsoph[os]</u> <u>auô</u> <u>enesbôôf</u>,
σοφὸς καὶ ἐπιστήμων.

In the NT, the periphrastic conjugation of these verbs
occurs only in Luke 6.35 (with <u>naše</u>): (6.23 <u>eis</u> <u>hêête</u>
<u>gar</u> <u>petnbeke</u> <u>našôf</u> <u>hn</u> <u>tpe</u> . . . πολύς <u>scil</u>. ἐστιν) . . .
<u>auô</u> <u>petnbeke</u> <u>našôre</u> <u>enašôf</u> (ἔσται . . . πολύς). Also
at Luke 6.23, MSS 111 114 read <u>našôre</u> <u>enašôf</u> against 37
87 and Gk.

39   <u>eei-</u>] II present emphasizing <u>hn-</u> etc.

40   <u>šoop</u>] Slight emphasis upon '<u>isn't</u>' (contradicting <u>39</u>);
        otherwise the verb could be simply omitted.

42   <u>efhêp</u>] Repredication after <u>ke-laue</u>.

43   <u>ptêrf</u> . . . <u>etbe</u> <u>pšôpe</u>] Split by an intervening word
        (cf. <u>15</u> <u>petešše</u> . . . <u>etbe</u> <u>tanastasis</u>, <u>33</u> <u>tapokatastasis</u>
        . . . <u>ahoun</u> <u>applêpôma</u>).

        <u>pšôpe</u>] Either 'being' (τὸ εἶναι) or 'becoming' (τὸ
        γίνεσθαι, ἡ γένεσις); no contrast between these two
        terms can be made when the infinitive is used as a nn.
        But Coptic <u>can</u> contrast <u>petšôpe</u>/<u>petšoop</u>: γίνεσθαι/εἶναι
        'what comes into being, comes about'/'what exists, is
        the case'. The nature of the literature transmitted in
        Coptic (excepting gnostic texts, which do not seem to
        have enjoyed wide or at least continuing circulation),
        as well as the general accessibility of Greek to the
        learned in Egypt, does not seem to have necessitated
        the development of such a distinction in the language,
        though surely one could have been found. A similar
        problem arose in Arabic when the Platonic and Aristotel-
        ian corpora were first translated: after unsuccessful
        initial attempts, convenient linguistic conventions were
        developed for contrasts like εἶναι/γίνεσθαι.

<u>44</u> Note the use of <u>variatio</u> in the Coptic translator's placement of the coordinating particles <u>mmen</u> . . . <u>nde</u>, first splitting the vb. and adverb from its genitive, next splitting the vb. from the adverb. <u>abal</u> goes with the infinitive in either instance.

<u>ppethau</u>] The definite article marks an abstraction ('evil' as such), as in <u>tmêe</u>.

<u>petsatp</u>] 'Whatever is . . .', 'the . . .', cf. on <u>15</u> <u>peteśśe</u>.

<u>mmen</u>] Like <u>nde</u>, <u>ngar</u>; forms in <u>n</u>- are the norm in this text, as in <u>AP</u> (Schm.). The origin of this <u>n</u>- is unknown. Class. Sa. (and with it the Subachm. John) uses the Greek forms; but so also our text at <u>33</u> <u>44</u> <u>de</u>, <u>72</u> <u>gar</u>.

<u>teei te</u>] The predicate is <u>teei</u>; <u>pbôl</u> . . . <u>pouônh</u> . . . stand to it in extraposition or topicalization: 'as for <u>pbôl</u> etc., the <u>probolê</u> is <u>this</u>', viz. <u>pbôl</u> etc.

<u>45</u> <u>ta tmêe</u>] <u>ta</u> is the possessive prefix (Stern 250), which alternates freely with <u>pô= tô= nou=</u> (<u>pêi mpnoute/pa pnoute</u> as <u>pefêi/pôf</u>). Three uses of <u>pa pô=</u> etc. must be distinguished:

  (1) Resumption (substitution in parallelism: Luke 22.42 <u>mare pekouôś śôpe</u>, <u>mpôi an</u>, μὴ τὸ θέλημά μου ἀλλὰ τὸ σὸν γινέσθω. Here repetition of the noun is avoided; only the possessor is of interest. So in <u>72</u>: <u>ptopos gar ntpistis pe auô pa prpeithe en pe</u>.

  (2) To predicate possession: as an identifying predicate of a nominal sentence (like <u>tai te</u>). This is the construction in <u>45</u>. Cf. 1 Cor.3.21, <u>ptêrf pôtn pe</u>, πάντα ὑμῶν, <u>omnia uestra sunt</u>; vs.23 <u>ntôtn de ntetn-na pekh(risto)s</u>, <u>pekh(risto)s de pa pnoute pe</u>, ὑμεῖς δὲ Χριστοῦ, Χριστὸς δὲ θεοῦ. So also in <u>107</u> <u>mê mpôk en pe</u>, 'is it not yours?'.

(3) To form a substantive (the most common usage); a Coptic substantivized relative clause of the binary nominal sentence is used. So <u>108</u> <u>pete</u> <u>pôk</u> <u>pe</u>, <u>mê</u> <u>nfšoop</u> <u>en</u> <u>nmmek</u>.

pete pôi <u>pe</u> = τὸ ἐμόν

    <u>-k</u>   σόν

    <u>-f</u>   ἴδιον (John 15.19)

  <u>etc</u>.   <u>etc</u>.

(Negative in Luke 16.12 = τὸ ἀλλότριον)

Relative conversion: here a ternary nominal sentence <u>ete</u> <u>pô=</u> <u>pe</u> . . . can also be used.

   = οὗ 'whose (is) . . .' Acts 21.11

   = ᾧ 'to whom belongs' Rom.16.27.

<u>46</u>   ômnk] Always spelled thus in the text.

<u>49</u>   ešaf-] Relative form of the habitual (i.e., Polotsky's 'aorist'), interchangeable with <u>ete</u> <u>šaf</u>-. Restrictive relative equivalent to adjective.

<u>48</u>-<u>53</u> The clauses group as follows:

    <u>afkôe</u> <u>ngar</u> . . . <u>afšft[f]</u>

    <u>auô</u> <u>aftounasf</u> <u>eafômnk</u>

    <u>auô</u> <u>afti</u>

<u>afkôe</u> is prob. for a Gk. aorist participle, formally subordinate to <u>afšftf</u>. See Grammatical Appendix V, 'The Asyndetic First Perfect'. <u>(e)afômnk</u>, probably also a Gk. aorist participle, represents a stage of the narrative prior to <u>aftounasf</u> ('once he had devoured', 'after he had devoured') and so must be translated in Coptic by a circumstantial of I perfect.

<u>49</u>   ešaftako] The opposite of <u>nattako</u>.

55   joof] And not joos, hence 'said about him' (or 'it'--
        but there is no likely impersonal antecedent). Cf.
        John 11.13: neumeeue je efje-penkotk mpôbš, ἔδοξαν ὅτι
        περὶ τῆς κοιμήσεως τοῦ ὕπνου λέγει, cf. Matt.24.25.

59-61   eišpe tnšoop] Answered below by a second tense,
        enrphorei mmaf (emphasis upon mmaf).

62   enšoop] II present emphasizing mpetmmau.

63   euemahte] Circumstantial.

65f.   eusôk] II present emphasizing nthe nni- etc.

        enseemahte en] Circumstantial.

        abal hitootf] Agential expression; note that when used
        before prê and laue, abal is not repeated. Avoidance
        of multiple ebol's in a single sentence is a stylistic
        rule generally observed in class. Sa. and related
        dialects.

        nthe nni-] Coptic formula of comparison, its Gk. (and
        English) equivalent saying 'as (does or is) a _____'.
        See Grammatical Appendix 1, sub (4).

67   teei te] The predicate is teei: 'It is this which
        is . . .'.

68   esômnk] Adnominal circumstantial, explaining why the
        preceding statement is true.

        mn tke-] 'And also the', a stock formula in Coptic
        for τε καί.

70   pisteue] Auxiliary r (used in this dialect before Gk.
       vbs.) is omitted randomly, as not rarely in Subachm.
       John. The other omissions of r in this text are all
       with pisteue: 77 80 (yet r is used at 75 84 85 and
       passim with other Gk. verbs).

71,73 pr peithe] Passive in meaning, 'the being persuaded'.
       The Gk. form is seemingly active (the active present
       imperative), but in the Sa. NT peithe often renders
       πείθεσθαι, whether middle (Luke 20.6, Acts 5.39) or
       passive (Acts 21.14, cum ei suadere non possemus,
       Vulgate). Cf. A. Böhlig, Lehnwörter 246 (wrongly
       terming all his examples 'passive').

74   petmaout natôôn] An independent clause, giving as an
       afterthought the topic of discussion. At 72, the pro-
       noun pe (in ptopos pe) does not yet have a referent;
       this is supplied by the present clause.

75   oun pet-] A common Copt. construction, postulating or
       (as here) inquiring about a typical instance of some
       activity. The actor of the substantivized relative is
       quantified (its quantity is specified, one typical
       instance), hence p- is used. But the actor is not
       specifically identified, hence ouref- or oua ef- is
       not used. The petsôtm form often shows semantic
       characteristics of nns. with a zero article, cf. on 15.
       Note that petsôtm is not the generic nn. (prefsôtm),
       i.e., it does not refer to all possible instances of
       something, but rather to anyone at all, identity
       unspecified. Bl.-D.-F. 413.1 note the Greek models:
       either 'the individualizing article ὁ' with participle
       or else a bare participle without the Gk. article.

75   hn-] After a zero article plus nn., the English equiva-
       lent is 'among'; after an indefinite article or

151

indefinite pronoun (<u>oua</u>, <u>laau</u>, etc.) 'of'.

<u>etnnima</u>] Restrictive relative.

<u>nphilosophos</u>] Class. Sa. <u>nephilosophos</u>. Subachm. texts
(as studied by Nagel, <u>Unters</u>. para. 37) generally use
the short form throughout, except before Greek words
(<u>AP</u>, GospTr regularly so), <u>th</u>- excepted; and the
Manichaean corpus generally not at all (except
<u>pekhr(-sto)s</u>, <u>pkhr(-sto)s</u> also occur). Our text
fluctuates between the Sa. rules (which make exception
for <u>ptref</u>- as at <u>32</u>) and the practice of Ma. (most of
the violations of the Sa. rule in this text occur with
Greek words): <u>pe</u>- before <u>Khrêstos</u> (<u>11</u> <u>143</u> <u>184</u>), <u>pneuma</u>
(<u>44</u>), <u>śta</u> (<u>160</u>), <u>houo</u> (<u>151</u>), <u>tekharis</u> (<u>45</u> <u>195</u>); but <u>p</u>-:
<u>plêrôma</u> (<u>33</u> <u>94</u>), <u>philosophos</u> (<u>77</u>); <u>t</u>-: <u>probolê</u> (<u>44</u>),
<u>psukhikê</u> (<u>68</u>); <u>n</u>-: <u>philosophos</u> (<u>75</u>), <u>hbêue</u> (<u>151</u> <u>156</u>).

<u>77</u>   <u>npôr</u> <u>a</u>-] Marker of the negative imperative, alternating
freely with <u>mpr</u>- and identical to it in meaning. Not
to be confused with the independent use of <u>mpôr</u> (Crum
178<u>b</u>.

<u>81</u>   <u>tôoun</u>] Earlier, <u>tôôn</u> was used (<u>57</u> <u>74</u> <u>76</u>); from this
point on, the text has <u>tôoun</u> (<u>81</u> <u>131</u> <u>133</u> <u>172</u> <u>174</u>).

<u>abal</u>] Probably goes only with <u>hn</u>, since <u>tôoun</u> most often
occurs without adverbial reinforcement.

<u>82</u>   Cleft sentence. <u>mmof</u> takes its gender and number from
<u>peei</u>.

<u>84</u>   <u>hôs</u> <u>ounac</u> <u>pe</u> . . . <u>hnnat</u> <u>ne</u> . . .] Class. Sa. uses ὡς
as follows:
A. ὡς with circumstantial.
        (1) 'On the supposition that' (not necessarily
contrary to fact): Matt.7.29, Rom.13.13, etc.

(2) 'As though it were the case that' (contrary to fact): Acts 3.12, 1 Cor.4.18, etc.

(3) 'When', like (eph)hoson: 2 Cor.13.2, Gal.6.10.
B. ὡς without circumstantial.

(4) hôs . . . tai on te the = sicut . . . sic et
. . . (Rom.5.18 only). This is the closest parallel; but our passage lacks tai te the with the second member.

petour pisteue araf] A generalization, 'whoever' or 'whatever'. The specifying equivalent would be pai etour pisteue erof, 'the one in whom they believe'.

85   nat] Clearly a form of Sa. noc (Subachm. nac, Bohairic niśti).

86f.   pmeue . . . pnous] The single definite article is meant distributively, English 'the thoughts . . . the minds'.

87   netah-] The Achm. relative marker, used characteristically when the subject of the following vb. is identical with the antecedent. Cf. Sethe ÄZ 52 (1914) 112ff. (ah a qualitative from w3ḥ, the Demotic auxiliary vb.), Steindorff, Lehrb. 313 (2c). Besides -etah (87 90 133), a form -ntah also occurs in this text (95 pentah bôl abal).

89   haeie hn-] Sa. he hn-. Either 'fall into' or 'fall in the manner of'. hn- rather than e- is often used as the directional preposition with he both because of Gk. usage and because he e- would also mean 'discover' (εὑρίσκειν).

90   ena-] II future, 1st person plural. In, e.g., the Subachm. John ena- coincides with the III future form. But from the parallel of 32 we can surmise that II future is the appropriate tense here. One of the many

syntactical features which Subachm. shares with Achm.
is its extensive use of affirmative II future where Sa.
has affirmative III future.

91   etou] Restrictive relative, 'that truth which
they . . .'.

95f.   pentah- . . . af- . . .] The asyndetic first perfect
construction (cf. Grammatical Appendix 5) very often
obtains between the members of a compound relative
clause.

pentah bôl abal] Generalization.

bôl abal] The basic meaning of bôl is loosen, untie, or
intransitive counterparts, become loose or untied.
There is no pre-Demotic etymology. See Crum, Dict. 32a:
besides the loosening of chains, cords, book-rolls etc.,
it figures in physical and alchemical expressions be
melted, i.e., loosen bond of solidity, and so by extension to various other realms. But the concept of a bond
which is broken or loosened is always inherent, even in
the extended meanings. Transitively, the vb. means to
break that bond; intransitively, to have one's bond
broken by an unspecified agent.

97   Normally it is the predicate of a nominal sentence which
preceeds pe, but in those with three members of which
both substantives have the definite article, only exegesis can distinguish subject (thème) from predicate
(propos). Since petouemahte mmaf (97) contrasts with
pentahbôl abal (95) and semantically alternates with it,
we may assume that it does so syntactically and that
ptêrf alternates with the predicate oukouei. ptêrf, be
it noted, will then be an identifying predicate (it
answers the question 'What is it that is what-is-held-
fast?'), while oukouei, like oujôre (94), probably is not.

101   śoop] 'Exist', not merely 'be', cf. on 18 and 22.
        Answering the question 'In what condition can you be
        said to have existed before?'

102   sarks] The zero article is used because sarks is con-
        ceived of as a substance, with neither particular
        identity or fixed quantity.

104   etbe eu] 'Why is it the case that . . .' See Grammati-
        cal Appendix VI for this and other instances of the
        phrase.

106   petsatp atsarks] Generalization.

        petśoop] Cleft sentence (=pe etśoop).

        nes] Dativus ethicus, 'exists as its cause', literally
        'for it as cause', or even 'belongs to it as cause'.

        pôônh] Sa. pônh; the definite article is used with the
        name of an abstraction.

107   mê n- . . . en] Expects 'yes' as an answer, i.e.,
        'surely it must . . .'.

        pôk . . . pe] Predicates possession, cf. on 45.

109   ek-] Circumstantial.

110   eu pe etk-] Cleft sentence. Here and at 162 (ntaf pe
        ettamio) the long form occurs. At 19 (henkouei nde
        netcine), 82 (peei petnjou mmaf), 106 (petsatp . . .
        petśoop) the usual form occurs.

114   <u>śoop</u>] Not 'are you' corruptible, but 'do you exist'
(like ὑπάρχεις), viz. perpetually exist, corruptible.

115   <u>ntapousia</u>] Direct object.

    <u>nouhêu</u>] Repredication. Note that <u>n</u>- alone, rather than
<u>n</u>- plus zero article, is the mark of the predicative
noun. It is the semantic context which usually elicits
the zero article.

117   <u>bôk</u>] I.e., <u>bôk ahrêi ahoun apaiôn</u>, 105.

118   <u>pethau</u>] Not <u>ppethau</u> as at 44, but bare <u>pet</u>- 'what(ever)
is . . .', for which English can say 'the inferior
(part)'.

119   <u>oun</u> <u>hmat</u> <u>araf</u>] The 'inferior' (<u>pethau</u>), i.e., the body,
is meant. For Till's 'es gibt Gnade dafür' we should
probably need <u>nef</u> rather than <u>araf</u>. 'C'est grâce pour
lui' is equally impossible, as the edd. note.
        Sa. <u>oun</u>- . . . <u>ero=</u> is a common expression from
the language of commerce and credit, to express the
existence of a debt. Two syntactic patterns must be
distinguished (evidence can be found in the <u>Concordance</u>,
ed. Wilmet, p. 89f.):
        (1) Bipartite sentences with <u>e</u>-/<u>ero=</u> as predicate.

            The subject = amount or item of debt.
            The object of the preposition = debtor.

(The substitution table of the subject position includes,
for non-specification of the amount or item, the pronoun
<u>ouon</u>.) When an indefinite pronoun, indefinite article,
or zero article occurs in the subject position, the
auxiliary <u>oun</u>- will precede it, as always in the
bipartite sentence pattern.
Gal.5.3 <u>serof</u>, ὀφειλέτης ἐστίν.
Mt.18.30 <u>peterof</u>, τὸ ὀφειλόμενον.

Mt.23.16 & 18 oun-ouon erof, ὀφείλει.

Lc.13.4 (where nobe is added interpretively by the
translator) oun nobe eroou para nrôme têrou, ὀφειλέται
ἐγένοντο παρὰ πάντας τοὺς ἀνθρώπους.

Shenute MIF 23:98.50 pai gar eron ntootf mpjoeis.

(2) Possessive verb ounte- ounta= plus actor
(plus dir. object) plus e-/ero=.

> Actor = creditor.
> Direct object = amount or item of debt (may
> be omitted).
> Object of preposition = debtor.

(Omission of the direct object corresponds to the use
of ouon in the first construction.)

Mt.18.28 neuntaf erof nse nsateere, ὤφειλεν αὐτῷ ἑκατὸν
δηνάρια.

Ro.1.14 nsophos mn nathêt, euntau eroi, σοφοῖς τε καὶ
ἀνοήτοις ὀφειλέτης εἰμί.

The construction in 119, then, is the first (1) of
the two constructions of debt just described, and it
means 'it (viz. pethau) owes hmat'. This is of course
Gk. χάριν ὀφείλειν, 'to owe gratitude', 'to be beholden'
(LSJ χάρις s.v., II.2). The zero article precedes hmat
for the same reason that it does in expressions like
ti-hap 'judge', r-hote 'be afraid' and śp-hmot 'be
thankful (for a gift)', literally 'receive presents'.

120   sôt] The usual Subachm. form (cf. Kasser, Compléments)
is sôte, as in Sa. and as above at 88. The form sôt
occurs in Achm. along with sôte; so in Sa. in the PS 83,
18 Sch.

abal] Very likely to be taken with nnima, which is for
hnnima, since λυτροῦσθαι is simply rendered by sôt.
For sôt ebol without preposition, Crum cites only
Bohairic texts (362ab).

121   pe] Always singular after independent pronouns in the

nominal sentence.

122   tn-] Plural by attraction to anan.

123   ha] L.Eg. r š3ᶜ (Erman²656.2), correctly spelled ša
    (as at 63). There is a confusion of ša (all dialects),
    r š3ᶜ 'up to, as far as'; ha ḫa (ⲍ ⳝ) Eg. ḫr 'under,
    away from'; and ha S (rare) B(!) of unknown etymology
    'toward' [Crum 634b], mostly referring to persons but
    not exclusively so. The difficulty in simply identify-
    ing ha with ša is of course the Bohairic contrast
    between ḫa:ha,

    Perhaps read jinn- or jinarêjf ha thê] The meaning is
    obvious, 'from one end to the other', but I know of no
    exact parallel to this expression. (Both Copt. nouns
    mean περας or εσχατον, and are virtually interchangeable.
    E.g., at Bar.3.25, the Bohairic reads ḫaie and the Sa.
    arêj=, while at Ps.7.6 just the opposite is the case,
    Sa. haê and Bohairic aurêj=.) Cf. PS 117.23 sena
    makarize mmo jin arêjf mpkah ša arêjf 'from one boundary
    of the earth to the other'.

125   hees] Obviously he is meant. The form occurs here, in
    the following line, and at 180, and nowhere else. No
    explanation is possible since the etymology of he
    'manner' is unknown, though the final s suggests that
    it is a nn. formed secondarily in a final pronoun, cf.
    Steindorff, Lehrb. 122.2.

126   mme] AA² = eime.

127   eišpe] Sa. ešje, 'if' (the Subachm. form also occurs in
    GospTr): mme . . . eišpe . . . fnaoujeei. The word
    'whether' (1 Cor.1.16; je ene Mark 15.44) is expected
    and possibly should be inserted before, or instead of,

158

eiŝpe. Stern (629 end) misquotes John 9.25 to illustrate such a putative use of eŝje, but the correct text
of this variant is actually je eŝje.

129   mpr tre laue r-] Here not causative but the negative
jussive, cf. Polotsky 'Modes Grecs en Copte?'.

130   nnes] for neŝ as at 21. The gemination of the particle
n- before vowels is a common phenomenon. Note that
Sa. naŝ nhe tends to be split by sentence-connective
particles; here it is not.

    etouaanh abal etmaout] Both are restrictive relatives.
The asyndeton is not unusual.

130f.   nnes nhe . . . je . . .] Here je = epexegetical (δι)ότι
'since', cf. Grammatical Appendix 3.   naŝ nhe 'how can
it be so that . . .': cf. Luke 1.34 naŝ nhe pai naŝ ôpe
mmoi ⟨e⟩mpisoun hout, πῶς ἔσται τοῦτο, ἐπεὶ ἄνδρα οὐ
γινώσκω; 6.42; 20.41.

131   neuna-] Elliptic: ('If what you said were true,) they
would arise', Coptic literally 'were going to arise'.
Greek potential optative.

133   nim] 'Any given', i.e., over and over again, at 'each'
occasion.

134   akr pmeue] Here present perfect, 'have considered the
fact . . . that'.

135   ek-] ôŝ, the normal word for 'read', means to utter an
audible sound (ἤχειν, βοᾶν, etc.). In Egyptian, as in
Gk. and Latin, reading apparently was performed aloud,
even in private.

136   auô Môusês] A slightly stronger articulation than mn
      Môusês. John 1.35 nere Iôhannês aheratf auô snau ebol
      hn nefmathêtês. Contrast John 4.12, 6.22, 8.52, etc.
      with mn-.

138   ouphantasia te] A Gk. adjective can be rendered thus in
      Coptic; so at 140 oumêe te (*ἀληθινή). Cf. Polotsky,
      'Nominalsatz'.

141   oupetesśe pe a-] Class. Sa. can use śśe e-, eśśe e-,
      peteśśe pe e-, and (2 Cor.12.11) eśśe pe e-.

      -sśe] As at 180. The etymology of Sa. śśe is here
      obvious, 'it goes'. The -e- between et- and sśe is
      presumably anaptychtic: it is normally written in
      class. Sa. orthography (old spelling etśe; for the
      Bohairic, cf. Stern 401).

143   abal hitoot-] The same agential preposition is used with
      both the Coptic passive and the vb. śôpe.

144   etbe eu] Request for the topic of conversation, cf.
      Grammatical Appendix 6.

145   nteunou] 'Suddenly' (ntounou 128): tinou (191) 'now'.

146   pôs] The πῶς of disbelief. The Gk. word is rare in
      Coptic, occurring only thrice in the Sa. NT (also in
      Bohairic NT OT and Shenute according to Böhlig), all
      Sa. NT instances being in Mark (4.13, 8.21, 9.12). In
      the Sa. NT it is usually replaced by naś nhe (interroga-
      tive) or other expressions with he. Several examples
      occur in the Gosp.Phil. however. Unfortunately their
      value is diminished by the lack of an extant Gk. model
      and by the generally odd style of the Coptic. At least

two of these provide parallels to our text in that they
are instances of the pôs of disbelief ('how can it be
that . . .'): CG II 52:10-13 <u>netmoout maurklêronomei</u>
<u>llaau</u>. <u>pôs</u> <u>gar</u> <u>petmoout</u> <u>fnaklêronomei</u> ('for how could
a dead man inherit?'); 77:6f. ('He purified liturgical
items') <u>pôs</u> <u>fnatoubo</u> <u>an</u> <u>mpkesôma</u> ('surely he will purify
the body, too'). The second tense in <u>146</u> presumably
emphasizes <u>hn</u> <u>ouphantasia</u> rather than pôs. Note that
at <u>130</u>, however, *πῶς is translated, as in the Sa. NT:
<u>nnes</u> <u>nhe</u> <u>ce</u> <u>nmelos</u> <u>etouaanh</u> <u>abal</u> <u>etmaout</u> <u>nsenaoujeei</u> <u>en</u>.

<u>anh</u>] Freely alternates with <u>aanh</u>, cf. <u>131</u> <u>145</u> (the
infin. is ôônh <u>106</u>). Qualitative, hence 'are alive'
rather than (in the sense of passing one's life through
a series of habitual acts) 'live'.

147   <u>au</u>-] Present perfect, 'have . . .'.

148   <u>nnraei</u>] Sa. <u>nerrôou</u>, plural of <u>rro</u>. For geminated <u>nu</u>
before a vowel (or as here, before syllabic resonance
r), see <u>130</u>. The manuscript has N̄N̄ⲣⲁⲉⲓ (the stroke
is slightly wider than the second <u>nu</u>) but probably
<u>n̥</u> - <u>nr̥</u> - (r)ai is meant; the supralinear stroke has been
written over the wrong <u>nu</u>.

<u>auśrśôrou</u>] Coptic passive.

149   <u>śareb</u>-] I.e., <u>śaref</u>- a common misspelling.

151   <u>jekase</u> etc.] Self-exhortation. See Grammatical
Appendix 3 <u>sub</u> 'Jussive (2)'.

<u>ni</u>] Short form of III future negative. (The -<u>i</u> desi-
nence is typical for Subachm.), Sa. <u>nna</u>. Cf. <u>182</u>.

<u>nhbêue</u>] Sa. <u>nehbêue</u>, yet <u>a-pe-houo</u> in the same line.

sa] Subachm. form of nsa. Omission of initial nu is
shared with Achm. (se), but the vocalization is Sahidic.
Like the Subachm. John, our text uses both this form and
nsa (179). All dialects agree on nsô= (127 186) as the
status pronominalis.

155-   Note variatio in the word order: First a long predicate
156   before pe (155), and then (156) intercalation of pe
early in the predicate. The latter is a normal position
in Coptic.

157   [.$^{4\frac{1}{2}}$.] A verb of motion is needed. The editors'
hetie (by analogy with 158) just fits the available
space; the restoration is also adopted by Barns, JTS N.S.
15 (1964) 165. Edd. also suggest sbôk; but for vbs.
of motion having both an infin. and a qualitative only
the qualitative can appear in bipartite sentences.
Hence only sbêk 'goes' would be possible; and surely
snêu 'comes' would be more likely than this.

162   Cleft sentence.

ppetnanouf] Definite article before the name of an
abstraction.

164   oute] For μητέ. Coptic does not use μῆτε, μηδέ, but
rather substitutes for them the forms in οὐ-.

politeuesthai] The Gk. imperative form is expected. Sa.
NT uses politeue (as it uses the active imperative in
the case of other middle vbs., listed by Böhlig, Lehnw.
136f.; this is also the practice of PS). But
rpoliteuesthai occurs in Gosp.Phil. at 86:10 and (mis-
spelled as though plural imperat.) rpoliteuesthe at
65:4 and 72:10. The middle imperative form is normal,
e.g., in Bohairic.

167-
175 For the tenses and periodic structure cf. Grammatical
     Appendix 7.

168 efnamou] The I future (here in circumstantial conver-
     sion) of mou regularly translates a present tense of
     the Greek vb. This was first noted by Lagarde's
     teacher, M. G. Schwartze, Das alte Ägypten, II (Berlin
     1847).

169 r] Usual verb for 'passing' time.

171f. neu arak . . . eaktôoun] eaktôoun is repredication
       after arak.

174 ptôoun] 'The uprising'. Perhaps translating a different
     Gk. word than tanastasis.

176 hôs ekna-] See on 84.

181 nse-] Conjunctive and passive. bal-f takes abal in the
     sense of 'release', and abal functions ἀπὸ κοινοῦ with
     n- (for hn-).

182 jekase] On the tenses see Grammatical Appendix 3.

183 peei et-] In apposition to mmaf ouaeetf as a restrictive
     relative, *ὅν or more likely *ὅντινα 'whoever . . .',
     'such a one as . . .'.

     etśrp nśoop] For the construction see Grammatical
     Appendix 8.

184 neei ntahi-] Extraposition, reṣumed as the prepositional

object of tsebak in 185 arau. 'As for these,
which . . .'.

185 naśêre] Apposition to neksnêu, as Peel has pointed out.

186 a ptajre têutn] Greek articular infinitive after *εἰς.

188 efśêk] Repredication after sêh, 'written deep' or '(too)
profoundly'. For the same metaphorical use, Crum 555a
cites C86 (Balestri-Hyvernat, Acta Mart.) 241 (Bohairic):
zêtima etśêk of scriptures.

189 balf] bôl in the sense of 'interpret' does not take ebol

191 rphthonei a-] Takes a personal object, 'regard (someone)
with envy'.

etêp] efêp is needed, since the antecedent is not
definite. The correct construction occurs in the
following line, euncam.

195 neei] Resuming hah. In extraposition to mmau.

atirênê] Although tamo n- pers. e- rem is one normal
construction of the verb, atirênê probably means 'for
the sake of . . .', as often before.

197 euoei] Circumstantial continuing the relative et- as
often; 'who love you and are *φιλάδελφοι'.

title tanastasis] As we learn from the argument of the
treatise, there is not one single resurrection; rather
it is a general and recurring phenomenon for each

individual of the saved (<u>133</u> 'at any given time').
Hence the definite article here is not cross-referential
but abstract: 'the treatise on <u>resurrection</u>'.

GRAMMATICAL APPENDICES

Grammatical Appendix 1:

Use of Forms Spelled pi-, ti-, ni-

As always, the orthography of the manuscript must be scrutinized. Confusion of pi- etc. with peei- etc. is not uncommon in early Coptic texts; even manuscripts as good as the Beatty Acts and Epistles (Thompson) sometimes show uncertainty (Phil.1.30, 2.2, Acts 24.21; also pekro for pikro). The use of pi- in class. Sa. has been worked out by Polotsky, OLZ 52 (1957) 230. But Subachm. is less consistent in its practice, though different groups of manuscripts can be seen to display more or less detectable patterns (P. Nagel, Untersuchungen zur Grammatik des subachmimischen Dialekts, diss. Halle 1964, p. 94ff. [not using our text]). The usage of our text may be summarized as follows.

1. The demonstrative pronoun peei, teei, neei is used as in class. Sa. [170 67 6 etc.], 'this' οὗτος etc. . Its correlate pê [ἐκεῖνος] occurs once at 177; so the synonym petmmeu [ἐκεῖνος] at 62: these forms are interchangeable in the Sa. NT.

2. The demonstrative article is attested at 64 169, both instances hm peeibios 'in the present life', and at 164 kata teeisarks.

3. There are, however, no examples in which a clear contrast in the context indicates the meaning of pi- to be 'that'. Possibly, 3 'they have piskopos ('the aforementioned goal')', but this is probably for Sa. peei- as the weight of the evidence below will indicate.

4. One example of the familiar 'pi- of simile' guarantees the existence of the form as such in our text: 'we are drawn up to heaven nthe nniaktin hitm prê'(65). As Polotsky (l.c.)

has noted, Sahidic Coptic will characteristically use a <u>plural</u> here when Greek has ὡς followed by a <u>singular</u>, <u>indefinite</u> noun or its equivalent; <u>ni-</u> is the correct form, not <u>neei-</u>.

    1 Thess.2.11 ὡς πατὴρ τέκνα ἑαυτοῦ (scil. παρακαλεῖ)
        <u>nthe</u> <u>nnieiôt</u> <u>etsops</u> <u>nneuśêre</u> (Beatty)
    Ps.72.22 κτηνώδης ἐγενόμην παρὰ σοί
        <u>air</u> <u>the</u> <u>nnitbnê</u> <u>nnahrak</u> (Budge)
    Lc.24.11 ἐφάνησαν ὡσεὶ λῆρος
        <u>aur</u> <u>the</u> <u>nnihôb</u> <u>nsôbe</u> (v.1. <u>nneihôb</u> <u>nsôbe</u>)
    Ps.31.9 μὴ γίνεσθε ὡς ἵππος καὶ ἡμίονος
        <u>mprr</u> <u>the</u> <u>nnihto</u> <u>mn</u> <u>nimas</u> (Budge)

Thus in our text the model was probably *ὡς *ἀκτῖνα etc.

    5. The form <u>pi-</u> often occurs in locative expressions, 'this':

    <u>60</u> <u>hm</u> <u>pikosmos</u>
    <u>103</u> <u>ahoun</u> <u>apikosmos</u>
    <u>25</u> <u>hn</u> <u>pitopos</u>, <u>peei</u> <u>etkhmast</u> <u>nhêtf</u>
    <u>181</u> <u>abal</u> <u>mpistoikheion</u>
    <u>35</u> <u>tisustasis</u> . . . <u>hn</u> <u>teei</u> . . . ('in which . . .')

Of special interest are phrases with the <u>plural</u> of <u>ma</u> 'place' (? = *ἐνταῦθα):

    <u>109</u> 'while you are <u>nnima</u>', 'here'.
    <u>75</u>, <u>77</u> <u>nphilosophos</u> <u>etnnima</u> 'the scholars here', 'worldly
        philosophers'
    <u>120</u> <u>abal</u> <u>nnima</u> 'from here' (from out of this world)

Somewhat similar examples of <u>pi-</u> occur in the Manichaean corpus though they are in the singular: <u>mpima</u> 'here' Psalmbook 84, 29; Kephalaia 160,12; <u>apima</u> 'hither' Kephalaia 79,18.

    6. The form <u>pi-</u> also occurs in expressions of manner, 'this', 'that'.

    <u>124</u> and <u>125</u> <u>ntihees</u> (= <u>ntihe</u>)
    <u>152</u> <u>pismat</u> <u>ntimine</u> (perhaps *τοιοῦτος *τρόπος), Sa. <u>peei-</u>
        . . . <u>nteeimine</u> (τοιοῦτος   ), cf. Mark 6.2, John
        9.16, 2 Cor.3.12, etc.

Uses (5) and (6) seem to be for Sa. <u>peei-</u>, <u>teei-</u>, <u>neei-</u>. It might, however, be thought that the examples listed in (5) bear relationship to what Polotsky calls 'affective <u>pi-</u>' in Sa.

for in the context of our treatise all of these expressions
are pejorative. Cf. pielakh(istos), pitalaiporos, self-
depreciatory epithets in Sa. monastic letters and colophons;
Crum, Short Texts 173, 233, 274 (scribe), 309, 343; colophon
to Beatty MS. A (Tho. Acts p. xvii, plate VI); Shenute ed.
Chass. MIF 23:99,2; Shenute Op. III Leip. pass.; Hall, p. 106;
yet Crum, ST 218 pei-, 375 nei-.

Grammatical Appendix 2:

Use of Connective Particles in the Text

Index of Particles

(Reference is made from the line number to the divisions of
the outline below.)

alla (ἀλλά)
                       15 : 6.b.i
                       40 : 6.b.i
                       41 : 6.b.i
                       43 : 2.b   (*μή . . . ἀλλά)
                       76 : 6.b.i
                       90 : 2.b   (*μή . . . ἀλλά)
                     109 : 6.b.i
                     119 : 6.b.i
                     121 : 6.b.i
                     126 : 6.b.ii
                     140 : 2.b   (*οὐ . . . ἀλλά)
                     152 : 6.b.i
                     165 : 2.b   (*μή . . . ἀλλά)
                     175 : 6.b.i
                     183 : 2.b   (*μή . . . ἀλλά)

auδ (καί)
                        6 : 3.a
                      14 : 1.b.i
                      18 : 1.b.i
                      23 : 1.b.i
                      30 : 1.b.i
                      51 : 1.b.i
                      53 : 1.b.i

```
 57 : 1.b.i
 58 : 1.b.i
 63 : 1.b.i
 73 : 1.b.i
 75 : 3.a
 77 : 3.a
 80 : 1.b.i
 82 : 1.b.i
114 : 3.a
136 : 1.a.ii
148 : 1.b.i
155 : 1.b.i
156 : 1.b.i
158 : 1.b.i
160 : 1.b.i
166 : 1.b.ii
173 : 1.b.iii
181 : 1.b.i (?1.b.ii)
```

gar, ngar (γάρ) [all ngar except 72]

```
 48 : 4.b.i
 72 : 4.b.ii
 79 : 4.c
101 : 3.c.i
116 : 3.c.ii
134 : 3.c.i
157 : 4.b.ii
167 : 4.c
```

de, nde (δέ) [all nde except 33 44]

```
  8 : 6.a.i
 19 : 2.a.i   (μέν . . . δέ)
 28 : 4.a     (*λέγω δέ)
 29 : 3.b
 33 : 2.a.ii  (μέν . . . δέ)
 44 : 2.a.i   (μέν . . . δέ)
 59 : 3.b
 69 : 3.b
 97 : 6.a.i
```

                    141 : 2.c   (*οὐ . . . *μᾶλλον δέ)
                    144 : 6.a.ii
                    187 : 6.a.i
                    191 : 3.b   (*νυνὶ δέ)

kaitoige (καίτοιγε) 177 : 7

mn (καί)   31 : 1.a.i
                     36 : 1.a.i
                     44 : 1.a.i
                     68 : 1.a.i
                     88 : 1.a.i
                    161 : 1.a.i
                    165 : 1.a.i
                    185 : 1.a.i
                    195 : 1.a.i
                    196 : 1.a.i

mmen (μέν)   18 : 2.a.i
                     32 : 2.a.ii
                     44 : 2.a.i

ngar, see gar

nde, see de

oute (οὔτε)   93 : 1.c   (*οὐδέ)
                    164 : 1.c   (*μήτε)

hôste (ὥστε)   100 : 5.b
                    163 : 5.b

ce (probably οὖν)   54 : 5.a.ii (τότε *οὖν ?)
                     91 : 5.a.iii
                    120 : 5.a.i
                    130 : 5.a.i
                    132 : 5.a.i
                    151 : 5.a.i
                    179 : 5.a.i

Use of Coptic Connective Particles

(Line references give the location of the particle in question.)

1. Sequential connection of cola (parataxis).
   Coptic dissimilates καί into several syntactically specialized morphemes, of which two belong here: (a) mn connects individual substantives when they are used with an article; auô does so only in certain cases [see l.a.ii]; (b) auô connects clauses, i.e., verbal kernels; with negatives, oute/oude can be used. mn is excluded from use (b).

   a. Connection of substantives. i. mn 'and'. 31 'having humanity mn divinity'; 36 'lordships mn divinities'; 44 'offshoot of the truth mn the spirit'; 88 'salvation mn ransom'; 161 'the symbols mn the likenesses'; 165 'the divisions mn the bonds'; 185 'to you mn your brethren'; 195 'peace mn grace'; 196 'you mn whoever love you'. Coordinated: 68 'the psychic resurrection homoiôs mn ('and likewise') the fleshly'.

   ii. auô in a compound subject (second member postponed). Also auô can be used to connect substantives, indicating, presumably, a slight colonic subdivision (which mn does not): 'X did so-and-so, and Y (did also)'. 136 'Elias appeared--and Moses--in Jesus' company' [compare John 1.35, nere Iôhannês aheratf auô snau ebol hn nefmathêtês; but John 8.52 Abraham afmou mn peprophêtês].

   b. Connection of clauses (auô). i. 'and'. Connecting a pair of clauses: 14 'obtained it when we gained acquaintance with the truth auô rested upon it'; 18 'it is a basic matter, auô many disbelieve' etc. [an adversative particle might be expected, but the author is enumerating the reasons why he has chosen to write to Rheginos]; 23 'while He was incarnate auô after He had revealed Himself . . . He walked' etc.; 30 'He was a son of man auô He was master of His circumstances in two respects'; 63 'we are His rays auô, being held fast : . ., we

are drawn up to heaven'; 73 'it is the domain of faith auô it
is not that of argumentation'; 148 'the rich have become poor
auô the kings have been overthrown'; 181 'practice auô be
released from this element'. Connecting three clauses: 57f.
'suffered with Him auô have arisen with Him auô have ascended
into heaven . . .'; 80-82 'through faith, knowledge; auô we
believed . . . auô He is the one of whom we say . . .' etc.;
155f. 'it is what is constant auô it is the revealing of what
truly exists auô it is . . .'; 158-160 'incorruption is streaming down . . . auô light is streaming down upon darkness . . .
auô the Fulness is filling up its lack'. Connecting pairs of
coordinated clauses. 51-53 'laying aside the perishable world
He exchanged it for an unperishing eternal realm auô He raised
Himself up . . . auô He gave us . . .'.

ii. auô introducing a loosely connected apodosis (parataxis):
'and then'. 166 'come out of the μερισμοί . . . auô ('and
then') you already have resurrection'. Cf. Bl.-D.-F. 471.3
for parallels. So perhaps 181, treated above [1.b.i].

iii. auô (καί) marking an additional comment, but without formal parallelism of clauses. 173 'the body is dead: why do you
not understand that the real you has arisen from it? auô
[almost: 'and indeed'] you are rushing towards this outcome,
since you possess resurrection'.

    c. οὐδέ, μηδέ [both Coptic oute]. i. Merely additive
'and . . . not'. 93 'truth cannot be brought to naught oude
it will not', Gk. οὐδέ.

ii. Coordinating negative clauses. 164 'do not concentrate
on particulars oute live according to flesh', Gk. μήτε.
Classically the forms are οὐδέ/μήτε, but confusion of οὔτε/
οὐδέ had already begun with Gk. authors and scribes of the
Imperial period; Coptic translators (who used both oude and
oute) understandably added even further to the confusion, cf.
Lefort, Concordance s.vv.

2. <u>Close coordination of cola</u> (<u>not</u> *καί).

    a. μέν . . . δέ . . . [Coptic <u>mmen</u> . . . <u>nde</u> or <u>de</u>],
English merely '. . . <u>and</u> . . .' or '. . . <u>while</u> . . .'.

i. <u>In contrast</u>. <u>44</u> 'the undoing <u>mmen</u> of evil, the manifestation <u>de</u> of the superior part'; <u>18</u>f. 'many <u>mmen</u> give it no
credence, few <u>nde</u> are they who find it' (adversative coordination imposed upon the condensation of a Biblical passage, Matt.
7.13-14).

ii. <u>Merely additive</u> (<u>holding together long clauses</u>). <u>32</u>f.
'that He might conquer <u>mmen</u> death . . . through <u>de</u> the son of
man might come to pass' etc.

    b. *οὐ (*μή) . . . ἀλλά . . . [Coptic: negative . . .
<u>alla</u> . . .] connecting clauses, English '<u>not</u> . . . <u>but rather</u>
. . .'. <u>41-43</u> 'so as not to leave anything hidden <u>alla</u> so He
might reveal everything' etc.; <u>89-90</u> 'might not stumble in the
folly of the ignorant, <u>alla</u> might enter into the wisdom of
those who have known the truth'; <u>139-140</u> 'resurrection is not
an apparition, <u>alla</u> it is something real'; <u>163-165</u> 'do not
think μερικῶς . . . <u>alla</u> come out of μερισμοί'; <u>182-183</u> 'that
he might not err <u>alla</u> recover his former state of being'.

    c. *οὐ . . . *μᾶλλον δέ . . . [Coptic: negative . . .
<u>nhouo</u> <u>nde</u> . . .] with clauses, '<u>not</u> . . . <u>rather</u> . . .'. <u>nhouo</u>
<u>nde</u> is stronger than <u>alla</u>. <u>139-141</u> [cf. sub 2.b] '<u>resurrection</u>
is not an apparition, but something real. <u>nhouo</u> <u>nde</u> ('instead',
*μᾶλλον δέ) one ought to maintain that the <u>world</u> is an appari-
tion'. Here two members 'resurrection' and 'world' are
contrasted by <u>nhouo</u> <u>nde</u>; within the first of these there is a
further contrast, 'apparition/something real' articulated by
<u>alla</u>.

3. <u>Sectional articulation without explicit contrast</u>.

    a. <u>auô</u> (καί) '<u>and</u>', <u>to indicate a new impetus in the</u>
<u>thought</u>. <u>6</u> 'there are certain persons who wish . . . <u>auô</u> if
they succeed . . .'; <u>77</u> 'the argumentation of scholarship

cannot save; yet a believing scholar will be saved. auô let him
not trust in one who has caused his own conversion' [we might
have expected an adversative particle instead of auô, but in
reality the author is beginning upon a new topic, the relationship of belief and salvation: auô marks this new beginning];
114 'surely you are not interested in the body, are you? auô
are you--the real you--mere corruption? Absence will be a
profit'. Moving from the general principle to a specific
example or problem: 75 ('that the dead arise is the assertion
of faith, not argumentation') auô is there any scholar here
[worldly practitioner of persuasion] who believes? Why then,
he will arise' [despite his profession].

b. Connective de. Consciously adding new points, 'and
what is more', 'moreover': 29 'Lord's career included incarnation, self-revelation as son of god and teaching ministry.
Moreover (nde), Rheginos, the son of god was a son of man' etc.
[expanding from a specific point]; 69 '(all the preceding
explains spiritual resurrection) Now (nde) if there is anyone
who is not a believer' etc. [an entirely new topic: the author
starts in again upon the uselessness of philosophy, cf. 1 sq.];
191 [a concluding exhortation] 'so, then [tinou nde, *νυνὶ δέ],
do not be hesitant to share with anyone'. Introducing a new
set of terms: 59 'He showed us immortality . . . then we arose
with Him . . . Now (nde), since we are manifestly present in
this world . . .' [stronger articulation than tote ce at 54,
where the same kind of terms continue].

c. Supplementive gar. i. Elliptical, stating the basis
of a possible or hypothetical objection, 'now'. 101 'do not
doubt resurrection. Now (gar 'you might wrongly suppose')
granted you did not preexist in flesh, then why . . .' etc.
[answered at 109 by alla 'Nay, rather, . . .']; 134 (after
various hypothetical objections have been sustained) 'Now
(ngar, 'for it may be the case that . . .') you might recall
having read . . .'.

ii. Anticipating an hypothetical objection (unstated). 116
'absence (i.e., death) is a profit. For (ngar, scil. 'even
though it might seem to be total annihilation') you will not
pay back the superior element (viz. the nous)'.

4. Expletive particles.
     a. Expletive de, in parenthetical explanation of a single
term. 28 'the law of the natural order, I mean (second tense,
eeijou nde), of death' [Greek λέγω δέ, id est; emphasis
entirely upon the gloss].

     b. Expletive gar, explaining a whole phrase or idea, just
as λέγω δέ explains a single term. i. 48 'Savior swallowed
death. You must not be unperceptive; for (ngar, scil. 'I mean
that') He laid aside the world'.

ii. Restatement in slightly different terms (pseudo-explana-
tion). 72 'now if there is anyone who is not a believer he
cannot be convinced. For (gar) it is the domain of faith and
not that of argumentation' [no real reason or explanation is
given]; 157 'resurrection is an exchange and a migration; for
(ngar) incorruption streams down upon corruption' etc. [but γάρ
is frequent and almost formulaic in Greek hymnic strophes].

     c. γάρ in logical exposition, moving from conclusion to
explanation. 167 'leave the state of dispersion and then you
already have resurrection. For (ngar: 'for my reasoning is
as follows') if the dying part knows' etc. 79 perhaps belongs
here; the preceding passage of the text is corrupt, obscuring
the train of thought.

5. Summarizing particles.
     a. ce [most often οὖν in Sa. NT], marking what follows
or can be concluded. i. Summarizing, 'then'. 120 'nothing
ce ransoms us while we are here, yet we are saved'; 130
[question, raising an earlier aporia for final reconsideration]
'how ce can it be that the dead, visible members will not' etc.;

the answer at 132 (which is introduced by a rhetorical question) also uses ce, claiming thereby to derive from what was said earlier: 'what ce ('then', 'pray') is resurrection? It is . . .'; 151 [here the author attempts to shut off the discussion] 'let me ce not deprecate the circumstances of this world too much'; 179 [question] 'why ce am I so lenient except because of your inadequate training?' [scolding: 'why, after all this, . . .'].

ii. At the articulation point within a sequence of items, reinforcing tote (τότε) [which is here used unclassically to mark a subsequent event rather than one occurring at a definite time, a usage common in the koine: probably τότε οὖν, as Sa. John 11.14, 19.1 (Beatty), 19.16, 20.8 (Be.)]. 54 'He swallowed death . . . raised Himself . . . gave us the way . . . tote ce . . . we suffered with Him' etc. Articulated again at 59 by nde (when a new set of terms is introduced).

iii. Resuming after digression. 91 'the minds of those who have known Him will not perish . . . Indeed (ce) that truth, to which they are wakeful, cannot be brought to naught'.

      b. hôste (ὥστε), 'so', stating a pointed conclusion; gives a command as though it followed logically from what had been said. 100 'hôste do not be doubtful . . .'; 163 'hôste do not think μερικῶς'.

6. Adversative (contrasting) sectional articulation: nde and alla.
      a. Adversative nde, 'but'. i. Marking a new and contrasting impetus of thought. 8 'there are some who wish to become learned . . . But (nde) I do not think their results lie within the truth' [assertion of an opposite point of view]; 97 'that which broke loose and became the universe is trifling, but (nde) what is held fast . . . did not come into being, it simply was [nde introduces a new topic with a contrasting attribute: permanent existence as opposed to breaking loose

and becoming]; <u>187</u> 'I have taught you everything necessary to
strengthen you. But (<u>nde</u>) if anything is too deep I shall
explain it [whatever is 'necessary' must be simple: <u>but</u> if it
is somehow difficult . . .]'.

ii. Because it is sometimes used to express contrast, <u>nde</u> can
introduce an authorial interjection designed solely to concentrate and direct the reader's attention. This is pseudo-
contrast; its purpose is really to keep the chain of thought
in vivid operation. So <u>144</u> 'and (<u>nde</u>) what am I telling you?'
[the author then elaborates].

   b. <u>alla</u> when a preceding negative correlate has not been
explicitly stated. This usage is a characteristic of our
author's style. i. <u>alla</u> brushing aside previously stated
objections or difficulties, '<u>despite all that</u>', '<u>nonetheless</u>',
'<u>and yet</u>'. <u>15</u> 'scholarly discussion is often ultimately fruitless. <u>alla</u> since you ask for basic doctrines, I am writing to
you'; <u>40f.</u> 'I am speaking in difficult terms; <u>alla</u> nothing
within the λόγος τῆς ἀληθείας is truly difficult; <u>alla</u> ('at
any rate') since the Savior came forward for the sake of
explanation . . .' (. . . scil. 'I shall now attempt to make
you understand')--[here we have minor and major <u>alla</u>. The
first <u>alla</u> attempts to brush aside the possibility of difficulty; the second <u>alla</u> brushes aside the whole question and
moves valiantly ahead ('but anyway . . .')]; <u>76</u> 'resurrection
is the domain of belief, not argumentation: and suppose there
is a scholar here who believes? <u>alla</u> ('why then', 'despite that
fact') he will arise', i.e., 'despite having professed an
occupation devoted to persuasion, his faith will suffice';
<u>119</u> 'the inferior element (i.e., body) takes a loss (scil. 'and
this might lead to its discouragement or discomfort'), <u>alla</u> it
owes thanks'; <u>121</u> [paradox] 'nothing, then, ransoms us while
we are here, <u>alla</u> we are saved'; <u>152</u> 'the world is illusory and
changing, <u>alla</u> ('what I shall now speak of is not thus, but
rather') resurrection has no such aspect'; <u>175</u> 'you (the mind)
possess resurrection, <u>alla</u> you persist as though you were

dying'. <u>Strong alla</u>: <u>109</u> 'for you might argue that you will
take your flesh with you to eternity, etc.' (arguing for
necessary immortality of flesh), answered by <u>alla</u>, 'Nay,
rather . . .'.

ii. <u>alla</u> introducing opponents who would brush aside the
author's claim to have settled matters. <u>126</u> 'let us think and
apprehend thus. <u>alla</u> certain persons desire to know whether
. . .'.

7. <u>kaitoige</u> (καίτοι γε). In contrast to the use of <u>alla</u> out-
lined above (6.b.i) in which the particle clears away objections or difficulties so that an assertion may be made,
<u>kaitoige</u> <u>introduces</u> such objections, inconsistencies, or
qualifications after some assertion or fact has already been
stated. <u>177</u> 'you persist as though <u>you</u> were dying, <u>kaitoige</u>
('even though') it is the body that knows it has died'.

Grammatical Appendix 3:

Clauses of Purpose, Cause and Command

Clauses of purpose (jekase, atre=)

II future is used for the affirmative, III future for the negative.
32f. jekase efnajro mmen . . . hitootf de . . . ere tapokatastasis naŝôpe.
182f. jekase nfrplana alla efnaji mmaf ouaeetf.

The syntactical equivalent of jekase + II/III future is atre=; negative atre=tm-.
89f. eahoutaŝn . . . atrntm haeie . . . alla enaei . . .

Clauses of cause

(a) Before the main clauses.
15 epeidê ekŝine mman apeteŝŝe.
41 alla epeidê etbe (Polotsky, etre cod.) pbôl ntaf ei abal.

(b) After the main clause, coordinating: (i) epeidê [Bl.-D.-F. 456.3]:
34 (amplifying) epeidê nŝarp efŝoop abal hm psa ntpe.
   (ii) je for epexegetical ὅτι or διότι [= διὰ τοῦτο ὅτι], 'for', cf. K.-G. 569 Anm. 5, citing Homer; the usage reemerges in the koine, Bl.-D.-F. 456, Coptic je. Often introducing scriptural citations.
17-19 (containing scriptural reference) je ouanagkaion te etc.
131 ('how can so-and-so not be the case') je ('and I ask this because') . . .

181

(iii) <u>ngar</u>.   Cf. Grammatical Appendix 2,   s.v.

<u>a- introducing the verbal complement of a governing verb</u>

<u>2</u> eu(ou)ôśe a sbô.
<u>43</u> ntaf ei . . . a tm ke laue efhêp alla atref ouônh abal
mptêrf.
<u>47</u> nkêp en a r atsaune.
<u>89</u>f. eahoutaśn . . . atrntm haeie.
<u>112</u> ntakr spoudaze asbo.
<u>141</u> oupetesśe pe a joos.
<u>180</u> sśe a poueei poueei a trefr askei.

Jussive: (1) maref-

For the Greek equivalents, see Polotsky, 'Modes Grecs en
Copte?'.
<u>marn-</u> (1 plural, Greek aorist subjunctive): <u>124</u>, <u>125</u>.
<u>mare</u> (usually Greek jussive): <u>20</u> mare plogos śôpe nen etbêts.

Negative: mprtre= and mpôr a tre= are interchangeable.
<u>129</u> mpr tre laue r distaze.
<u>77</u> philosophos . . . mpôr a trefpisteue.

(2) jekase independent

Greek negative subjunctive, cf. Philemon 19.
<u>151</u> jekase ce nirkatalalei sa nhbêue apehouo.

Imperative

<u>165</u> amou abal hn nmerismos.

Negative: mpr and mpôr a are interchangeable.
<u>100</u> mpôr a rdistaze.
<u>137</u> mpôr a meue.
<u>163</u> mpôr a rnoei merikôs.
<u>164</u> mpr rpoliteuesthai.
<u>191</u> mpr rphthonei.

Grammatical Appendix 4:

pśêre n-

The alternation of attributive and genitive constructions
following the nn. śêre is noteworthy. This is probably not
controlled by the form of the Coptic article which appears
before śêre; rather, by the syntax of the phrase (i.e., that
of the Greek model): the second noun (noute, rôme) appears in
the Copt. attributive construction when the phrase is predicate
and in the Copt. genitive construction when not predicate.
This parallels a rule for use of ὁ θεός etc. in the Gk. NT,
whereby the article (which is regularly used before θεός to
designate the Christian God) 'is sometimes missing, especially
. . . with a genitive which depends on an anarthrous noun
(especially a predicate noun)', Bl.-D.-F. 254.

The evidence of the Sa. NT is not sufficient to clarify
the situation, since the NT use of these terms in their two
possible meanings (epithet, characterization) does not supply
material for a complete paradigm; also, the phrases tend to be
formulaic.

In our text, the choice of article before śêre is governed
only by meaning: ou- is used when introducing a new topic of
conversation, p- for cross-reference thereto, the zero article
in predicative expressions:

24 (new topic of conversation) 'revealed himself, euśêre nnoute
   pe'.

29 (cross-reference) pśêre nde mpnoute . . . (new topic)
   neuśêre nrôme pe.

32f. conquer mmen death abal hitm ptrfśôpe nśêre nnoute,
   hitootf de mpśêre mprôme there might come to pass the
   return . . .

79 [a]hnsoun pśêre ngar mprome.

Grammatical Appendix 5:

The Asyndetic First Perfect Construction
(afsôtm afŝtortr)

In Coptic, two (sometimes more) main clauses of the I
perfect that occur in asyndetic series (i.e., unconnected by
a clause conjunction) most often recount events that are
closely related within the sequence of the narrative. Absence
of conjunction (zero conjunction) is in Coptic a mark of their
close sequential connection; in contrast, connection with auô
(etymologically 'add!') indicates a new impetus in the narrative, and a less close sequential connection. The decision
when to use auô and when to use zero conjunction must have been
a very delicate matter: the Greek models for these constructions did not resemble their Coptic counterparts; the formal
resources of Greek and the stylistic interests of Greek authors
were very different from those of Coptic; thus the Greek model
did not always clearly show which events in a narrative were
thought of as being especially closely related. Such a discrimination was more rigorously applied in Coptic (despite
Greek's possession of a participial subordination) and is
perhaps more typically Coptic than Greek. Thus it fell to the
skill and artistic aims of each Coptic translator to use the
device as he saw best. The principle of choice was analogous
to that of auô versus mn when translating a series of substantives connected by καί.

There are basically two (or at least two) Greek models
which can be translated by the asyndetic I perfect construction:
      1) finite aorist plus καί plus finite aorist;
      2) aorist participle agreeing with finite aorist.

184

These same Greek models are sometimes rendered by a quite different Coptic translation: af- auô af-, indicating that the two events are distinct in the narrative; or nteref- af-, stressing the dependence (almost causally) of the second event upon the first. Note that if the Gk. participle is in the present tense, ef- will normally occur. Genitive absolute becomes nter(ou)-.

The details of this basic Coptic construction (the asyndetic first perfect) have never been worked out systematically. Indeed it hardly receives mention in the grammars (Stern 592; Till, Sah.[2] 371; Till, Achm. Gram. 196; clearest, Steindorff[2] 451 sq.). It may be of service then to illustrate the construction by an extensive piece of prose narrative (Sa. Matt. chap. 2). Within the scope of this discussion, the general stylistic practices cannot be described in detail.

2[1] . . . ᾽Ιησοῦ γεννηθέντος	nterou-		
[1-2]παρεγένοντο λέγοντες	au-	eu-	
[2]εἴδομεν γὰρ καὶ ἤλθομεν	an-	gar	an-
[3]ἀκούσας δὲ ἐταράχθη	af-	de	af-
[4]καὶ συναγαγὼν ἐπυνθάνετο	af- (= καὶ συναγ.)		af-
[5]εἶπαν	pejau		
. . .	. . .		
[7]τότε καλέσας ἠκρίβωσεν	tote af-	af-	
[8]καὶ πέμψας εἶπεν	af- (= καὶ πέμ.)	ef- (sic)	
[9]ἀκούσαντες ἐπορεύθησαν	nterou-	au-	
καὶ . . . προῆγεν	auô . . . af-		
[10]ἰδόντες δὲ ἐχάρησαν	nterou- de	au-	
[11]καὶ ἐλθόντες εἶδον	auô nterou-	au-	
καὶ πεσόντες προσεκύνησαν	au-	au-	
καὶ ἀνοίξαντες προσήνεγκαν	au-	au-	
[12]καὶ χρηματισθέντες ἀνεχώρησαν	au- de (sic)	au-	
[13]ἀναχωρησάντων δὲ αὐτῶν	nterou-		
φαίνεται (historical	af-		
present) λέγων	ef-		
[14]ἐγερθεὶς παρέλαβεν	af-	af-	
καὶ ἀνεχώρησεν	af-		
[15]καὶ ἦν	nef- de (sic)		

[16] τότε ἰδὼν ἐθυμώθη   <u>tote</u> <u>nteref-</u>   <u>af-</u>
καὶ ἀποστείλας ἀνεῖλεν   <u>af-</u>   <u>af-</u>

. . .   . . .

[19-20] τελευτήσαντος δὲ τοῦ   <u>nteref-</u> <u>de</u>
    'Ηρῴδου φαίνεται   <u>af-</u>
    (historical present)
    λέγων   <u>ef-</u>

[21] ἐγερθεὶς παρέλαβεν   <u>af-</u>   <u>af-</u>
    καὶ εἰσῆλθεν   <u>af-</u>

[22] ἀκούσας δὲ ἐφοβήθη   <u>af-</u> <u>de</u>   <u>af-</u>
    χρηματισθεὶς δὲ ἀνεχώρησεν   <u>au-</u>   <u>af-</u>

[23] καὶ ἐλθὼν κατῴκησεν   <u>af-</u> (= καὶ ἐλθ.)   <u>af-</u>

This is quite a good rendering of the Greek model. By participial subordination, the Gk. can formally bind a certain event
of the narrative to one which follows it: Coptic uses the zero
conjunction analogously, but applies stricter discrimination as
to the relative importance and the interconnectedness of the
events in question. It is noteworthy that καί + Gk. aorist
participle at the beginning of a clause (Matt.2.23) can be
rendered simply <u>af-</u> (and not <u>auô</u> <u>af-</u>) if the asyndetic first
perfect construction is employed.

Grammatical Appendix 6:

etbe eu . . . ?

This interrogative phrase has three distinct logical uses
in the Sa. NT. Each occurs in our text.

First, and statistically the most common, is a request for
purpose, i.e., for the conscious human motivation of some deed
past (Matt.19.7), or simultaneous (Acts 15.10), or contemplated
(Mark 5.35): 'why?'. [Cf. the Concordance; I cite complete
references for the other uses below.] This is illustrated at
179 and, in malam partem, at 171.

Second, and quite frequent, is the request for the
external cause of an event, thought of as lying outside the
volition of those involved or being in the nature of things:
again, 'why?'. [Matt.17.19 (Mark 9.28), Luke 12.56, 24.38
(paralleling ahrôtn 'what is the matter?'), John 8.43 (posed
as a problem outside immediate human volition), 8.46 (ditto),
Acts 26.8, Rom.9.32 (bare etbe ou: contrast 2 Cor.11.11, a
request for purpose), 1 Cor.6.7. A special case is Mark 10.23
(MS 120), admirative πῶς: 'from what cause could it be . . .'].
This second use is well illustrated at 104: '(It is claimed
that) you will not take your flesh with you: Why is that so?'.

Third, and only occurring twice in the Sa. NT, is the
request for the topic of a conversation: 'about what?' [Mark
9.16, 9.33]. This is the construction in 144.

Syntax: First tenses are used, except (a) in indirect
questions (Luke 8.47, Acts 19.32, in both of which the position
of etbe ou is post-verbal); and (b) to request the topic of a
conversation. Both NT instances of the latter employ a second
tense; so 144. But this part of the evidence is statistically

slight. Furthermore, Matt.5.35 (a request for motivation) is a second tense; contrast John 14.22. Apparently the second tense in the latter usage is facultative [Beatty MS A reads ek- at John 14.22 joined by m[1]; Thompson's Subachm. reads etbe eu ek- at John 18.23, elsewhere agreeing with Sa].

Word order: the interrogative phrase stands first if a first tense is used; and in the NT (though not in 144, perhaps because of nde) it is post-verbal whenever a second tense is used.

Grammatical Appendix 7:

The Periodic Structure of Lines 167-175

In view of the great difficulties that translators have
experienced in grouping these clauses correctly, I append the
following detailed analysis. For the sake of demonstration it
is easiest to proceed backwards from the end.

175 alla kceet. The conjunction alla followed by I present
can be expected to begin a main clause (although εἰ . . .
ἀλλά . . . is also possible).

174 eiŝpe, Sa. eŝje (*εἰ or *εἰ plus particle) marks the
protasis of some conditional sentence. If 175 begins a
new sentence, the protasis must follow its apodosis; for
this (with eŝje) see Matt.27.43, John 1.25.

171-173 The edd. bring both eaktôoun and auô seeine mmak under
the governance of kneu arak: this is impossible. For a
construction such as edd. propose (τί οὐχὶ ὁρᾷς σεαυτὸν
ἀνάσταντα καὶ ἀγόμενον εἰς τοῦτο) we should need two
circumstantials and *ektôoun rather than the circumstantial of I perfect. auô seeine must begin a main clause.

173-174 Therefore auô seeine is probably the apodosis to which
174 belongs as protasis, and eiŝpe almost means 'since',
as εἰ often does in Greek.

171 etbe eu . . . kneu (I present) must be a main clause,
172   to which a circumstantial (eaktôoun) is subordinated
as a predicative. auô of 173 excludes the possibility
that eaktôoun is subordinate to seeine.

170 seeine (I present), a main clause.

168-169, both marked for subordination to some other clause:

189

190

169 <u>kan</u> <u>efšan-</u> (concessive);

168 <u>efnamou</u>, = <u>present</u> participle of ἀποθνῄσκειν. <u>je</u>
    (<u>168</u>) must govern some other verb than <u>efnamou</u> or <u>kan</u>
    <u>efšan-</u> as it must introduce a main-clause verb of the
    <u>oratio</u>, this being its function as a particle.
Thus,

168-169 <u>kan</u> <u>efšan-</u> is subordinate to the pronoun 'it' in the
passive construction <u>seeine</u> <u>mmaf</u>, which is also modified
by the participial <u>efnamou</u>. <u>kan</u> <u>efšan-</u> etc. is as it were
parenthetical: 'dying (even though it may have passed
many years in this life), it is being brought to this'.

167 <u>eišpe</u> (*εἰ or *εἴ <u>plus</u> particle, 'if') <u>fsaune</u>: introduces
a protasis. Because of <u>ngar</u> it must also be at the
beginning of a clause-complex. <u>je</u> . . . <u>seeine</u> is subordinated to <u>saune</u> <u>araf</u> as <u>oratio</u>. The apodosis corresponding to <u>167</u>ff. is <u>171</u> <u>etbe</u> <u>eu</u> etc. 'If so-and-so . . .,
why not so-and-so?' [For this <u>etbe</u> <u>eu</u>, see Grammatical
Appendix VI.] <u>173-174</u> is completely separate from this
complex, note its <u>auô</u>: 'And indeed so-and-so, since so-
and-so'. For this <u>auô</u> see Grammatical Appendix 2, <u>sub</u>
1.b.iii.

A final remark: In Greek, the mixed construction εἰ . . .
ἀλλά . . . 'If <u>X</u>, yet <u>Y</u> (is also the case)' exists, and thus
<u>174</u> might be subordinate to <u>175</u> rather than <u>173</u>; in fact this
would not affect the remainder of the analysis. And the con-
text and flow of argument indicate that it is not.

For a Coptic reader, the organization of these sentences
would have been immediately clear on first reading.

Line 183: etŝrp nŝoop

The qualitative is disallowed in all constructions but
bipartite conjugation. It is also forbidden where the infinitive can stand independently (psôtm) or is governed by another
verb as infinitival complement, e.g., after na futuri, ouôŝ,
etc.

An apparent exception is formed by a small class of
auxiliaries or verbal pre-extensions, r houe, r pke, ke, n ŝrp
n, ŝrp, and ŝrp n. Somehow these extensions must stand outside
the conjugation, for a glance at the following examples will
show that a qualitative here only follows such an auxiliary
when the auxiliary itself is in bipartite conjugation. I use
examples from Crum, Quecke in Le Muséon 75 (1962) 291-300, and
a few others taken at random:

r houe: ShA 1.266 (Crum 737b) 'men etr houe shouort'.

r pke: ShC 73.6 (Crum 92a) 'hard to escape sin sr pke mokh
                de on nhouo to escape God's wrath'.
            ShC 73.80 esr pke ouoj an.
            Sh MIF 23 (Chassinat): 124,51 ser pke cont eroou
                têrou.

ke: Va 57.126 (Crum 92a) eretenke oi nŝrôis (καὶ μετὰ
(Bohairic) ἀγρυπνίας).

r ŝrp n: Gosp. Tr. CG I 39:31-32 'who will name him, peei ete
                nefr ŝrp nŝoop ha thê mmaf, cf. John 1.15.

191

śrp: Nicaeanum (Zoega 243) [Spiegelberg, Hdwb. 206] kata
           the esśrp sêh. Noted by Quecke op. cit.
           Basilius-Anaphora, ed. Doresse-Lanne, Témoin
           archaique etc. (1960) fo. III^V 13-15 (p. 20).
           neidôron etśrp kê ehrai. τὰ προκείμενα ταῦτα.
           Noted by Quecke.

śrp n: The present text, 183.

       Quecke's notion (followed by edd., p. ix) that such
examples illustrate 'occasional' use of the qualitative where
only an infinitive is allowed by the language, is unfounded,
for the examples belong to a small and isolatable construction.
The mistaken conclusions of Sethe, ÄZ 57 (1922) 138 to the
same effect, cited by Quecke, were laid to rest in 1925 by
Jernstedt, Comptes Rendus de l'Académie des Sciences de l'URSS
(série B) 1925, 74-77, apparently unbeknownst to Quecke. [The
reading emeaeit of Zeph.3.20 (Achm.) there discussed, has now
been improved by Till's new edition, with the correct reading
e nsaeit: this does not affect Jernstedt's argument.]

Grammatical Appendix 9:

Inflection of Conjugations and

Suffixed Pronouns

A. Bipartite Sentence.

I Present: <u>ti</u>, <u>k</u>, <u>f</u>, <u>s</u>, <u>tn</u>, <u>se</u>, <u>(o)un</u>/<u>mn</u> (before non-definite
  nouns). Negative: <u>nti</u> . . . <u>en</u>, <u>nk</u> . . . <u>en</u>, <u>nf</u> . . .
  <u>en</u>. Circumstantial: <u>ek</u>, <u>ef</u>, <u>es</u>, <u>en</u>, <u>eretn</u>, <u>eu</u>, <u>eun</u>
  (before non-definite noun). Negative: <u>emf</u> (sic) . . .
  <u>en</u>, <u>ense</u> . . . <u>en</u>. Relative: <u>etk</u>, <u>etn</u>, <u>etou</u>, bare <u>et</u>
  (as in Std. Sahid.). Preterit: <u>nef</u>. Negative: <u>nek</u> . . .
  <u>en</u>.

II Present: <u>eei</u>, <u>ek</u>, <u>ef</u>, <u>en</u>, <u>eu</u>.

I Future: <u>tina</u>, <u>fna</u>, <u>sena</u>, ∅ . . . <u>na</u> (subj. a noun).
  Negative: <u>nkna</u> . . . <u>en</u>, <u>nfna</u> . . . <u>en</u>, <u>nsena</u> . . . <u>en</u>.
  Circumstantial: <u>ekna</u>. Relative: <u>etna</u> (as in Std.
  Sahid.). Preterit: <u>neuna</u> . . . <u>pe</u>.

II Future: <u>efna</u>, <u>ena</u>, <u>ere</u> . . . <u>na</u> (subj. a definite noun).

B. Tripartite Sentence. (a) Sentence Conjugations.

I Perfect, base <u>a=</u>: <u>aei</u> (?), <u>ak</u>, <u>af</u>, <u>an</u>, <u>au</u>, <u>a</u> (before noun).
  Circumstantial: <u>eak</u>, <u>eaf</u>. Relative: <u>ntaei</u>, <u>ntak</u>, <u>entas</u>.
I Perfect, base <u>ah=</u>: <u>ahi</u> (?), <u>afh</u> (read <u>ahf</u>?), <u>ahn</u>.
  Circumstantial: <u>eahou</u>. Relative: <u>ntahi</u>, <u>ntahn</u>, <u>ntaha</u>
  (before noun). Substantivized Relative: -<u>entah</u>/ -<u>etah</u>
  (like bare <u>et</u>).

Negative I Perfect: <u>mpef</u>. Circumstantial: <u>empi</u>.

II Perfect, base <u>nta=</u>: <u>ntaf</u>.

194

II Perfect, base ntah=: ntahn, ntaha (before noun).

"Not Yet". Circumstantial: empate (before noun).

Aorist: šareb, šau. Relative: ešaf.

III Future Negative: ni, nf, nes.

Imperative: Special form amou.

Negative Imperative: mpr & mpôr a.

Causative: marn, mare (before noun).

Negative Causative: mpôr a tref, mpr tre (before noun).

(b) Clause Conjugations.

Conjunctive: nse.

Temporal: ntarek, ntaref, ntaren.

Conditional: ekšan, efšan, enšan.

(c) Causative Infinitive: tref/trf, tre (before noun, but
     error 41). Negative: trn-tm.

Suffixal Pronoun Inflection

(Attested Forms)

A. **Suffixed Pronouns** After Infinitive, Preposition, or
    Verstärker.

1 sing.	-ei (after ô, 186)
2 masc. sing.	-k (16 etc.)
2 fem. sing.	(not attested)
3 masc. sing.	-f (11 etc.)
3 fem. sing.	-s (14 etc.)
1 plur.	-n (14 etc.)
2 plur.	-tn (after arô= 189, mmô= 196 [stem-final a > ô])
	-têutn (after tajre- 186).
3 plur.	-u (after a 30 etc., e 3 etc.)
	-ou (after ô 37, after consonant 7 etc.)

195

B. Possessive Articles.

pa-	pn-, pen-	--	tn-
--	--	tek-	--
--		--	
pef-	peu-	--	--
--		--	

	na-	--
	nek-	--
	--	
	--	--
	--	

For Possessive Articles see also the index.

COMPLETE INDEX TO THE

COPTIC TEXT

Transcription of Demotic letters: ś f h j c ti.
Theta is transcribed th, ksi is ks, etc.

    * after an entry (e.g., 131*) means "key word(s) partly
restored or read from uncertain letter traces."

    Words found in the critical apparatus also have been
indexed here, and these entries are marked by ap. (e.g., 76ap.).
Forms given in round brackets--e.g., ('Ηλιας) or (aïaï)--do not
actually occur in the text; Crum's main entry is used when a
Coptic form must be so supplied.

    A certain number of cross-references from equivalent
Sahidic forms have been given for the convenience of users
unaccustomed to the Subachmimic dialect.

    Abbreviations: dir. obj. = direct object (accusative),
which in Coptic must either be suffixed to the infinitive or be
introduced by n-, mmo=.   vb tr = transitive verb, one which
demands a dir. obj.; all the instances listed under a "vb tr"
are constructed with a dir. obj. except those marked "no dir.
obj." or "med."   med. = middle voice, in which a vb tr without dir. obj. describes the entry of the subject into the state
otherwise described by the qualitative of that verb (e.g.,
af-ouanh-f [reflexive dir. obj.] "he revealed himself,"
f-ouaanh⁺ "he is manifest," but med. af-ouônh "he became manifest").   vb intr = a verb that can never take a dir.
obj.   vb intr motion: one whose infinitive is excluded
from the bipartite pattern.   p c = participium
conjunctum.   attrib = attributive construction, or attributive complement after śôpe or the like. w. = with.   Ver-
stärker, see Polotsky in Orientalia 30 (1961) 294-313. And
the other usual abbreviations.

A. PROPER NAMES

('Ηλίας), h̲ê̲l̲e̲i̲a̲s̲.   136.   Μωυσῆς.   136.

('Ιησοῦς), abbrev. I̅H̅C̅, [1] I̅C̅.   ‛Ρηγῖνος, voc. [1] ‛Ρήγινε.
   143, [1]184.   1, [1]29, [1]100, [1]163.

B. GREEK WORDS

αἴτιος   nn masc.   βίος   nn masc. 64, 169.
   n̲-̲a̲i̲t̲i̲o̲s̲ attrib 106.
αἰών   nn masc. 50, 105.   γάρ, [1]n̲g̲a̲r̲   connective
ἀκτίν   nn fem. 65.   particle.
   n̲-̲a̲k̲t̲i̲n̲ attrib 62.   see Grammatical Appendix
   classical form, ἀκτίς.   2 for analysis.
ἀλλά   connective particle.   [1]48, 72, [1]79, [1]101, [1]116,
   see Grammatical Appendix 2   [1]134, [1]157, [1]167.
   for analysis.
   15, 40, 41, 43, 76, 77a̲p̲.,   (γυμνάζω), r̲-̲g̲u̲m̲n̲a̲z̲e̲   vb.
   90, 109, 119, 121, 126,   m̲n̲t̲-̲a̲t̲-̲r̲-̲g̲u̲m̲n̲a̲z̲e̲ nn fem
   140, 152, 165, 175, 183.   179.
(ἀναγκαῖος), -ον   adj.
   as nn masc: 17.   δέ, [1]n̲d̲e̲   connective
ἀνάστασις   nn fem. 15, 67,   particle.
   100, 132, 137, 142, 152,   see Grammatical Appendix
   161, 166, 198.   2 for analysis.
ἀπαγγελία   nn fem. 188.   [1]8, [1]19, [1]28, [1]29, 33, 44,
ἄπιστος   adj.   [1]59, [1]69, [1]97, [1]141, [1]144,
   o̲e̲i̲ n̲-̲a̲p̲i̲s̲t̲o̲s̲ a̲r̲a̲=̲ 18.   [1]187, [1]191.
(ἁπλῶς), h̲a̲p̲l̲ô̲s̲   adverb. 43.   (διστάζω), r̲-̲d̲i̲s̲t̲a̲z̲e̲   vb.
ἀποκατάστασις   nn fem.   -- e̲t̲b̲e̲- 100, 129.
   -- a̲h̲o̲u̲n̲ a̲- 33.   (δύσκολος), -ον   adj.
ἀπόστολος   nn masc. 55.   n̲-̲d̲u̲s̲k̲o̲l̲o̲n̲ attrib 39, 40.
ἀπουσία   nn fem. 115.
(ἀσκέω), r̲-̲a̲s̲k̲e̲i̲   vb.   (εἰρήνη), †p̲H̲N̲H̲ (coalescing
   -- (no dir. obj.) 180.   w. definite article)
                                             nn fem. 195.
                        199

ἐπειδή   conj. 15, 34, 41.
εὐαγγέλιον   nn neut. 135.

ζήτημα   nn neut. 4.

ἤδη   adverb. 166.

καίτοιγε   connective
  particle.
  see Grammatical Appendix 2
  for analysis.
  177.
κἄν (καὶ ἐάν)   particle.
  kan efśan 169.
κατά   preposition. 164.
(καταλαλέω), r-katalalei   vb.
  -- sa- 151.
κόσμος   nn masc. 48, 60, 103,
  142, 150.
  m-kosmos (i.e., n-kosmos)
  attrib 96.

λόγος   nn masc. 9, 20, 40,
  188, 198.

μέλος   nn neut. 130, 131*.
(μέν), mmen   connective
  particle.
  see Grammatical Appendix 2
  for analysis.
  18, 32, 44.
μερικῶς   adverb. 163.
μερισμός   nn masc. 165.
μεταβολή   nn fem. 156.
μή   interrogative particle.
  107, 108.

(νοέω), r-noei   vb. 163.
νόμος   nn masc. 27.

νοῦς   nn masc. 87.

(ὁμοίως), homoiôs   adverb.
  homoiôs mn-tke- 68.
(ὅριον)   nn masc.
  see Exegetical Commentary
  on 112, end.
οὔτε   conj.
  see Grammatical Appendix 2
  for analysis.
  93, 164.

(πείθω), r-peithe   vb.
  as nn masc 71, 73.
(πιστεύω), pisteue,
  [1]r-pisteue   vb.
  -- (no dir. obj.) 70, [1]75,
  77, [1]85.
  -- a-, ara= 77ap., [1]84.
  -- je- 80.
πίστις   nn fem. 72, 79.
(πλανάω), r-plana   vb. 182.
πλήρωμα   nn neut. 33, 94,
  160.
πνεῦμα   nn neut. 44.
(πνευματικός), -ή   adj.
  n-pneumatikê attrib 67.
(πολιτεύομαι), r-politeuesthai
  vb.
  -- kata- 164.
προβολή   nn fem. 44.
πῶς   interrogative particle.
  -- w. II Present.

(σαρκικός), -ή   adj.
  as nn fem (scil. ἀνάστασις)
  68.
σάρξ   nn fem. 22, 101, 104,
  106, 164.

ji-sarks 102.

σκοπός   nn masc. 3.

σπέρμα   nn neut.

n-sperma attrib 34.

(σπουδάζω), r-spoudaze   vb.

-- a- + infinitive 112.

στοιχεῖον   nn neut. 181.

σύμβολον   nn neut. 161.

σύστασις   nn fem. 35.

σύστημα   nn neut. 94.

σῶμα   nn neut. 112, 127.

σωτήρ   nn masc. 11, 46, 143.

τόπος   nn masc. 25, 72.

τότε   conj. 54.

φαντασία   nn fem. 138, 139, 142, 146, 150.

(φθονέω), r-phthonei   vb.

-- a- 191.

mnt-at-r-phthonei nn fem 184.

φιλόσοφος   nn masc. 75, 77.

(φορέω), r-phorei   vb.

-- mma= 61.

φύσις   nn fem. 27.

χάρις   nn fem. 45, 195.

χόριον   nn neut. 112.

(χράομαι), r-khrô   vb.

-- n- 21.

χρηστός   adj. 11, 143, 184*.

(ψυχικός), -ή   adj.

-- as nn fem (scil. ἀνάστασις) 68.

ὦ   interjection. 163.

(ὡς), hôs   particle of comparison.

-- + nominal sentence (not converted) 84.

-- + circumstantial 176.

(ὥστε), hôste   conj.

-- + imperative 100, 163.

(ὠφελέω), r-ôphelei   vb.

-- (w. out complement) 192.

C. NON-GREEK WORDS

A reference to Crum's Dictionary is given in round brackets, e.g., (50a).

a-, a=   conjugation base of I Perfect.

aei (or ?ahi) 185ap.;
ak 102, 134; eak 172; af 25 (ahf ?), 46, 48, 50, 51, 53, 81, 83, 96, 178; eaf 52; an 14, 56, 57, 58; au 9, 147, 148; a (before nn) 36, 136.

see also: mp(e)=.

a-, [1]e- (error), [2]ara=, [3]arô= (2 pl)   preposition (e-, 50a). 2, 6, 7, 10, 15, [2]18, 27, [2]30, 32, 41, [2]52, 58, 65, 77ap., [2]84, [2]91, [2]112, [2]119, 137, 156, [2]167, [2]171, 180, [2]185, 186, [3]189, 191,

bôk   vb intr motion (29a).

-- (w. out complement) 117.

-- a-tpe nmme= 58.

-- ahrêï ahoun a- 105.

bal, see abal.

bôl, [1]bal=   vb tr (32a).
[1]189.

as nn masc: 5, 39, 41.

-- med. abal 95.

-- abal as nn masc: 44;
n-bôl abal attrib 83.

-- abal m- [1]181 (= abal
abal m-).

for derived nn bal, see abal.

.brre   nn masc fem (43a).

mnt-brre nn fem 156.

(e-, preposition), see a-.

e-, e=   converter of
Circumstantial.

expressing [1]attendant
circumstance; as [2]relative;
as [3]complement; [4]oun- (nn)
ef-:

(a) I Present ek [1]109, [1]135;
ef [1]22, [1]27, [3]42, [1]159,
[3]188, [2]191ap.; es [1]68; en
[3]60; eretn [1]190; eu [4]2, [1]4,
[2]5, [1]63, [1]197; eun- (before
nondefinite nn) [1]192; negative emf (sic) . . . en [4]70;
ense . . . en [1]66.

(b) I Future ekna [1]168,
[1]176 (hôs ekna).

(c) I Perfect eak [3]172; eaf
[1]52; eahou [1]89; negative
empi [1]186.

(d) "not yet" empate (before
nn) [1]35.

(e) nominal sentence e
. . . pe [3]24.

(f) suffix vbs enašô= [3]37;
eunte= [1]31.

e-   converter of relative
Aorist, forming eša=. 49.

(ebol), see abal.

emahte   vb tr (amahte, 9a).
4, 63, 66, 97.

-- (no dir. obj.) 30.

en, see n- . . . en.

en w. out n-, see n- . . .
en.

enta=, see nta-.

-entah-, see ntah-.

(ere-, converter of
Circumstantial), see e-.

(ere-), e=   conjugation base
of II Present.

eei 28, 39, 144; ek 15; ef
34; en 61, 62; eu 10, 65,
146.

ere- . . . na, e=na   conjugation base of II Future:
after [1]jekase; [2]continuing
clause of purpose;
[3]insistent future;
[4]emphasizing adverb:
efna [1]32, [4]128, [3]168, [1]183;
ena [2]90; ere . . . na (w.
nn subject) [1]33.

(eršan-), e=šan-   conjugation base of Conditional.
ekšan 105, 117; efšan 127,
169; eušan 6.

es, see eš.

et-   bare converter of
relative.

follows nn antecedent; also

preceded by [1]definite
article or by [2]peei and in
[3]cleft sentence:
(a) I Present [3]19, [1]44bis,
[1]52, [1]62, [1]74, 75, [1]75, 77,
[1]81, [1]85, [1]86, [1]89, [1]106,
[3]106, [1]107, [1]116, [1]118, [1]127,
130bis, 131bis, [1]145, [1]154,
[1]155, [3]162, [2]183, 191
(error for ef?), [1]196.
(b) I Future [1]167.
(c) nanou= [1]162, [1]167.

et= converter of relative I
Present: follows nn
antecedent; also preceded
by [1]definite article or by
[2]peei; in [3]cleft sentence.
etk [2]26,[3]110; etn [3]82; etou
[1]84, 91, [1]97, [1]126.
etes in petesśe [1]141,
netesśe [1]186; peteśśe [1]15.

ete- converter of relative.
-- w. nominal sentences 64,
113, 121.
-- preceded by definite
article 108.

etbe-, [1]etbēt= preposition
(61a). 15, 20, [1]20, 41ap.,
43, 79, 88, 100, 104, [1]107,
126, [1]126, 129, 144, 164,
171, 179, 198.

etah- bare converter of
relative I Perfect.
always preceded by definite
article: 87, 90, 133.
see also: nta- (converter),
ntah-, ntaha- (converter).

eu interrogative pronoun
(ou, 467b, 31). 110, 132.

etbe eu 104, 144, 171, 179
(see Grammatical Appendix
6).

eś, [1]es interrogative
pronoun (aś, 22a, 1).
n-eś n-he 21, [1]130.
(eśje), see eiśpe.

êp, see ôp.

ei, imperat (masc sg) [1]amou
vb intr motion (70a, 7b).
-- abal a- 41.
-- abal hn- (= abal abal
hn-) [1]165.
-- ahoun a- 90, 103.
(eime), see mme.
eine vb tr "bring" (78b).
-- ahoun a- 170, 173.
(eire), r- [+]oei vb tr (83a).
r- auxiliary before
following Greek vbs: ἀσκέω
(180), γυμνάζω (179),
διστάζω (100, 129),
καταλαλέω (151), νοέω
(163), πείθω (71, 73),
πιστεύω (75, 84, 85; also
w. out r-), πλανάω (182),
πολιτεύομαι (164), σπουδάζω
(112), φθονέω (184, 191),
φορέω (61), χράομαι (21),
ὠφελέω (192).
r- w. following nns:
atsaune 47, hêke 147.
r-pmeue je- 134.
[+]oei n-, m- [+]18, [+]89, [+]197.
r- "pass (time)" 169.

itn nn masc (87b).
apitn 157, 158.

(mpe-), mp(e)=   conjugation
  base of I Perfect negative.
  empi 186; mpef 98*.
  see also: a-, a=.
mpôr, [1]mpr-   mark of
  negative Imperative.
  (a) negative Imperative:
  mpôr a- 100, 137, 163;
  mpr- [1]164, [1]191.
  (b) negative Causative (cf.
  mare-): mpôr a-tref 77;
  mpr-tre [1]129.
mpate-   conjugation base
  "not yet."
  empate (before nn) 35.
(mour), for derived nn see
  mrre.
mare-, mar=   conjugation
  base of Causative.
  marn 124, 125; mare (before
  nn) 20.
  see also: mpôr.
mrre   nn fem (182a). 165.
meete   vb tr (mate, 189a).
  -- (no dir. obj) a- 6.
mête   nn fem (190b).
  a-t-mête 41.
mtan   vb tr (193b).
  -- (refl.) ahrêï ajô= 14.
  as nn masc: 10.
meu, see mmeu.
meue   vb intr (199a).
  -- (w. out complement) 124.
  -- a- 7; a- . . . je- 137.
  -- je- 8.
  -- as nn masc: 86; r-pmeue
  je- 134.
(moośe), see mahe.
mahe, perhaps hmahe   vb intr

(moośe, 203b).
afhmahe 25 (error for
either ahf-mahe or af-mahe
[under influence of hmast,
26]).
correct form is mahe.

n- is classified in the
following entries by
meaning rather than
etymology.
n-, [1]m- (by assimilation)
preposition of genitive.
9, [1]9, 27, [1]29, [1]33, 34bis,
40, 44, [1]44bis, 53, [1]62,
65, 72, [1]79, [1]83, 86, 87,
89, 90, [1]94, [1]106, [1]112,
133, 152, [1]155, 156, 161,
[1]184, [1]188.
n- + bare nn, see n-
preposition of attrib.
n-, [1]m- (by assimilation)
preposition of attrib.
(a) forming attrib construction proper: 24, 29, 32,
39, 50, 67 (n-pneumatikê).
(b) partitive: ou-aps n-
180; eś (es) n- 21, 130;
laue n- 40; hah n- 169.
(c) introducing predicative
after oei, śôpe, śoop: 18,
32, 34, 62, 83 (śôpe n-bôl),
89, [1]96 (śôpe m-kosmos,
?error), 106, 114, [1]197;
after dir. obj. 115.
(d) resuming obj. of
preposition with equivalent
nn [1]33 (hitootf m-pśêre),
[1]52, [1]143.

[7]21, 27, [3]27, 28, 29bis,
[1]30, [3]31bis, 32bis, 33ter,
[3]33, 34, [3]34bis, 39, 40, [3]40,
41, [3]41, 43bis, 44ter, [1]44,
[3]44bis, [3]45, [4]45, 46bis, 48,
52, [4]53, [5]54, 55, [3]58, 65,
[3]65, [5]65, [3]67, [3]68bis, 71,
72, [3]72, 73, [7]75, 77, 79bis,
83, 86, 87, 88bis, [3]89,
[3]90bis, [3]91, 94*, 94, 97,
[3]100, [3]104, 105, 106, [3]106,
112bis, [3]113, [3]115, 118,
123, [5]123, 126, [3]128, [7]130,
[7]131*, [3]132, 133, 134, 135,
[3]137, 142, [3]142, 143, [1]143,
[4]145, [7]147, [7]148 (? [8]nn-),
149, 150, [1]151, [7]151, [3]152,
[3]153, 155, 156, [7]156, 157bis,
[3]157, 158ter, 160, [1]160,
[3]161, [7]161bis, 162, [3]164,
[7]165bis, [3]166, 174, 180bis,
[1]184, [3]184, 186, 188, [3]188,
[4]195, [6]195, 198, [3]198.
(b) forming substantivized
relative: masc sing 15, 44bis,
52, 62, 74, 75, 84, [1]95, 97,
106, 107, 108, 116, 118, 127,
141*, 154, 155, 162, 167;
plur 81, 85, 86, 87, 89, 90,
126, 133, 145, 186, 196.
note that this n- does not
assimilate to m- (cf. 75,
130, 131, 165).
pa- possessive article,
inflected "my" etc. (258b).
pa 1, 72, 100, 184, na 185;
tek 179, nek 185; pef 127;
pn 11bis, 63, tn 53, 79,
pen 64, 143; peu 5, 10.

pa-, [1]pô= absolute
possessive pronoun,
inflected "that which
belongs to . . ." (259a,
260b).
pa- 73, ta- 45; pôk [1]107,
[1]108.
(pai), see peei.
pe nn fem (259a).
sa ntpe 34.
a-tpe 58, 65.
pe mark of the Preterit
(260a, 24). 99, 131.
pe, [1]te, [2]ne copular
pronoun (260b, 21).
(a) in binary nominal
sentence [1]17, 24, 29, 72,
73, 77ap., 107, 108, 111,
121, 133, [1]138, [1]139, [1]140,
141, 153 (error), [1]153,
154*, 155, 156.
(b) in ternary nominal
sentence [1]44, [1]45, 64, [1]67,
84, [2]85, 94, 95, 97, 113,
[1]132, 142, 150, [2]161.
(c) in cleft sentence [2]19,
82, 106, 110, 162.
peei masc sing demonstra-
tive pron, [1]teei fem sing,
[2]neei plur (259a). [2]6, 20,
[1]36, [1]44, 64, [1]67, 82, 88,
111, 113, 129, [2]161, 170,
173, 193, [2]195.
-- introducing relative
converter 11, 26, [1]143,
183, [2]184, 194.
see also: peei-, pi-.
peei- demonstrative article
masc sing, [1]teei- fem sing

(259a, 19). 64, [1]164, 169.
see Grammatical Appendix 1.

pê   demonstrative pron masc
sing (260b). 177.
see also: pe te ne.

pi-, [1]ti-, [2]ni-   article
(259a, 20). 3, 25, [1]35, 60,
[2]75, [2]77, 103, [2]109, [2]120,
[1]124, [1]125, 152, [1]152, 181.
nthe n-ni- [2]65.
see Grammatical Appendix 1.

pô=, see pa- (absolute
possessive pronoun).

(ra), ra-   nn masc (287a).
perhaps in expression
jin-rarêjf (ra-arêjf ?)
ha-thaê 123.

rê   nn masc (287b). 65.

raei, see rro.

rôme, [1]rm- in compounds   nn
masc (294b). 33, 79.
n-rôme attrib 29 (but see
Grammatical Appendix IV).
mnt-rôme nn fem 31.
mnt-rm-hêt nn fem [1]90.
see also: ref-.
for derived nn see: rmmao.

(rmmao), plur rmaaei   (296a,
19). 147.

rampe   nn fem (296b). 169.

(rro), plur (r)raei (? or
nraei)   nn masc (299a).
148.
see Grammatical Notes on
148.

raeis   vb intr (300b).
-- ara= 91.

ret=, see aret=.

ref-   prefix forming nn
masc fem (295b).
refkto mmaf ouaeetf nn 77.

sa   nn masc (313a).
sa ntpe 34.
forming preposition sa-,
[1]nsa-, [2]nsô=: [2]127, 151,
[1]179, [2]186.

sbo   vb intr (435a).
-- a-, ara= 2, 112.

sôk   vb tr (325a).
-- a- 65.

smat   nn masc (340b).
pi-smat ntimine 152.

san, plur [1]snêu   (342b).
[1]185*.
m-maei-san (cf. maeie)
attrib 197.

soun-, see saune.

sneu   nn masc (snau, 346b).
30.

snêu, see san.

sap   nn masc (349b).
n-ke-sap 183.

sôt, see sôte.

sôte, [1]sôt   vb tr (362a).
[1]120.
as nn masc: 88.

(sôtp), [+]satp   vb tr (365a).
petsatp 44, 106, 116.
-- ahoun a- 88.

souôn-, souôôn=, see saune.

saune, [1]soun-, [2]souôn-,
[3]souôôn=   vb tr (369b).
[2]13, [1]79, [3]87, [2]90.
-- (no dir. obj.) je- 38,
177.
-- (no dir. obj.) ara=

in expressions with sśe,
¹śśe "it is necessary":
peteśśe etbe ¹15.
neteśśe a- + infinitive 186.
-- a- pers. atref- +
infinitive 180.
oupetesśe pe a- +
infinitive 141.
(śibe), śbeie, ¹śft= vb
tr (551a).
-- med. 149.
-- (reflexive) ahoun a- ¹50.
as nn masc: 156.
(śôk), ⁺śêk vb tr (555a).
⁺188.
śine vb tr (569a).
-- (no dir. obj.) 190;
etbēt= 126.
-- (no dir. obj.) a-, ara=
10, 196.
-- n- (pers.) a- (rei) 15.
as nn masc: 126.
(śôp), śp- (574b).
śp-hise 56.
śôpe, ⁺śoop vb intr (577b).
-- (w. out complementary
phrase) "exist" ⁺99, ⁺155,
⁺183 (śrp-n-śoop).
-- (of events) "happen, come
to pass" 33, 93.
-- (of things) "come into
being, be" 35, 98, 107, 143.
-- ne= (dative) 20.
-- n- attrib "be, become"
32, 83, 96.
-- + circumstantial, as
periphrastic conjugation
śôpe enaśô= 36.
-- n- attrib "exist as"

⁺34, ⁺62, ⁺106, ⁺114;
similarly + circumstantial
⁺59.
-- w. various other prepo-
sitions, "be, exist, dwell"
⁺22, ⁺40, ⁺101, ⁺108, ⁺131.
as nn masc: 43.
(śare-), śa=, ¹śare= conju-
gation base of Aorist.
śareb ¹149; eśaf 49; śau 7.
śêre nn masc (584a). 1, 24,
29bis, 33, 72, 79, 100, 185.
n-śêre attrib 32 (but
see Grammatical Appendix
4).
śrp- verbal infix (588a).
-śrp-n- + qualitative 183.
see Grammatical Appendix
8.
śarp nn masc (587a).
n-śarp adverb 34, jin
n-śarp 89.
see also: śrp-.
(śôrp), see śarp, śrp-.
(śorśr), śrśôr= vb tr
(589a). 148.
(śôôt), ⁺śaat vb tr (590b).
-- med. m-, mma= "fall
short of" 5, 110.
see also: śta.
śta vb intr (593b, ult.).
as nn masc: 160.
śśe, see śe.
śeje vb intr (612b).
-- a- (res) 27.
ścam, see cam.

ha-, see śa-.
(hae), fem haê   nn

66.
abal hitn-, hitoot= [1]32, [2]52, [2]63, [2]65, [2]143.

hôtp vb tr (724b).
  as nn masc: 63.

hau[+] qualitative of vb (hoou, 731a, penult.). pethau 44, 118.

hêu nn masc (729a). 115.

houo nn masc (735a).
  a-pehouo 151.
  nhouo 10, 141; nhouo a- 142.

hah nn masc fem (741b). 2, 18, 193.
  hah n- 169.

je- conj (746b, 3). introducing discourse after following vbs: mme 127ap.; meue 9, 138; pisteue 77ap., 81; r-pmeue 136; saune 39, 178; joos 142. amplifying after a dir. obj.: 28, 56, 83, 168. causal conjunctive ("for . . .") 17, 131, 153.

ji, [1]ji-, [2]jit= vb tr (747b). [2]11, [2]12, [1]102, 104, 123, 125, [2]184.
  ji mmaf ouaeetf (reflexive) nkesap peei etŝrp-n-ŝoop 183.

jou, [1]joo= vb tr (745a).
  joos je- "say" [1]141.
  jou mma= (joo=) je- "say about (something)/utter (words), namely" 28, [1]55, 82.

jô= (nn), see ajn-.

jôk vb tr (761a).
  -- abal 160.

jekase conj (jekaas, 764a). w. II Future affirmative 32. w. III Future negative 151, 182.

jin- preposition (772b). jin-rarêjf ha thaê 123. as conj: jin-n-ŝarp 89.

jro vb intr (783a).
  -- a- 32.
  for derived nn see: jôre.

jôre nn masc fem (784b). 94.

jaeis nn masc (787b). 11, 21, 143, 184.
  mnt-jaeis nn fem 36.

ce connective particle (802a). see Grammatical Appendix 2 for analysis. 54, 91, 120, 130, 132, 151, 179.

(cô), [+]ceet vb intr (803a). [+]175.

côlp vb tr (812a).
  -- abal, as nn masc: 133.

cam nn fem (com, 815b, 9 up). oun-cam mma= n- + infinitive 192. ŝ-cam as nn: mn-ŝcam n- + infinitive 92.

cine vb tr (820a). 19.

côŝt vb intr (837a).
  -- ahoun a- 193.

côjb vb tr (841b).
  as nn masc: 118.

SYNOPSIS OF REFERENCE SYSTEMS

edition	manuscript		edition	manuscript
1	= 43: 25-26		27	= 44: 19-20
2	26		28	20-21
3	27		29	21-23
4	28			
5	29		30	23-25
6	29-30		31	25-27
7	30-32		32	27-29
8	32		33	30-33
9	33-34		34	33-35
			35	35-36
10	34-35		36	37-38
11	35-37		37	38-39
12	= 44: 1		38	39
13	1-2		39	39-45:2
14	2-3			
15	3-6		40	= 45: 2-4
16	6-7		41	4-6
17	7-8		42	6
18	8-9		43	7-9
19	9-10		44	9-13
			45	13-14
20	11-12		46	14-15
21	12-14		47	15
22	14-15		48	16-17
23	15-16		49	17
24	16-17			
25	17-18		50	17-18
26	18-19		51	19

217

edition	manuscript				
52	= 45: 19-22		87	= 46:	23-24
53	22-23		88		25-26
54	23-24		89		26-29
55	24-25				
56	25-26		90		30-31
57	26-27		91		31-33
58	27-28		92		33-34
59	28-29		93		34
			94		34-36
60	29-30		95		36-37
61	30-31		96		37-38
62	31-32		97		38-39
63	32-34		98		39-47:1
64	34-36		99	= 47:	1
65	36-38				
66	38-39		100		1-3
67	39-46:1		101		4-5
68	= 46: 1-2		102		5
69	3		103		5-6
			104		6-7
70	3-4		105		7-8
71	4-5		106		9-10
72	5-6		107		11-12
73	6-7		108		12-13
74	7-8		109		14
75	8-9				
76	10		110		14-15
77	10-13		111		15
78	13		112		15-17
79	14-15		113		17-18
			114		18-19
80	15		115		19-20
81	16-17		116		21-22
82	17-18		117		22
83	18-19		118		22-23
84	19-20		119		24
85	20-21				
86	21-23		120		24-26

edition			manuscript
<u>121</u>	=	47:	26-27
<u>122</u>			27
<u>123</u>			27-29
<u>124</u>			29-30
<u>125</u>			30
<u>126</u>			30-33
<u>127</u>			33-35
<u>128</u>			35-36
<u>129</u>			36-37
<u>130</u>			38-48:1
<u>131</u>	=	48:	1-3
<u>132</u>			3-4
<u>133</u>			4-6
<u>134</u>			6-7
<u>135</u>			7-8
<u>136</u>			8-10
<u>137</u>			10-11
<u>138</u>			11-12
<u>139</u>			12
<u>140</u>			12-13
<u>141</u>			13-14
<u>142</u>			14-16
<u>143</u>			16-19
<u>144</u>			19-21
<u>145</u>			21-22
<u>146</u>			22-24
<u>147</u>			24-25
<u>148</u>			25-26
<u>149</u>			26-27
<u>150</u>			27-28
<u>151</u>			28-30
<u>152</u>			30-32
<u>153</u>			32-33
<u>154</u>			33
<u>155</u>			34-35

edition			manuscript
<u>156</u>	=	48:	35-38
<u>157</u>			38-49:2
<u>158</u>	=	49:	2-3
<u>159</u>			3-4
<u>160</u>			4-6
<u>161</u>			6-7
<u>162</u>			8-9
<u>163</u>			9-11
<u>164</u>			11-13
<u>165</u>			13-15
<u>166</u>			15-16
<u>167</u>			16-18
<u>168</u>			18-19
<u>169</u>			19-20
<u>170</u>			20-21
<u>171</u>			22-23
<u>172</u>			23
<u>173</u>			23-25
<u>174</u>			25-26
<u>175</u>			26
<u>176</u>			26-27
<u>177</u>			27-28
<u>178</u>			28
<u>179</u>			28-30
<u>180</u>			30-32
<u>181</u>			32-34
<u>182</u>			34-37
<u>183</u>			37-50:1
<u>184</u>	=	50:	1
<u>185</u>			1-3
<u>186</u>			3-4
<u>187</u>			5
<u>188</u>			6-7
<u>189</u>			7

edition	manuscript
<u>190</u>	= 50: 7-8
<u>191</u>	8-10
<u>192</u>	10-11
<u>193</u>	11-12
<u>194</u>	12-13
<u>195</u>	13-14
<u>196</u>	15-16
<u>197</u>	16
<u>198</u>	17-18